D1503572

WHEN PREGNANCY FAILS

To Steve and Kim,
   Whose little lambs have
gone to be part of the eternal
flock of the Good Shepherd,
in the sincere hope and prayer
that this book can help to bring
some peace to your grieving hearts.
Jesus loves you, and so do we!

                  Pastor Jim and Kathy

St. John 10: 11-16, 27-29

A REVISED AND UPDATED EDITION

WHEN PREGNANCY FAILS

Families Coping with Miscarriage,
Ectopic Pregnancy,
Stillbirth, and Infant Death

Susan Borg and Judith Lasker

BANTAM BOOKS
TORONTO · NEW YORK · LONDON · SYDNEY · AUCKLAND

WHEN PREGNANCY FAILS

A Bantam Book / published by arrangement with the authors

PRINTING HISTORY
Beacon Press edition published 1981
Bantam revised edition / January 1989

Grateful acknowledgment is made to F Magazine for permission to quote from "C'est quoi, une maman sans bébé?" by M.A., F Magazine, No. 26, April 1980. Copyright 1980. Reprinted by permission. Grateful acknowledgment for reprinting material is also made to the New York Times: © 1980 by the New York Times Company. Reprinted by permission.

We gratefully acknowledge Barbara Crooker for the use of her poem, "The Lost Children." We also thank Margie Gaffron for the use of her poem, "I Am a Woman Who Carries a Child."

All rights reserved.
Copyright © 1981, 1988 by Susan Borg and Judith Lasker.
Cover design copyright © 1988 by Rich Rossiter.
No part of this book may be reproduced or transmitted
in any form or by any means, electronic or mechanical,
including photocopying, recording, or by any information
storage and retrieval system, without permission in
writing from the publisher.
For information address: Bantam Books.

Library of Congress Cataloging-in-Publication Data

Borg, Susan, 1947–
    When pregnancy fails : families coping with miscarriage, ectopic
pregnancy, stillbirth, and infant death / Susan Borg and Judith
Lasker.—Rev. and updated ed.
        p.   cm.
    Bibliography: p.
    Includes index.
    ISBN 0-553-34594-X
    1. Miscarriage—Psychological aspects.   2. Pregnancy, Ectopic-
-Psychological aspects.   3. Still-birth—Psychological aspects.
4. Infants—Death—Psychological aspects.   5. Loss (Psychology)
6. Adjustment (Psychology)   I. Lasker, Judith, 1947–
II. Title.
RG648.B67   1989
155.9′37—dc19   88-21671
                                                        CIP

Published simultaneously in the United States and Canada

Bantam Books are published by Bantam Books, a division of Bantam Doubleday Dell Publishing Group, Inc. Its trademark, consisting of the words "Bantam Books" and the portrayal of a rooster, is Registered in U.S. Patent and Trademark Office and in other countries. Marca Registrada. Bantam Books, 666 Fifth Avenue, New York, New York 10103.

PRINTED IN THE UNITED STATES OF AMERICA

FG   0 9 8 7 6 5 4 3 2 1

In memory of
Daniel Borg, December 25, 1978–January 9, 1979
and
Elana Lasker Siegel, June 24, 1978

Contents

Acknowledgments

We can never adequately express our gratitude to the many, many people who helped us in writing this book. More helpful friends, family members, and acquaintances than we could possibly list here gave us ideas and suggestions of articles and books to read, made contacts with bereaved families to interview, and encouraged us with their enthusiasm.

This book would not have been the same without the vital contributions of hundreds of men, women, and children who were willing to share their tragic experiences with us. We have promised them anonymity and have changed their names in the book, but we hope that they will know how much their accounts, their insights, and their feelings have enriched our understanding and our writing.

We thank Dr. John Kennell for writing the foreword and for what we have learned from him about the ways in which professionals can help families after infant loss.

We would also like to thank the professionals who gave of their time and experiences, providing crucial information and insights into the professionals' perspectives at the time of a birth tragedy.

Thanks to the attorneys:
Steven A. Bergstein, Richard E. Brennan, David Gross, Linda B. R. Mills, Clifford Rieders, and David F. Shrager

health planners:
Jan Bishop and Nancy Erickson

members of the clergy, funeral directors, and scholars of religion and ethics:
Father Barbone, Reverend Ronald Cadmus, Rabbi Earl Grollman, C. Stuart Hausmann, Reverend Paul Irion, Dr. Joseph LaBarge, Reverend

O. Allen Lumpkin, Dr. Russell L. McIntyre, Harry Rishel, and Rabbi Mark Urkowitz

nurses, nurse-midwives, and childbirth educators:
Barbara Bordner, Joan Butasek, Judith Goodkin, Laura Martin, Nancy O'Donohue, Gloria Opirhory, Donna Schlicher, Pat Turoczy, and Rozalyn Yannacone

physicians:
Dr. Jack L. Fairweather, Dr. Edward Goodkin, Dr. Howard C. Schlachter, Dr. Catherine Sladowski, Dr. Robert Spahr, Dr. Andrew Unger, Dr. Ilana W. Zarafu

social workers:
Christel D'Agostino, Jane M. Dronick, Barbara Hemmendinger, Nancy Kilstrom, Joan A. Odes, and Lynne Witkin

In addition, Dr. Robert Echenberg, a good friend and physician who was one of the pioneers in providing help to grieving parents, has been very helpful with the revisions.

Many people contributed to the research effort reported in the new Section VII of this revised edition. Thanks to Elaine Aivaliotis, Janice Alhadeff, Gail Arbeiter, Dr. Donald T. Campbell, Lynn Cawthray, Deborah Coulter, Sally Donches, Pat Gerstenberg, Dr. Roy Herrenkohl, Carolyn Hittinger, Charis Hughes, Florence Gabriel Hughes, Hiranthi Jayasuriya, Carole Reese, Sandy Kelly, Alice Mesaros, Sally Novack, Linda Pegalis, Louise Potvin, Carol Remmel, Lori Rogora, Mary Scott, Steven Sherback, Debbie Shin, Lynn Sinnott, June Stephen, Aileen Wells, Jackie Young, and April Young.

We received important information and ideas from demographer Dr. William Mosher of the National Center for Health Statistics and social scientists Dr. Caryl Goodman and Dr. Bryon Good. We are also appreciative of the numerous support group organizers who shared with us information about their groups and their experiences in helping bereaved parents. Sister Jane Marie Lamb of the SHARE organization has been a wonderful source of support and information.

We thank Gail Gulliksen, who read and commented on the entire manuscript, and Nicholas Borg, Sidney Borg, Katie Griffiths, Kim Scheppele, and Alison Wachstein, who read portions of earlier drafts. All of them offered important suggestions for changes. We appreciate the time and effort Brenda John and Ina Saltz gave in helping us with design aspects of the book.

Ann Dainoff typed the first drafts of parts of the manuscript, and Yvonne Wetzel completed the typing and retyping of the entire book. Judy Specht typed portions of the revised manuscript. We are grateful to all of them for their promptness and accuracy, their ability to decipher our changes and additions, and their enthusiastic support of the project. The Sociology Department and the administration at Bucknell University gave invaluable support to the original book, and Lehigh University has assisted with the revisions, particularly with a grant from the Unsponsored Research Fund.

Because we live 110 miles from one another, it was necessary to find a midway point at which we could meet regularly and work comfortably. The public library in Washington, N.J., has provided a welcoming atmosphere in which to work.

Two very special women, our mothers, helped and encouraged us in many ways. Ruth Oransky provided both emotional support and much practical assistance. Miriam Lasker gave her time and interest to the expert reading and editing of several drafts.

A very special thanks to John McKinney for spending countless hours on careful review and editing of the drafts. We learned a great deal from him about the organization and expression of ideas.

Rabbi Arnold Lasker generously shared his wisdom and professional experience in helping with both ideas and writing. His strong support and extensive comments on several drafts were extremely valuable.

We thank the staffs of Beacon Press and Bantam Books and especially our editors, Jeffrey Smith and Linda Loewenthal, who have been most helpful in seeing this book to its completed form. Their cooperative spirit and attentive editing are very much appreciated. We would also like to thank Tom Walter for his initial support and his early perception of the importance of this book.

Our husbands, Andrew Borg and Barry Siegel, read and commented on portions of the manuscript and contributed their professional expertise. They also had to live with our many absences from home, our constant talk about the book, and increased child care responsibilities. We thank them for their love and understanding, for being with us during our times of tragedy, and for being patient with us while we worked on the book.

Our daughters, Laura and Shira, arrived while we were writing the first edition, and since then we have celebrated the births of Margo and Ariella. Their cheerfulness and adaptability made it possible for us to continue working, even if they often complicated our schedules. Their presence in our lives makes everything so much more worthwhile.

About the Revised Edition

Eight years have passed since we wrote the original version of this book, eight years that have brought many changes into our lives. As we read over again what we wrote then, it is hard for us to believe that two tiny babies whose deaths inspired those words would now be almost ten years old. Yet we often imagine how different our lives would be now if they were alive.

During those eight years, medical information and technology have continued to change. New legal precedents and national policies have been set which affect many parents. Fortunately, there is a great deal more support for bereaved families now, both within the medical care system and through parent support groups. All of these changes are reflected in this new edition. Rather than simply add a new introduction or conclusion, we have rewritten each chapter as needed. In addition, a new chapter has been added on ectopic pregnancy because of the lack of information about this important and growing tragedy. The references and appendices are updated to reflect the vastly increased number of articles, organizations, and resources now available. In a new section at the end of the book, we have summarized results from a large follow-up study of bereaved families which was based on the conclusions of the first edition. Funded by The National Institutes of Health, this study gives strong scientific support to the significance for parents of a loss in pregnancy.

Eight years, many changes. But the feelings we described in this book have not changed. Grief is a universal human response, a painful reaction to loss that needs to be expressed. Hundreds of bereaved parents and caring professionals have shared their feelings with us over these past years and have confirmed the validity of what is expressed here. We are grateful for their openness and their insights. We hope that this new book will continue to be a comprehensive resource for parents who suffer the terrible loss of a baby and for all those who seek to help them.

Foreword

As I contemplated how best to introduce the reader to this book's compelling and important subject, I decided it would be wise to use the words and experiences of bereaved parents. They, like the authors, are in the best position to describe how parents feel after a miscarriage, selective abortion, stillbirth, or infant death.

For years I have attended the monthly meetings of a group of parents whose babies died without even leaving the hospital. Over the years the composition of this group changed, but the themes expressed at meeting after meeting are fairly constant. At one meeting, the parents were discussing how difficult it was to have others appreciate what they are going through and listen to them as they struggled through weeks and months of excruciating and painful grief reactions. One mother said, "I feel like throwing open my bedroom window and shouting out to the world: 'My baby has died! My baby has died!'" The other parents nodded in agreement. These parents discussed the need for a visible sign to the world, such as wearing a black armband or placing a black wreath on their door, that would let everyone know what had happened to them. These signs might give parents the understanding and support they desperately need for many months after their loss.

A universal concern of parents at these meetings has been that the world will forget their baby. If the baby was stillborn or lived for only an hour, they realize there may be no one other than the parents who really knew the baby. They are concerned that not only will others forget about the baby but even they themselves may forget as the intense preoccupation with the loss eases. Yet parents who lost their baby several months ago reassure the more recently bereaved parents that they will never forget. This concern in part explains the angry reactions of nearly every parent when well-meaning relatives and friends say, "It's time for you to stop grieving. It was just a little baby and you can always have another." Or "It is just as well she died because she probably would have been damaged." Or "The thing you should do is to have another baby right away." The parents, especially the mothers, have known their babies intimately for seven to nine months of intra-uterine life. After the baby dies, they want to keep the memory of this unique infant alive. They are exquisitely sensitive to any words or actions that seem to depreciate the importance of the baby because their own self-esteem has been shattered as well as their faith in God, their doctor, science, and medicine.

At every meeting parents complain that their friends and relatives avoid discussing the baby and the death. One group discussed how close friends and relatives who were supportive in the beginning later were anxious to find some evidence that the bereaved couple were feeling a bit better or were coming out of their mourning period. Bereaved parents continue to have periods of ups and downs and need help as the weeks pass just as they did in the first few days after their infant's death. But now even their closest friends eagerly restrict conversations to happier subjects. These parents feel there is no one who will listen to the stories they desperately want to tell: the baby's appearance and behavior, the detailed account of the events leading up to the death, and their own subsequent physical symptoms and mental aberrations.

The personal tragedies of Susan Borg and Judith Lasker have led them to write this book to provide valuable insights and understanding for the thousands of parents who lose a baby each year and for those who attempt to help them professionally or as friends and relatives. Many articles have been written about the mourning reactions of parents, and the subject has been discussed in a large number of professional meetings. In our community we have seen major changes in the management of parents after a stillbirth, the abortion of a defective fetus, or a neonatal death, but there appears to have been little impact on the general public as reflected in the reports of bereaved parents attending group meetings or the parents whom we have counseled individually.

I want to congratulate and thank Susan and Judith personally for collecting this information and writing this book so that the bereaved parents and friends of the bereaved, professionals and nonprofessionals, can appreciate the overpowering reactions of parents who have lost a baby. I expect that the information they have supplied will guide many readers so that they can work through the mourning process or enable them to help a close friend or relative get through this time. On several occasions the parents in the group have agreed that it is almost impossible for any of us to say the right words to parents who have lost an infant. The important point is to attempt to understand what the bereaved parents and family are going through and then to show our continuing concern and availability.

This book should give a large number of individuals an opportunity to understand the long and painful journey many parents have had to travel alone. With understanding, the healing properties of improved communication should benefit many more of the bereaved and those who wish to assist them. Pain cannot and should not be removed from the long arduous trail of mourning, but it can be endured better when understanding spouses, relatives, friends, and professionals travel along with parents.

JOHN H. KENNELL, M.D.
Professor of Pediatrics
Case Western University School of Medicine

I
PROLOGUE

Prologue

We met as young children, we grew up together, and together we almost became mothers. We were both thirty when we became pregnant, and we shared with each other the joyful anticipation of motherhood. But nothing in our experience had prepared either of us for what actually was to happen. Childbirth is supposed to be a natural, a blessed event. But not all stories have happy endings. Neither of ours did.

Judy's experience:

> My pregnancy was an easy one. Although I had the usual fears and worries of any expectant mother, I felt healthy and confident. I had read a number of critiques of present-day childbirth practices in America, and I looked for a physician who believed, as I did, that delivery should not be assisted with potentially harmful drugs and machines, unless necessary. Since I lived in a small town, my choices were limited. But I found the physician I wanted, and in long and friendly discussions during prenatal visits we planned for the baby's arrival.
>
> My husband, Barry, participated with me in both Lamaze and hospital classes, and I took a prenatal exercise course at the Y. Besides reading and rehearsing and planning for the big day, we also took great delight in shopping for baby clothes, bedding, furniture, and all the supplies. We bought a secondhand crib and refinished it lovingly. We decorated the nursery with colorful mobiles and pictures. We even addressed the birth-announcement cards and drew up an invitation list for the party we were planning.

3

On a sunny June day I went into labor. At the beginning, since the contractions were still at least ten minutes apart and I was not really uncomfortable, we spent the day walking and working in the garden. We even commented on how considerate and gentle this baby must be to begin its arrival so easily and on such a pretty day. That evening we went to the hospital, calm but excited, and began our familiar and very helpful Lamaze routine.

At 10:00 P.M. the doctor told us the baby was in a breech position. He brought in the obstetrician who was on call that night to assist with the delivery. Our hopes for a labor room birth vanished, and for the next several hours the possibility of a Caesarean was considered.

I was wheeled to X ray, then hooked up to an intravenous, and had a blood sample taken. I began to feel poked and prodded from every direction. The doctors decided, on the basis of the X ray and the progress of labor, not to perform a Caesarean.

Hours later, I was wheeled into the delivery room. When I saw myself in the overhead mirror, I experienced a sudden feeling of panic. I felt as if I were watching some strange theatrical production, with elaborate costumes and scenery and myself at center stage. It seemed like the baby inside me was being ignored while three doctors performed their rituals: the masks, the sterile field, the anesthesia, the forceps, the episiotomy.

Then a nurse checked the fetal heartbeat and said it was low. (Later my doctor told me that she might have been hearing the beating of my own heart.) When the time came, I felt no desire to push; but I pushed when finally told to. The baby emerged easily, without the use of forceps.

To everyone's surprise, both the baby and the cord were still. While the resident worked at sewing up the episiotomy, causing me pain, Barry and I watched the obstetrician who was trying to breathe life into our baby girl. Each of us kept an eye on the clock, desperately wanting the baby to live but fearful that she would be revived too late to be healthy. We held tightly to each other, numb with shock, telling each other that everything would be okay, and knowing it would not.

Abruptly the drama was over. The obstetrician stopped. There was no more hope for our baby. A hug from my own doctor; then suddenly the room was empty. The one nurse who remained encouraged Barry and me to hold our baby. She was beautiful, surprisingly clean of the slimy vernix we had expected, looking very much like me, we thought. We held her gingerly, never having been so close to death before. And we wondered at such a beautiful, gentle child, who all of a sudden was dead.

Susan's experience:

A few days after Judy told me her tragic news, I discovered I was pregnant. My husband, Andy, and I had been trying to conceive for over a year and had begun to fear that there might be some fertility problem. So when the results of the pregnancy test came back positive, we were ecstatic.

For the first three months, everything seemed normal. At the end of the fourth month, my obstetrician said that by my next appointment I should be feeling the baby kick. But two months and two more visits to the doctor passed and still I didn't feel any movement at all. My doctor didn't seem concerned, but I began to worry. Finally, I asked her if anything could be wrong. She said that the baby seemed small for my due date, which was only three months away. She recommended that I have an ultrasound test to determine the age of the fetus. The results indicated that the baby was four weeks younger than I had thought, and this probably accounted for my small size and the lack of movement as well. (Later the test results were proved wrong—the original date had been correct.)

I was somewhat relieved for a while, thinking that everything was fine, but then a new problem developed, this time with my back. I was so uncomfortable that I had trouble walking and sleeping. Finally it became so painful that I had to quit my job.

As my pregnancy progressed, Andy and I were attending classes in childbirth at the hospital. We were looking forward to a natural childbirth experience, now to be in March, the new due date for our baby. But in mid-December my amniotic fluid began to leak. I met my obstetrician at the hospital. She recommended that I remain at home and stay in bed, to delay the labor as long as possible.

As each day passed, I became more fearful, yet I could not really believe that anything could be wrong with my baby. After two anxious weeks of lying in bed, I went to a specialist in New York City to get a second opinion. He felt that I should be hospitalized. He said there was a seventy percent chance that I would go into labor soon and that my condition was serious. The two opinions were so contradictory that I didn't know which to believe. I weighed the many factors and finally decided to remain at home—but I was increasingly anxious about the situation.

Two days later, on Christmas Eve, I went into labor. Everything happened very quickly once we got to the hospital. My contractions were three minutes apart. Since the baby was in a breech position, a Caesarean section was decided upon. A resident made three unsuccessful intravenous attempts. I was in pain and emotionally in a state of shock. They wheeled me into the delivery room and administered a local anesthetic. Then I began to watch the clock.

Finally, I heard my baby crying weakly. Nobody said anything, so I asked, "Is it a boy or a girl?" My doctor responded that there were problems and she couldn't tell. I was confused; I must have heard wrong. I asked her again. She repeated the same answer with no other explanation. No one showed me my baby.

In the recovery room Andy said that our baby was dying. My body began to shake so violently that I wondered whether I would recover.

The neonatologist present in the delivery room did not know immediately what was wrong with the baby, but he told us that there were a number of severe deformities. He found the syndrome in a textbook and recommended that we not operate, that we let our baby die. We were shocked; we were scared—but we accepted the doctor's advice. We thought we had no other choice. Tests showed that the baby was a boy. We named him Daniel.

The next day relatives came. They mentioned seeing the baby and told me how beautiful he looked. I could only imagine a deformed monster, and I didn't believe them.

By the following day I was determined to see my baby. The nurses were encouraging and wheeled me to the special care nursery. I was frightened and didn't know what to expect. I scrubbed and put on a sterile mask. Then they brought him to me. Daniel. He was a beautiful baby!

While Daniel still lived, Andy and I spent as much time with him as we could emotionally bear, holding him and crying with him. We watched him lose weight and grow weaker. A week after his birth, I went home reluctantly, without him, but I continued to visit him every day in the special care nursery. On January 9, at 4:30 A.M., Daniel died.

Although our individual experiences differed in detail, we began to discover in our long discussions together just how similar our feelings were. We were both shocked, grief-stricken, and depressed. We had been ready for a normal birth, but totally unprepared to handle what did happen. We both felt angry about our powerlessness, our lack of choices in the medical setting. We wondered what we would have done differently. But in one very important way, we two were fortunate: we had each other to share our grief afterward.

We began to exchange the many stories we had heard about others who had suffered similar misfortunes: the grief of miscarriage, the shock of stillbirth, the trauma of deciding to abort a deformed fetus, the pain of watching a sick baby die. Families like us had shared the excitement, anticipation, and sometimes ambivalence of beginning a pregnancy. Yet none of us had that new baby to take home, to love, to plan the future with. For all of us, pregnancy had ended in failure.

Any pregnancy is a time of major emotional and physical changes. Psychologists consider pregnancy—especially the first—an important life crisis, a turning point in the individual's development as significant as puberty. Ordinarily this crisis is resolved by the birth of a healthy child. When this does not happen, the crisis deepens. Parents may feel they have suffered a major setback in their lives. They wonder if they will have to live their lives without children or without as many as they wanted.

These parents suffer a loss of self-esteem. The plans and dreams they shared during the pregnancy have been destroyed. They experience the pain of failure, the failure to fulfill one of the most fundamental of human acts: to give birth to a healthy child.

They experience these feelings alone, isolated from others. Most of their family and friends do not understand what sort of emotional support is needed. "At least you never knew this child," they will say, hoping to ease the pain. Or "It could have been worse." Or "You'll have another one." In their own way they might be trying to offer hope for the future, but to the bereaved parents it often seems that these people do not comprehend the enormity of what has happened.

What others do not understand is that the parents are grieving for the loss of a very real person. As pediatricians Marshall Klaus and John Kennell have shown, "bonding" between parent and child begins early in pregnancy. Long before the actual birth, parents are readying themselves for the arrival of their son or daughter. An image develops of how the infant will look and act. Parents may talk to the baby and even call him or her by name. The mourning after an unsuccessful pregnancy may be different from the mourning for the loss of an older child, but it is still grief for someone who already exists in the parents' minds.

Many professionals who come in contact with the mourning couple—medical people, clergy, funeral directors—often fail to provide appropriate support and counseling. This is true in many situations of death and dying—these are still difficult subjects to talk about. But when a miscarriage, an ectopic pregnancy, a stillbirth, an abortion of a deformed fetus, or an early infant death occurs, it is especially important for professionals to assist parents in beginning to grieve. They can do this by helping to create concrete memories for the parents to hold on to. Yet in too many hospitals, still, all reminders of the baby are removed quickly, and parents are not encouraged to consider a funeral or other formal mourning practices.

These parents are further isolated because they seldom know anyone else who has experienced a birth tragedy. They have no assurance that their own feelings and reactions are normal. Hardly a word is written about unsuccessful deliveries in any of the numerous books about childbirth for consumers.

And yet birth tragedies are not as rare as we like to think. In one year, in the United States alone, according to the National Center for Health Statistics, close to one million families are affected. Of the 3.67 million infants born alive, over 25,000 (one in 144) die during the first twenty-eight days of life and are counted as neonatal deaths. An additional 30,000 babies (about one in every 123 deliveries) are stillborn, having died between the twentieth week of pregnancy and the time of birth. These rates have been declining steadily, yet they are still higher in the United States than in many other countries. And no matter how rare a tragedy, when it happens to you, it is 100 percent.

In contrast to the drop in stillbirths and neonatal deaths, the number of ectopic pregnancies has been rising sharply, almost quadrupling since 1970. This is probably due to the increase in pelvic infections and in some cases to IUDs. Seventy thousand women each year experience this life-threatening condition, in which the embryo grows in the fallopian tube instead of in the uterus.

The most common pregnancy failure of all is miscarriage, which is estimated to occur in fifteen to twenty percent of all recognized pregnancies. Miscarriages are not uniformly recorded, but there is no evidence that this rate has changed. However, as the total number of pregnancies has risen, so has the number of miscarriages. Up to 900,000 families each year may be affected.

When these figures are combined with the many thousands of infants who die in their first year (e.g., from congenital abnormalities, crib death, or accidents), the tens of thousands who survive but with severe deformities, the millions of couples who experience infertility, and an unknown number of women who abort a wanted baby because of deformities (selective abortion), the number of people grieving for the lack of a healthy child is even more astounding.

Statistics do show that the problem is widespread, but they tell nothing about the tears, the regrets, the feelings of guilt, the long process of rebuilding hope. They hide the loneliness of those who feel they are the only ones in the world who have failed to become parents. We have written this book in an attempt to help grieving parents break through the barriers of their isolation; to offer them reassurance, information, encouragement, and advice. Our book is also for those professionals who want to understand and help them and for the families and friends who wish to console them.

In preparing to write this book, we interviewed many bereaved parents. We talked to some mothers and fathers whose tragedies had occurred a few weeks earlier, some after several years, and others after more than thirty years had gone by. Almost all parents were eager to share their experiences with us. For some, it was the first time they had ever talked about what happened.

Although the people interviewed were not chosen by any scientific sampling method, they represent a wide variety of social and economic backgrounds and of experiences with their pregnancies. There were many feelings these parents shared in common, but each of them found his or her own unique way of coping. No one approach worked for everyone. No one set of feelings was more appropriate than any other.

We also interviewed other family members and the professionals most often involved—doctors, nurses, social workers, midwives, clergy, lawyers, funeral directors, and childbirth educators. At the same time we read the literature on the subject, both the scientific research and the personal accounts. And from our own experiences, our interviews, and our readings, the ideas in this book emerged.

Since writing the first edition, we have spoken to many groups of professionals and bereaved parents. We have participated in creating hospital programs to help bereaved parents and have started and been part of support groups. All of these experiences have contributed to our thinking about loss and about the needs of bereaved parents.

The death of an infant is a great tragedy, but often the pain that the parents feel is greater than it needs to be. A better understanding of their feelings and the problems they face can help spare them that needless suffering. We hope our book will help accomplish this.

II
THE PARENTS' EXPERIENCES

1

The Parents' Grief

"A marriage just as I wished. A pregnancy just as I hoped.... And I feel good.... The apartment is bathed in sunlight, and in my head the baby is, too.... Everything is perfect.

"I see him, this baby. He is there a little more at each dawn.... I touch him, I feel him, I breathe him ... I wait for the first awakening more and more feverishly, the first smile, the first tooth....

"And then, one night, hemorrhage. Panic.... Here's the taxi, the hospital ...

" 'Madam, you must not think any more about the child.'

"Not think any more about the baby? About 'my' baby? About the one I waited more than eight months for?

"... I think I'm going to die of pain. My husband is there, close ... He kisses me ... I want to cry. Or to sleep. All I want is to sleep. Sleep so I won't have to think anymore, sleep so I won't see my husband cry anymore.... I want to bury my dreams and my sorrow.

"When I wake up, sympathetic faces walk past me, but ... they will never understand what I feel. It was a girl, they say. She should have lived, but ... she is dead. It's an 'accident.' No.... For me, it's failure. And jealousy.... Why all the others and not me?

"When I returned to the house, there was no more sun, no toys, no colors. The silence of the hours to come. An empty room. What is it, a mommy without a baby?"

M.A.
F Magazine
April 1980

The sunlight, the dream, the embrace of a baby—long before an infant is born, he or she is already a real person, one who is known, experienced, and loved.

Many couples create an image of their child even before conceiving. When pregnancy begins and the baby starts to grow, this image becomes clearer. Noticing the first signs of pregnancy, listening to the heartbeat, feeling movements—each plays a part in the bond between parents and child.

As the fetus grows, a personality and characteristics also develop in the minds of the parents and their friends. They speculate at length about the sex and seize upon a variety of signs for evidence. They may be carrying around with them a picture of the baby taken by ultrasound. When there have been tests to detect possible birth defects, the sex actually becomes known. People ask if the baby is a strong kicker or quiet, large or small. Parents identify limbs—a foot pushing out here, a head felt there. The baby may even have a bank account, often a special sleeping area, clothes and furniture, a name, and a future filled with specific friends, relatives, and activities.

This creation of a person, with an identity and life of his or her own, is a typical part of pregnancy and is encouraged by society. Maternity shirts now often say "under construction" or "baby" with an arrow pointing to the abdomen; commercial interests bombard a family with special offers and samples; friends give a shower, collect clothes to pass along, and treat the expectant parents like members of a special club. But suddenly, instead of being members of the club, they stand outside it, pitied and isolated.

Others may not understand that the parents grieve for their baby just as they would grieve for a person who has lived. They grieve for the person whom they feel they already knew well and for the dream of what that person would become. They grieve whether the pregnancy was planned or unplanned, whether wanted or unwanted, whether tragedy occurred after nine months or after only three. The death of a child can be particularly frightening for parents who begin to have children in their thirties, since the time available for a second chance is limited. But whether the bereaved parents are young, single teenagers or longtime married couples, parents with many children or couples expecting their first, all feel a sense of loss.

When pregnancy ends in tragedy, there is profound disappointment, the collapse of hopes and plans. Dreams are destroyed and worst fears realized; the preparations become useless. The bereaved parents experience the pain of putting away the crib and clothes and shower presents. They have lost not only a fantasy, not only the infant who was seen for a few days or who lived as an image in their minds, but a part of themselves, the companion knocking and moving about inside, their heir, their look-alike, their stake in the future.

Besides the disappointment and grief, there is also a strong sense of failure. The parents have failed to accomplish what every "normal" couple presumably does with ease, what some do without effort or even without desire. Their bodies can no longer be relied on. Their sexuality is challenged. They fear they will never be able to have a normal child.

They have failed to fulfill the expectations of others—their parents who were eager to be grandparents and their friends with children who encouraged them to share the experience. They are embarrassed at having disappointed those excited friends and relatives who waited with them for good news and at having to announce to them that there is no baby. And they are jealous of others—especially those in their own family—who have had no problems in bearing children.

In almost every society, men and women are urged to reproduce. Births are celebrated, and children are surrounded with favor. The biblical command to "be fruitful and multiply" is still a powerful message. It is not surprising that many couples who have lost an infant feel like outcasts. Like M.A., they wonder, "Why all the others and not me?"

When first-time parents experience the loss of a child, their very sense of identity may be threatened. After all, for most people, becoming a parent is part of being an adult. Having a child makes a statement to the world, to one's parents, and—more important perhaps—to oneself that he or she is grown-up, a responsible individual and an accepted member of society. A couple's failure to have a child may make them feel they have returned to being the children in their parents' families and not yet the heads of a new family.

For many women, becoming a mother represents the fulfillment of their own adult role and of other people's expectations. As poet Adrienne Rich wrote about her own experience of being pregnant:

> The atmosphere of approval in which I was bathed—even by strangers on the street, it seemed—was like an aura I carried with me . . . *this is what women have always done.*

When the pregnancy is unsuccessful, this sense of being approved of by others can quickly turn into disapproval, a feeling of having failed to do what a woman is expected to do. After her miscarriage, one woman said:

> You are a woman first and you have all these feelings of really not making it and fulfilling the role you want to fulfill. I mean I wanted to be a mother and couldn't be.

Some women who had forgone career aspirations or given up a job for the sake of motherhood feel despair and a loss of purpose. When their pregnancies fail, they are not only without children, they are without work as well.

Fathers also grieve. Although having children may not be considered a primary goal for men in American society, it is still one of major importance to most of them. The father develops a bond with the expected infant early in the pregnancy. He may envy his wife's closeness to the baby and ability to feel his or her presence from inside; he is eager to see and hold his baby for himself.

Not having carried the baby, the father may not feel quite as intense an attachment as the mother. This may be why studies of parents after stillbirth have found that the father's grief is usually somewhat less severe than the mother's, although it is much greater than most of his friends or relatives suspect.

If the baby survives for a while, the father has the opportunity to create a strong attachment, especially if the mother is still hospitalized and the baby transferred to another hospital. The circumstances of the pregnancy and birth, therefore, and the father's feelings about parenthood influence his response to the tragic loss.

For men and women both, there can be a loss of confidence and self-esteem. After all, they had embarked on one of the most important endeavors of their lives, and it ended in tragedy. As one woman said after a stillbirth:

> All my life I have believed that if I worked hard at something, I would succeed, and that has almost always happened. And here's something I prepared for so carefully, yet I failed miserably.

Because of the advances in modern medical technology and the continuing decline in the infant death rate, most couples begin their efforts to conceive with great confidence that they will have a favorable outcome. They feel that they are largely in control of their future; although they may have some fears during pregnancy, they expect to be among the large majority who give birth to healthy children. They are shocked when it turns out otherwise and frightened to discover that they have no control over what happens. Their youthful sense of invulnerability is shattered. They are faced, often for the first time in their lives, with the reality of death and a sense of their own mortality. Tragedy no longer happens only to other people.

Sometimes parents think they are "going crazy"; their emotional reaction is so strong that they become disoriented, depressed, bitter, and withdrawn for many months and maybe even years. Friends may expect them to bounce back quickly, have another child, and try to forget the past. But they cannot forget.

The great majority of bereaved parents are not going crazy. In addition to having the feelings that are specific to the loss of a baby, the parents are also experiencing a normal grief reaction that occurs in anyone who has lived through the death of someone close. Psychiatrists now recognize a pattern in these reactions and talk about the stages of grieving through which the bereaved person must almost inevitably pass before regaining peace of mind. These stages are *shock, denial, sadness, despair, guilt, anger,* and eventual *resolution and reorganization*. What the bereaved and their friends often do not realize is that the grief process is not restricted to the loss of a person who lived.

It occurs after a birth tragedy precisely because the expected infant already was a person for the parents, and that person is being mourned.

The grieving process can last from a few months to a few years. The stages may overlap, and their ordering and degree of intensity may vary for different people. During this period, as psychiatrist Colin Parkes writes, "For the bereaved, time is out of joint. He may know from the calendar that a year has passed since his loss, but his memories of the lost person are so clear it seems like only yesterday. . . . The first year of bereavement [is] looked back upon as a limbo of meaningless activity."

Physical symptoms are not uncommon. Dr. Erich Lindemann, one of the first psychiatrists to study grief reactions of people whose relatives had recently died, noticed that insomnia and loss of appetite were almost universal.

When a loss is expected, stages of grief can begin even before the death has actually happened. This "anticipatory grief" may occur under a variety of conditions: when the first signs of miscarriage appear, when the movements and heartbeat of an infant stop before birth, when a decision is made to abort a deformed fetus, or when a child is born with little chance of survival. Because of the terrible uncertainty of the outcome, a major aspect of anticipatory grief is the strong temptation to deny the reality of the situation and to bargain with God or oneself in an effort to make things right again. As one woman said about her stillbirth:

> The baby didn't move for about a week before my delivery date. I kept telling myself that maybe the baby was sleeping, and thinking that if I just stayed in bed everything would be all right. I was depressed and scared, and just didn't want to believe that anything could be wrong. But at the same time I couldn't help talking with my husband about what we'd do if our baby were dead.

In this case there was time to begin preparing for the worst, even to begin grieving. Once the miscarriage is over or the baby's death is confirmed, parents may feel relieved that at least the uncertainty has ended, but they also start to grieve all over again.

By contrast, those parents whose pregnancies end in tragedy without warning have no time for anticipatory grieving. In such cases, there is no hope, and the reaction is one of shock.

Shock, the first stage of the grieving process, is a natural response; it is beneficial in that it gives the individual time to absorb the gravity of the tragedy by delaying the impact. Feelings of numbness are common during the first minutes and sometimes hours or even days after a death. After her baby died, one woman recalled:

> I felt paralyzed and was amazed at how calm I must have appeared right after delivery. I wondered if the nurses thought I was being callous. I was totally numb.

This reaction can be deceptive to others who are unaware of the grieving process. They may falsely assume that the bereaved is an insensitive person, that the experience is not of major significance to the parents, or that the mother is strong and bearing up well. Some may take this calm to confirm their belief that miscarriage or infant loss is only a minor event.

Some professionals try to shield parents from seeing their baby or from receiving any detailed information about what happened. They are afraid their patients might become hysterical. They fail to take into account the fact that shock usually enables the parents to get through the tragic situation initially without losing control.

Although it is essential that bereaved parents express their emotions over time and talk about their loss, some degree of *denial* is a normal part of grieving. It is a form of self-protection, a way of not having to face up to the pain. "This didn't happen to me" is a common feeling.

Many parents say that it was difficult to face the reality of the situation and to accept the fact that the tragedy had happened. One woman said, "After the miscarriage was over, I had this crazy feeling that I would go home and continue with the pregnancy. I knew the reality, but somehow I didn't believe it." Another talked about her fantasy that the baby was still alive somewhere. Although these are normal reactions, the parents must ultimately distinguish between fantasy and reality and confront the very real tragedy that has occurred.

There is an overwhelming *sadness* as there is after any tragedy. Some parents feel sad for the baby. They say that it seems particularly unfair for a baby to die. It is expected that an old person who has experienced life will die, but an infant is thought to deserve a chance at life. As one father expressed his feelings: "She seemed so innocent. What did she ever do to deserve this? It just doesn't seem fair, and it makes me feel so sorry for her."

They are sad for themselves as well, sad because of the emptiness and the disappointment. Their wish to be parents—to have someone to nurture, to love, to teach, to care for, to play with, someone who would care for them in their old age and inherit the benefits of their work—has not been granted.

In a very real sense, children are a perpetuation of oneself into the future, a symbol of immortality. When the hopes for children are not fulfilled—especially under circumstances that suggest a possibility of never having children—there is a terrible feeling of pain, a deep sense of despair and of the meaninglessness of life. The parents mourn not only for the dead infant, but also for all the future possible children, a kind of mourning that is even less recognized and supported.

For certain parents, *despair* may become focused on the fact that the baby's sex was the one they had wished for. Perhaps they had wanted to balance the family, if there are already children of one sex; a father may have been anxious for a son to identify with, to pass along his name or his skills and his livelihood to. Other parents may have pinned their hopes on having a girl. As one mother said after a late miscarriage:

> Lord, I wanted that girl so bad. I do everyone else's hair; I wanted my own little girl so I could do her hair and dress her up so nice! When I go to Main Street, I look in the windows and see the little girls' clothes and they're so cute I just can't help myself—I have to run and get away.

Guilt is one of the strongest emotions bereaved parents feel. Many parents blame themselves for the tragedy and wonder what they did to cause it. After all, the baby was part of them, a product of their bodies. If their infant was deformed or too weak to survive, it is hard for them not to think that something was wrong with themselves. Perhaps it was a deficiency in their physical makeup, their "bad genes" or bad blood, that caused the problem. They wonder what they might have done to prevent the tragedy. For example, a woman who had a miscarriage in her fourth month said:

> I always minimize my pains. Maybe if I had not downplayed the symptoms when I called the doctor after the first pains started—if I had said I have terrible, severe pain—then he would have acted differently by hospitalizing me, and I would not have lost the baby. This is something I feel very guilty about.

Many parents review in their minds the times they had sexual intercourse during the pregnancy, wondering if this had an effect. A mother may think about the medications she swallowed, the alcohol or diet soda she drank, the extra trip she took, or the possibility that she was exposed to harmful chemicals. Parents scrutinize every activity, looking for a clue. They study every news item reporting the discovery of possible causes of damage to unborn children.

Some wonder whether the outcome would have been different if they had picked another doctor or hospital. "If only I had done this . . . If I hadn't done that . . . If only . . ." These thoughts predominate. But usually the cause of death cannot be known, which makes it difficult to resolve the feelings of guilt or to erase the lingering doubts and questions. The parents' search for answers is a normal part of the effort to regain control over their lives, to give sense and order to a chaotic situation even if it also contributes to the feeling they might have been responsible.

What some parents feel most guilty about is the ambivalence they had experienced in response to the idea of becoming parents, and this memory is one of the sources for the strong feelings of guilt and depression that assail parents whose infants die. As one man recalled:

> When I found out my wife was pregnant, quite frankly I wasn't all that thrilled. The idea of having a child and losing Jan's

income when we weren't really on our feet was very frightening for me.

So I never really wanted the baby. Then, when she was still-born, all sorts of guilt welled up. I felt that somehow I was being punished for having such negative thoughts. I know it's irratio-nal, but I can't shake the feeling.

For some, a sudden and somewhat surprising sense of relief that they will be spared the burdens of parenthood can quickly turn into a feeling of *guilt*. They ask themselves how they could dare have positive feelings about such a tragedy.

Guilt is by far the most serious problem for those parents who decide to abort a wanted baby when they learn that there are serious deformities: guilt for conceiving an abnormal child, but, much worse, guilt for deciding to end the pregnancy. One mother in this situation expressed her feelings about what she had done:

I couldn't help but feel that I was killing this child. Not that I don't believe in abortion, but this baby had been moving for some time, and at twenty-three weeks there are some babies that live. I'm sure we made the right decision, but I still feel guilty.

Parents do not limit their blame to themselves. Their feelings of guilt and frustration also turn into *anger* toward others. They blame God, the doctor, and even the baby for causing them so much heartache. They are angry that they have gone through a pregnancy and then have nothing.

It may seem surprising to feel anger toward a baby, especially one so longed for, so innocent. Expressing this hostility overtly may be impossible, but the feeling is still there—how could you have left us and made us so miserable? Why couldn't you have been stronger?

The husband and wife may blame each other, putting a severe strain on their relationship. Each may question the other's ac-tions and reactions and motivations for having a child. They seek consolation from each other but may be angry if they do not receive as much as they would like.

Frequent targets of the parents' anger are the doctor and

other hospital staff. It is not unusual for parents to be angry at them for not having been able to do the impossible—save their baby. In some cases, however, the tragedy may actually have been caused by neglect or inappropriate procedures. The doctors are blamed most frequently for their lack of attention and caring, for failing to provide information, for not having warned the parents of possible problems, or for not having taken the signs of trouble seriously enough. The parents' lack of control over the medical setting and the absence of choices or of understanding what is taking place may intensify this anger.

Some parents are angry at their friends because they don't know how to be supportive, or perhaps they say foolish and thoughtless things in an effort to be kind. If friends talk of their own children, their complaints of problems seem petty and their mention of pleasures thoughtless. It may cause the bereaved parents to reevaluate their friendships and even turn away from people they were once close to.

Some are angry with God for allowing so senseless an event to occur. When one man's baby died at the age of two months from a severe malformation, he felt furious: "Every day I think, why is God punishing me? Why should a baby die who did nothing in this world to deserve this? I feel so bitter."

Some may even direct their anger toward the funeral director. One mother remembered: "When I arrived at the funeral parlor, I saw they were going to bury him in a white styrofoam box. That was the last straw. I thought, after two months of suffering, so this is what you get. But I tried to keep this feeling inside so I wouldn't upset everyone else."

Some are angry at the world in general—at all those other people who have babies and don't even seem to want them. Some get angry with acquaintances who ask excitedly if they had a boy or a girl and then do not know what to say when they learn the bad news. Some become angry at phone calls from photographers and others soliciting business and offering congratulations.

Studies indicate that men usually express their hostility more easily and quickly than women do. Women who express no anger may experience greater depression instead. As with other feelings of grief, expressing anger can be an important step toward eventual resolution and peace of mind.

For many parents, there is a fear of breaking down in front of others, of losing control. As one woman said when her baby died shortly after birth: "I was afraid of facing it, afraid of letting go. So instead I covered up my feelings and acted like nothing happened. I went on a vacation and tried to act normal, but I couldn't."

While men may express their anger, they may feel that they must repress their other feelings of grief and appear to be "the strong one." They concentrate their energies instead on taking care of their wives and all the difficult details. According to Harriet Sarnoff Schiff, author of *The Bereaved Parent:* "The stoicism, the insistence in our culture that men suffer in silence when faced with disaster, although slowly changing, is very much evident during bereavement."

The father who appears busy and in control often will only express his grief in private. One bereaved father, who never shed a tear in front of anyone, spent many hours crying outside in the snow by his rose bush the night his baby died.

Some parents have such great difficulty in expressing their feelings, on occasion even to themselves, that they need professional help. They may deny what has happened completely and retreat into fantasies where they really believe the child is still alive. They may be consumed by anger and a desire for revenge that paralyzes them and prevents a move into other activities, or they may be severely depressed for a long period of time, unable to think about or do anything else. These cases are exceptions, but some studies do warn of the potential for psychological problems following unsuccessful pregnancies. For those parents who do have greater difficulty in achieving resolution of their grief or who simply need more support for coping with normal grief, professional counseling can be helpful for expressing and understanding their feelings.

For all parents, preoccupation with the events of the pregnancy and with the baby may continue for a long time. Memories may plague the bereaved parents, who review every detail over and over again. There are memories of particularly difficult times—leaving the hospital, milk coming into the woman's breasts, seeing other babies. This preoccupation is a normal part of grieving. It may intensify the sadness, but it also helps the parents make sense of what happened.

There are positive memories, too, for some parents. They remember the joy of conceiving the baby, the excitement of their plans, the beginnings of fetal movement, the sensations of swelling breasts and growing belly. If the infant survived for a while, there may be memories of holding and feeding, admiring and hoping. All of these recollections are now mixed with pain.

Many parents have few such memories. This is especially true in the case of an early miscarriage or ectopic pregnancy. They may be relieved about this and feel it is easier to get over their loss if there are no concrete memories.

For many, however, the lack of special images or mementos makes grieving more difficult. If they have no pictures, no gravestone, no treasured thoughts of a baby's individual characteristics, they may wonder why they're feeling so bad, what it is they are mourning for. That is one reason why parents are now encouraged to have as much contact as possible with a dead or dying infant.

Grieving seems endless for most people while they are going through it, but eventually the feelings change and the pain lessens. The memories blur a little, and it becomes possible to give up some of the constant preoccupation with the details of the tragedy.

Holiday times and anniversaries (of conception, of the birth, of the death) bring painful reminders even when the process of grieving is almost completed. Other events may surprise the bereaved and cause some renewed depression in moments of calm. Seeing other babies—particularly those who appear to be about the same age as theirs would have been—may continue to be difficult, although in time it becomes easier as the impact diminishes. As the mother of a stillborn girl remembered:

> I thought I had really recovered. Then one day, pow! I saw a commercial on TV which started "Remember the day you brought your baby girl home from the hospital?" It really threw me for a

while, and I cried like I hadn't cried in months for the baby girl I never got to bring home. But then it was over, and that hasn't happened to me again.

Most people find the strength to cope with a tragic situation, even without consciously realizing they are doing this. Talking, crying, dealing with the pain are ways of letting out the hurt.

Whatever the difficulties, human beings are fundamentally very adaptable. They seek a new balance after disruptive events. It is not surprising, then, that most parents try to put their experience in the best possible light. One woman who learned when she arrived at the hospital in labor that her baby was already dead is glad she found out then and did not have it come as a surprise at the moment of birth. On the other hand, another woman, who thought all was well until her baby was born dead, is grateful she did not have to go through labor knowing she was carrying a dead child.

The very effort of trying to make sense of the event, to find a meaning in disaster, can strengthen the bereaved parents. Some may find new meaning in their religious faiths. Others may devote their energy to political or environmental action to prevent future birth tragedies. Some become involved in support groups to help themselves and others. Many become more attuned to the needs of people who are bereaved and feel they can offer them a special understanding.

Having learned how fragile a life can be, they may treasure their other children, their spouse, or their parents even more. They also come to appreciate more deeply the love and friendship of those who understand their needs and were there to help.

They may plan for future children and discover a stronger commitment toward parenthood than they had ever felt before— convinced, perhaps for the first time, that they really do want children. For most of them there will be another child or children, and they will understand how truly miraculous is the life of a breathing, crying, laughing, healthy child.

They have survived. Their emotions, their relationship, their ability to cope were all tested, and they know now that they can get through a crisis and survive. They find strengths they did not know they had and often begin to think about other interests. They take up new activities, new jobs. They change, they grow, they begin to laugh again. They do not forget, but eventually the pain subsides.

2

Miscarriage

"A miscarriage is nature's way of sparing you from having an imperfect baby." "It's all for the best." "You can always have another baby."

These comments are heard over and over again by couples who experience a miscarriage. They represent the common view that it is a minor event or even one to be welcomed. This is only one of the many misunderstandings that surround miscarriage. For an event that occurs so frequently (in ten to twenty percent of all recognized pregnancies) there is a remarkable degree of ignorance, among both parents and physicians, about the causes, the process of miscarriage, and the feelings of those involved.

A miscarriage, or spontaneous abortion as it is called by physicians, is the unintended ending of a pregnancy before the time the fetus could survive outside the mother. This is usually considered to be the twentieth week of pregnancy.

Many attempts have been made throughout the world to explain why a miscarriage occurs. Men in some parts of the Philippines go to great lengths to satisfy the cravings of their pregnant wives, even traveling many miles to find a desired fruit, in the belief that a woman will miscarry if her desires are not fulfilled. Ancient Greek women were thought to miscarry if they were frightened by a clap of thunder. Certain psychologists in Europe and the United States have attributed miscarriage to fear of pregnancy, marital conflicts, neurosis, or hostility toward one's mother.

Misunderstandings about the causes of miscarriage persist because of lack of sufficient medical information and because of the general tendency to see women's health problems as having psychological origins. Many Americans still believe that a miscarriage results from strenuous physical activity, nervousness, intercourse, or emotional shock. But physical and emotional trauma are now considered to be very unlikely reasons. Although many women remember a recent fall or shock, neither one is usually the cause of a miscarriage.

The evidence that does exist shows definite medical reasons for most miscarriages. The timing of a miscarriage gives the first clue as to possible cause. Seventy-five percent occur within the first twelve weeks, and about one half of these "early" miscarriages are due to an abnormality in the embryo or in the process of its implantation in the uterus. The fetus may be deformed because of genetic problems inherited from the parents, but more often a chance mutation has occurred during fertilization or the early growth of the embryo. Endometriosis, a condition in which pieces of the uterine lining locate themselves anywhere outside the uterine cavity, is a cause of early miscarriage.

In "late" miscarriages (from the thirteenth to the twentieth week) the fetus is usually normal but there are problems in its attachment to the placenta or to the uterus. There may also be abnormalities in the structure of the uterus itself, such as a double uterus. Sometimes the cervix is overly weak ("incompetent") and dilates too early. This may be a result of previous surgery on the cervix. In addition, if a woman's mother took the drug DES (diethylstilbestrol) while pregnant with her, she has an increased risk of having an incompetent cervix.

Either an early or a late miscarriage may occur if a woman contracts a serious disease or infection or suffers from severe malnutrition during the pregnancy. There is evidence that exposure of either the mother or father to radiation, to toxic chemicals, and to other environmental and occupational hazards increases the risks of both early and late miscarriage. Smoking, excessive alcohol consumption, and the ingestion of medications, including birth control pills, contribute to problems in some pregnancies.

The risk of miscarriage increases as a woman gets older, especially as she approaches her late thirties. Although many women who miscarry have deficiencies in certain hormones such as progesterone or estrogen, this may not be the actual cause of the miscarriage but a sign of some other medical problem that is the real cause of the miscarriage.

In the majority of cases, early or late, the woman is shocked by what her miscarriage entails. Few couples expect a miscarriage to occur at all. When it does, they are surprised by the event and frightened and overwhelmed by its intensity. In general, people expect it to involve some bleeding, perhaps some pain, and the expulsion of tissue—and then be over. Each woman's experience is different, and there is considerable variation in the amount of pain and bleeding and in the time it takes for a miscarriage to be completed. For most couples, however, the event is very different from anything they might have anticipated.

Carol and Richard are one such couple; their first pregnancy ended in a late miscarriage. They lived in Philadelphia in a restored townhouse and shared a successful law practice. Although they were both involved with their work, they wanted children too. When they were ready to start a family, Carol became pregnant quickly and felt wonderful for the first three months. They carefully chose a well-known obstetrician, associated with a leading medical center, because they wanted the best medical care possible.

Then one morning at the end of her fourth month, Carol woke up and noticed a few drops of blood on her nightgown:

> Somehow I was really not concerned about it. I thought everything would be fine for me. I called the doctor and felt the first jolt of fear when he told me to stay at home since it could be serious. However, after I spent a couple of days in bed, the bleeding stopped and I went back to work. That week I began to feel the baby move and I was sure everything was fine. We were really excited.
>
> A few days later, on a beautiful summer Sunday, Richard and I decided to go to an outdoor concert. Maybe that was a mistake, because when I got home I started to bleed again. I called the doctor and he said to stay in bed and drink some whiskey.

That night I had severe abdominal pain. The cramping was about every minute and a half, but I was not aware that these were really labor pains. I did keep in close touch with my doctor, but he didn't mention that this was probably a miscarriage. The pain went away the next day but started again the following evening. It continued for eight hours, until I finally fell asleep.

I woke up the next morning and I felt good—exhausted but fine. I was lying in bed, waiting for my husband to wake up. Then my bag of water burst. That was when I knew it was all over. I was surprised because I had only heard about that happening at the time of birth. I thought miscarriages would only consist of blood and a few clumps. I ran into the bathroom and a little fetus was expelled. The umbilical cord was still attached to the baby and me. The baby was alive! I knew I had to cut the cord. I felt I was killing the baby, but I knew it could not survive anyway. It was a little baby, very well formed and it was clean because it came out with the water. I could see the eyes and the tiny fingers and toes. I called my husband, and he nearly fainted when he went to get something to cut the cord with and something to put the fetus in.

I went back to bed and started bleeding profusely. When I called my doctor, he told me to go to the hospital immediately and he would meet me there for an examination. By the time I got to the hospital I was very faint from either the loss of blood or the trauma. They took me to the operating room, gave me a local anesthetic and performed a D & C [dilation and curettage, a procedure to remove tissue from the uterus].

Carol stayed in the hospital twenty-four hours. She was able to return to work a few days later. Physically, she was fine, but both she and her husband were emotionally very shaken. As Richard recounted:

In all the books we read we were not prepared in any way for what actually happened. If we had been prepared, if the doctor had told us what to expect, it would have been a little easier. We were very angry at the doctor for not explaining what was happening—all he could say was "drink whiskey."

The uncertainty during that whole time was really difficult—you don't know how to act about whether you're expecting a baby or not. I kept saying it's just spotting and it will clear up. Then when Carol was having the contractions, I kept thinking it's going to stop and be all right, but it didn't. At that point the biggest problem was hoping, hoping. If it had occurred right away and not dragged on for so long, it might have been easier to take.

Richard's reaction is not unusual, since the symptoms of a miscarriage are often ambiguous. It is easy to interpret the contractions as gas pains and the light bleeding as a minor problem that will go away. The physician may not be able to predict what will happen either. Feelings of anxiety and denial are therefore very strong during the early stages of a miscarriage.

The surprise Richard and Carol felt was all the greater because the miscarriage occurred so late in pregnancy. Most parents feel that after the first three months they can be more confident, announce the news of the pregnancy, and begin to enjoy the sight of a growing abdomen and the sensation of a moving infant. Carol and Richard's shock was intensified by the experience of seeing a fetus and a placenta; they had no idea that even in the fourth month one could go through what seemed like a delivery.

Even in an early miscarriage there is a strong element of surprise. The pain of contractions and the amount of bleeding are much greater than most women expect, especially since the pregnancy is barely obvious. Although they have not felt the baby move and might not see a formed fetus, the experience is still very frightening. Some might be surprised to see the fetus in the sac all expelled intact. The feelings afterward—the guilt, the anger, and the depression—resemble those of parents whose babies die at a later time in pregnancy.

Brenda and Don's experience is an example of an early miscarriage. They already had one child and were fully confident, when Brenda conceived a second time, that all would proceed normally. They had always wanted a large family, since both of them grew up in neighborhoods where having many children was valued. Don regretted being an only child, so even more than Brenda he looked forward to having a house filled with children. When their first child, Greg, was born after two years of marriage, they were delighted.

Brenda's second pregnancy, however, was a difficult one. She had had much more trouble conceiving than she had the first time. She also felt sick during most of her pregnancy and began to wonder if it was worth all the discomfort:

I'm really active. I like to bike ride and swim, and I really felt a little guilty. Although I wanted a child, there were times when I thought: "What did I get myself into? This is awful!" I was so sick to my stomach that I couldn't eat and yet I felt guilty about not eating. Then, when I had the miscarriage I felt bad about it. I'm sure it goes through everyone's mind, that guilt trip that you wished it upon yourself.

In my third month, I started bleeding lightly. This went on for four days. Then one morning I woke up with severe diarrhea and heavy bleeding. The bleeding was so heavy that I had to sit on the toilet to catch all the blood—it was really scary. I thought that something was seriously wrong with my body and that there was a good chance I might die. I also began to have strong contractions. The pain was tremendous, much worse than I remembered from when I had Greg; that really surprised me since I was only three months pregnant. I found myself crawling on the floor with pain; I couldn't even stand up.

I knew it was over when after many hours a little clump came out. I knew enough to collect it for the doctor. That was very difficult, but Don, who was at home, handed me a jar and asked if I wanted him to do it. I said no and didn't even let myself think about it. I reached in the toilet and collected what I could and didn't look.

I think the miscarriage was more painful than childbirth because there was so much anxiety and anger mixed up with it. Why is this happening to me? I did everything I thought I was supposed to do. I ate the right things and I didn't take aspirin, and I even took powdered milk with me on vacation to make sure I'd eat right.

I went over all the things I did before and during the miscarriage. I even wondered about the prenatal vitamins I was taking, since someone said that if you take them for a long period of time you can develop deficiencies in other vitamins. My doctor reassured me about that. But what bothered me the most was that the night before I started spotting I had had sex with my husband. I felt great; it was the best I had felt since I had been pregnant. That's always in the back of your mind—I thought, if I hadn't had sex, it might have been different.

When we were in the hospital, the doctor told me that the fetus had been dead for four weeks. I wanted to know the sex, but he said they couldn't tell. I really appreciated his honesty. He spent a lot of time with us and answered all our questions.

At least I knew that making love had nothing to do with it. It was strange; during my pregnancy my breasts had gotten bigger, but a few weeks before the miscarriage they seemed to get smaller, and I wasn't feeling sick anymore. At the time I didn't think about it, but now I know that my body was going back to its normal state.

A very common reaction to miscarriage is nagging fear and continual questioning—"How did this happen? Did I do something that caused it?" Brenda felt relieved that sexual intercourse was not the cause, but she continually looked for a reason. Unfortunately, a reason cannot always be found.

Frustrated at not being able to find any concrete explanation, many people blame themselves, even though they know they are not responsible. For instance, ambivalence about being pregnant is extremely common, and since a miscarriage usually occurs early in pregnancy, the couple may still be uncertain about whether they want a baby. Perhaps the pregnancy was an accident. Perhaps they had considered the possibility of having an abortion. If a miscarriage occurs, they may feel a strong sense of guilt about this ambivalence.

Often a woman feels guilty, wondering if she might have been able to prevent the miscarriage by going to the hospital earlier or by staying in bed. Many physicians do recommend bed rest, vitamins, restrictions on activity and intercourse, or changes in diet when the first signs of a possible miscarriage appear. This is sometimes done in the case of an early miscarriage simply to reassure the woman who is bleeding and to allay potential feelings of guilt should a miscarriage occur. According to a leading textbook, *Williams Obstetrics:* "Most women who are in fact actually threatening to abort probably progress into the next stage of the process no matter what is done." Dr. Alan Guttmacher in his book, *Pregnancy, Birth, and Family Planning*, agrees: "It is not possible to shake a good fertilized human ovum loose from the uterus any more than you can shake a good unripe apple loose from the apple tree."

Myths about the prevention of miscarriage are common in many societies. In the Philippines, one treatment for a woman about to have a miscarriage consists of giving her a boiled mixture of matted fiber from a particular palm tree and roots of another tree, while at the same time laying banana skins across the lower abdomen to cool the uterus. This approach is probably as effective as most others that have been tried.

It is very hard to do nothing if one is bleeding or has had a miscarriage in the past. Women may urge their doctors to give them something. But in general the best way to reduce miscarriages is by eating a well-balanced diet and avoiding smoking and exposure to drugs and toxic influences in the environment. These precautions would require a more comprehensive and accessible system of prenatal care as well as major changes in our approach to environmental and occupational hazards. Such actions, however, would only eliminate a small portion of miscarriages. Most simply cannot be prevented.

When a miscarriage does occur, the feelings of the couple resemble those of people in any bereavement situation. Even at an early stage of pregnancy, the fetus has become a person. Both Carol and Brenda felt this way. Carol remembers:

> By the end of three months of my pregnancy the baby was already going through college in my mind. During that period I had such an active fantasy life; I fell in love with that baby. When I saw the fetus, the fantasy became a person and it was more than the death of a fantasy: it was a real baby I lost.

Brenda recalls:

> We had a name for the baby already. We called it Jennifer and pretended she was already with us. When I was upstairs at home, Don would call up and ask if Jennifer wanted to come down and play with him. She was a real person to us already, even in that short amount of time. After I left the hospital, I felt so empty and lost. I really missed our little Jennifer—she was no longer there. I found myself crying for no particular reason for a long time.

For some expectant fathers, concern about the wife's physical and emotional well-being outweighs the feelings of grief. There is relief that she is not in danger after so much pain and bleeding, and there is hope for another child.

In one of the few studies of the emotional reactions to miscarriage, however, Dr. Albert Cain and his colleagues found "disturbed reactions" among some men, including filing for divorce, suspicions about the origins of the pregnancy, guilt due to relief that the pregnancy was over, and blaming their wives or themselves for causing the miscarriage.

Many men also express feelings of emptiness and sorrow. Richard, for instance, was very distraught after Carol's miscarriage. He asked the doctor about the sex of the child and learned that it was a girl, just what he had wanted. He remembers:

> When I left the hospital that first day and I passed the nursery, that was when it hit me that I had lost a child. The feeling of leaving the hospital with nothing. It was so empty. Nothing there. It was a waste. I had this rotten feeling; I felt I had lost everything. What a waste; I lost my kid. I lost my kid. I had a bad time getting home; I was crying. In the car I just focused on the word girl. Girl, girl. I didn't picture blond hair or a naked little baby. Just the word "girl."

Although miscarriage is the most common type of failed pregnancy, the grief associated with it is probably the least understood. Studies of the phenomenon are almost nonexistent. One study, in which undergraduate students, nursing students and faculty, and hospital personnel were asked about their attitudes toward miscarriage, revealed their recognition of the parents' needs for emotional support. The authors call this recognition "the silent sympathy" because it is so rarely expressed. Most interesting is their finding that the undergraduates were considerably more sympathetic than were the health care professionals. They suggest several possible explanations: the needs of women patients are generally misunderstood, the professionals may realize that most women who miscarry will soon bear a healthy child, nurses and other hospital staff may be reacting to their own inability to do anything about a miscarriage. As Dr. Cain writes about the medical response to miscarriage, "[It] has almost consistently been viewed as an isolated medical problem and treated in a mechanical, physical manner."

Even efforts to offer comfort may be unsuccessful, as Brenda discovered:

> The doctor talked to me and tried to say reassuring things like, "This is nature's way of getting rid of imperfect fetuses; it's really better this way." Later that helped me to understand what had happened. At first, though, when he said it, it seemed sort of ridiculous, like you should really be happy this happened.

Whatever the source of the failure of others to express sympathy, it leaves couples feeling alone and confused about their emotions. Many people never speak about their miscarriage at all and have a very difficult time resolving their grief. They may find it hard to tell people who didn't even know they were expecting that the pregnancy has ended. Often, however, they find comfort from talking with others who have themselves been through a miscarriage and who can understand the sadness, the fears, the anger, and the disappointment.

Talking about the experience helps make it seem more real. Since a pregnancy may end fairly abruptly with bleeding and then a D & E (dilation and evacuation), usually done under general anesthesia, it may be very hard to grasp what has happened. Some physicians recommend that parents see whatever is expelled or removed from the uterus so they know for sure the pregnancy is really over.

As can be seen from the experiences of Carol and Richard and Brenda and Don, miscarriage is not always the same. In fact, physicians distinguish among several types.

A threatened abortion (miscarriage) is the term used when a woman bleeds and may have cramps but the cervix is still closed; the process could stop and the pregnancy continue. At least half the women who bleed early in pregnancy will not miscarry and are in fact bleeding for reasons unrelated to the condition of the fetus. If the bleeding becomes heavy and continues for several days, and if the cervix opens and severe contractions begin, the miscarriage becomes an *inevitable abortion*. Hospitalization may be necessary, especially if all of the fetus and placenta are not expelled.

When these tissues remain, the term used is *incomplete abor-*

tion. Carol's late miscarriage was of this type. A D & E is performed in these cases to remove the contents that were not expelled. If a D & E is not performed, the uterus cannot contract, the placenta will continue to pump blood, and the cervix will not close. Hemorrhaging or infection may occur, posing a danger to the life of the woman.

A *complete abortion* is one in which all the afterbirth comes out and the cervix closes. The physician will usually determine that a D & E is not needed in these cases.

Another type of miscarriage is known as a *missed abortion.* This occurs when the fetus dies at least four weeks before being expelled. In cases of missed abortion, such as Brenda's, the fetus degenerates and emerges in the form of bloody clumps of tissue; in other cases it is a small embryo. Some women who have early miscarriages expel such an embryo at home. Usually a woman no longer feels pregnant, her breasts return to their normal size, the uterus does not grow, and a pregnancy test is negative. Most often the embryo aborts naturally; sometimes, however, labor has to be induced or a D & E performed.

If a woman has three or more consecutive miscarriages, her condition is called *habitual abortion.* If the miscarriages all occur early (in the first twelve weeks), indicating that the fetus may be abnormal each time, genetic counseling should be considered. If the miscarriages occur after the twelfth week, there may be a defect in the woman's cervix. A cervix that dilates too soon can be corrected eighty-five to ninety percent of the time by using a stitching procedure called cerclage to strengthen it until the time of delivery. Other problems such as a double uterus or immune system problems can also be the reason for repeated miscarriages. These conditions can be treated.

Since the reason for repeated miscarriages may be discovered about sixty percent of the time, physicians usually encourage a woman who miscarries more than once to have a complete medical examination to determine whether there are any treatable conditions. Both she and her partner may also choose to undergo genetic testing.

Whatever the cause, the experience of several successive miscarriages creates new and painful emotions. Nancy and Tony talked about how their feelings changed after their second miscarriage—the increased panic and belief that something could be medically wrong.

When they married, Nancy was working as a secretary but planned to quit and raise a family. She and Tony, an electrician, saved for several years to buy a home; then they decided to have their first child. When Nancy's first three pregnancies ended in miscarriages, they felt they had to reconcile themselves to the possibility that they might never have children. This was especially difficult for Nancy to accept since she had never thought about what she might do if she weren't a mother.

Nancy's first miscarriage happened immediately after she discovered she was pregnant:

> We hadn't even had a chance to be happy about being pregnant. It all happened so suddenly and left us speechless. We were both depressed for a few days but talked about it and decided to follow the doctor's advice and try again as quickly as we could.
>
> Six months later I became pregnant again. And again very soon after I found out I was pregnant I had a miscarriage. This time I was beginning to panic, and I told Tony I just couldn't face another pregnancy. But he wanted me to try again, and the doctor told me that it could simply have been a matter of chance and that I had a good likelihood of success the next time.
>
> The third one just about destroyed me. I felt my body had betrayed me. It was not working the way it was supposed to. I couldn't stop crying. I was terrified. I thought I would never have a baby. I didn't know how to handle it. It's really scary that your body is betraying you. Three in a row. It seems like this will be my fate in life, that all my pregnancies will end in miscarriage.
>
> Sometimes I wonder even now after four years, and despite the fact that we have a child, which ones were boys and which ones were girls, and if they had gone to term what I would have called them.
>
> But we had had studies done on the fetuses and found out that they would have been abnormal. If one of them had been born retarded, then maybe I would not have gotten pregnant again, and I wouldn't have my daughter, Janie, who is perfectly healthy.
>
> But we always look for a reason why. I had allergies and thought that might be connected. Sometimes I began to wonder if I had a psychological problem. Did I do something wrong? Had I been too selfish? Was I being punished?

It seemed like I was either pregnant or recovering half the time; I was always sick, and my period was almost nonexistent. So when Janie was conceived, I wasn't even trying to get pregnant. What a joy when she was actually born! I couldn't believe it!

Habitual miscarriage means repeated physical and mental trauma. It also signals the possibility that there may never be children. As with couples who experience fertility problems, those who have several miscarriages must not only cope with their grief but also face difficult questions about their future plans.

Anyone who has been through a miscarriage is likely to fear that it will happen again, that pregnancy will always mean failure. Yet a woman who has had one miscarriage is probably no more likely to miscarry during the next pregnancy than anyone else. It is only after the second miscarriage that the odds of another one begin to increase somewhat. With each successive miscarriage, the chance of a successful pregnancy is further reduced.

Nancy and Tony were fortunate; after three miscarriages, they are now delighted with their daughter and are talking about having another baby. They are apprehensive about another pregnancy, but Janie's birth gives them hope for a successful pregnancy.

On the other hand, two years after her miscarriage, Carol is still depressed and plagued by feelings of guilt. Even though she has since had a healthy child, she had suppressed her feelings about her miscarriage and is not coping well. She has finally sought counseling to help her since she worries about the effects of her depression on the new child.

Brenda and Don recovered more quickly and planned to try again. They discovered she could not conceive, and they worried about Greg's being an only child and their not having the big family they wanted. After several years of anxiety and considerable help from a fertility specialist, they now have two more children and feel their troubles have faded into the past. Like almost all couples who experience a miscarriage, they were eventually able to have children.

The experiences of these couples represent some of the physical and emotional reactions involved in a miscarriage. The impact on some was more significant than on others; the length of time it took for them to recover also varied considerably. But it is evident that all six individuals felt the pain of loss and the need for sympathetic understanding. They were all surprised at the intensity of their emotions after an event that had once seemed insignificant to them when they had heard about it happening to others. Even though they all had children after the miscarriages, they still recall the details of their experience very clearly. They still wonder why it happened and whether it will happen again.

3

Ectopic Pregnancy

"I hadn't the faintest idea what was wrong with me, but I thought I was going to die. The pain in my stomach was so bad that I couldn't stop screaming. I finally fainted. An ambulance took me to the hospital, and the next thing I remember is being in the recovery room. They told me I had an ectopic pregnancy and had lost three pints of blood and one of my tubes. I couldn't believe it—I didn't even know I was pregnant. I remember hearing my husband say, 'God's been good to us. We almost lost you.' "

Ectopic pregnancy is a life-threatening condition which has almost quadrupled in number since 1970. It is difficult to diagnose and can destroy a couple's chance of ever having children. Yet even though seventy thousand women have an ectopic each year in the United States, its enormous emotional impact is rarely discussed.

An ectopic pregnancy is one that occurs when the embryo develops outside the uterus. In ninety-five percent of all cases, the embryo grows in the fallopian tube. As it becomes bigger, it exerts pressure on the tubal walls, which do not have the ability to expand and stretch as the uterus does. Unless detected and treated early enough, the tube will burst, leading to internal hemorrhaging. The other five percent of the time, the embryo implants in the ovary, the abdomen, or the cervix, also causing serious complications as it grows. In the past, death often resulted from ectopic pregnancy. One report published over one hundred years ago indicated that sixty-nine percent of women with ectopics died as a result. With better diagnostic and treatment techniques, the death rate has fortunately dropped sharply, to less than one in a thousand, even though the number of ectopic pregnancies continues to rise.

The experience is still a traumatic one for most families. Maria and Joe are one couple who described what happened to them. They had been about to leave on vacation to celebrate Maria's thirtieth birthday, when they found out that Maria was pregnant after three years of trying. They were both high with excitement as they flew off for a week by the ocean. Maria recalls:

> When we arrived at the hotel, I noticed that I was spotting and started feeling scared. I called my doctor back home, and he said not to worry, just to take it easy. I tried to stay in bed and lie quietly on the beach. But the next day the spotting was heavier and I began to fear I might be having a miscarriage. Joe became very alarmed and insisted that we fly home immediately since I would be better off in my own home and with my own doctor.

Joe explains what happened next:

> When the plane landed, we drove directly to the emergency room. The doctor there examined Maria and said her cervix was not dilated, so he reassured us that everything was all right. I began to feel foolish about spoiling our vacation, but we had wanted this baby for a long time and I didn't want to take any chances.

Maria continued:

> I was getting dressed the next morning to go see my own doctor when I began to feel a lot of pain and passed a very large blood clot. I thought, This is it. My heart sank. I was exhausted from the trip and very upset about losing the baby. The doctor sent me to the hospital for an ultrasound which showed that my uterus was empty. They admitted me and did a D & C that night. The doctor said he had considered that I might have an ectopic but because of the clots and my cervix dilating he decided it wasn't.
>
> I was relieved at least to think it was over, and I kept thinking

about the doctor saying I shouldn't have any problems with another pregnancy. At least I could get pregnant again. But I was still very upset.

Two days later I was driving home from work and began to feel pain in my stomach. It kept getting worse, and I realized I wasn't going to make it home. I pulled over to the side of the road by a telephone booth and tried to get out of the car. The pain was so bad I almost passed out. I was terrified that I would collapse by the road and no one would find me. I hung onto the car door until I could finally see straight again. I made my way slowly to the phone, overwhelmed by excruciating pain. Miraculously, someone saw me and realized I needed help. She called my husband, while I went and lay down in the back seat of the car until Joe finally arrived.

Joe had never been so frightened. He drove Maria straight to the emergency room, and the staff there called her obstetrician. He arrived within a few minutes and was clearly shaken. Joe describes what happened then:

Maria was rushed to surgery and they wouldn't let me go with her. It seemed forever until the doctor came out again. Losing the baby was hard, but I began to realize that Maria might not make it. I felt like my life was falling apart.

Finally the doctor came out and told me he had done a laparoscopy to look inside her tubes and found an enormous amount of blood in Maria's abdomen. Her tube had burst from an ectopic pregnancy—it hadn't been a miscarriage after all. He had to remove what was left of the tube. I was so relieved that Maria was going to be okay. But at the same time I was angry. I couldn't understand why he hadn't done the laparoscopy days before and avoided all this.

Maria and Joe's experience is not that unusual, since ectopic pregnancies are often difficult to diagnose. Many times a woman does not even realize that she is pregnant, and the doctors may think that the pain is from pelvic infections or appendicitis. As in Maria's case, where the pregnancy is known, it may be assumed at first that the woman is experiencing a miscarriage. In very rare cases, an ultrasound shows a sac in the uterus suggesting a normal pregnancy, while a twin embryo is still caught in the tube.

Part of the difficulty with making a diagnosis is that the

symptoms of an ectopic pregnancy are not always the same. Some women have bleeding, others do not. The type of pain varies and may occur in different parts of the abdomen and even in the shoulders. Pregnancy tests are sometimes inaccurate. Recently developed tests are more sensitive and are able to pick up the low levels of the hormone HCG which are present with an ectopic pregnancy. Physicians now rely on the combined use of these newer sophisticated pregnancy tests and on ultrasound to see if there is a sac growing in the uterus. However, these tests may have to be repeated several times before a diagnosis is confirmed. Laparoscopy is an invasive procedure carried out under general anesthesia which allows the physician to visualize the tubes and obtain the most definitive diagnosis. It isusually done only when a uterine pregnancy is ruled out and anectopic pregnancy strongly suspected.

Because diagnostic techniques have improved and physicians are much more likely now to be checking for ectopic pregnancy, the chance of a tube rupturing has declined somewhat. If a rupture occurs, being able to assess quickly what is happening has greatly improved the chances of survival. Even so, misdiagnosis is a major reason that as many as forty women a year die from ectopic pregnancy in the United States.

Maria realized that her life had been in danger and felt fortunate to be recovering well from the surgery. She had many questions that bothered her, though:

> I couldn't stop asking myself why this had happened to me, why the baby hadn't been able to grow in my uterus. What had gone wrong? My doctor explained that ectopic pregnancy is often a result of an earlier pelvic infection. I may have had an infection at some time and not even realized it. Maybe that's why I had a hard time getting pregnant, but no one seems to know for sure. I always felt so healthy, I couldn't believe this was happening to me. It's ironic—the doctor said that just two inches further and the embryo would have made it to the uterus and I would have had a healthy baby. Just two inches!

A good explanation of why an ectopic pregnancy might occur appears in Alan Guttmacher's book *Pregnancy, Birth, and Family Planning:*

The interior of the tube is a complex labyrinth with many folds in its lining. It is not surprising that an occasional embryo loses its way, becomes stuck in the maze, and makes efforts to implant there. However, the association of ectopic pregnancy with previous tubal infection makes it likely that adhesions among the folds of the lining of the tube, due to the infection, create pockets in which the embryo is trapped.

The rise in ectopic pregnancy has been blamed in part on the national increase in PID—pelvic inflammatory disease—which is linked to sexually transmitted diseases such as gonorrhea. Infection may come from other causes as well, for example, previous abdominal surgery or intrauterine devices.

In the past, undiagnosed or untreated infections often resulted in tubes being totally blocked. With better diagnosis and the rise of antibiotics, tubes are now likely to be saved, but the scarring that remains increases the chance of ectopic pregnancy.

Other conditions besides PID may cause ectopic pregnancy: having a mother who took DES during her pregnancy, trying in vitro (test tube) fertilization, or having endometriosis. Sometimes a woman who had her tubes tied (tubal ligation) becomes pregnant and the embryo gets caught in the tube. A growing number of women are attempting to reverse tubal ligations, and this may also contribute to the increased rates. Various hormone treatments may increase the possibility of an ectopic pregnancy. As women get older, they have more time to be exposed to one of these causes, and their chance of having an ectopic pregnancy increases. Black women have almost twice the rate of white women. In fact, black women thirty-five and older have five times the rate of white women under the age of twenty-five.

All of the factors which contribute to ectopic pregnancy have increased in the last two decades. It is not surprising, then, that the rate of ectopics rose from one-half of one percent in 1970 to almost two percent in 1983, the latest year for which the numbers are available. This represents a dramatic increase from 17,800 a year to 69,600 in one year.

With the growing concern about the dangers of ectopic pregnancy, people may lose sight of the feelings of loss experienced by the parents. It is a confusing time for many people; especially if they were not even aware of the pregnancy, the loss of a baby may seem less important than the trauma of the actual event. For some, the worries about fertility are foremost in their minds. Maria explained her reaction:

> For many months after the ectopic I had a very hard time. Although Joe was sympathetic, I still felt totally alone. I just cried and cried. Everyone else was so relieved that I had survived that they didn't want to think that there was a baby there. I feel so empty now, missing that baby I could have had, still wondering what I might have done to cause this. I had slept with other men before I met Joe. Was God punishing me for what I thought was fine then?

Joe was quiet but he had strong feelings about the loss:

> My first reaction was to want to run away. When I left the hospital, I thought, I have money in my pocket and a full tank of gas, I'll just take off. But I knew I couldn't do that. For a while I thought I was going crazy. It was too much to take—within a week we had gone from being completely happy to a feeling of despair. What kept me going was the gratefulness I felt that Maria's life had been spared and the hope that some day we might be able to have another child.

Worries about being able to become pregnant again are a major concern for families who have been through an ectopic pregnancy. In some cases both tubes are removed. Even when one remains, the chances of a normal pregnancy are greatly reduced, and the possibility exists for an ectopic pregnancy to occur in the other tube. There are no exact numbers, but the studies which have been done found that between one-third and one-half of women who have had an ectopic pregnancy eventually have a baby. The possibility becomes smaller with each subsequent ectopic pregnancy. These numbers may improve somewhat due to the availability of *in vitro* fertilization, but the success rate of this procedure is still low.

Newer surgical methods such as salpingostomy are making it possible to save the fallopian tube if it did not rupture. So far it has not been established whether this method increases the chances of a successful pregnancy compared to those of women who have had one tube removed (in a procedure called salpingectomy). Some physicians are trying drugs to dissolve the embryo in order to avoid surgery. However, this is still experimental.

An ectopic pregnancy is a traumatic event, both physically and emotionally. It often leads to infertility and all of the stresses associated with fertility decisions and treatments. At the same time, the parents are grieving for their baby, just as other parents do who have experienced a loss. They are sad for the past and fearful for the future.

Maria and Joe consider themselves to be very fortunate. After a year of treatment to help her ovulate, Maria conceived again. She watched carefully for any sign of pain or bleeding, and Joe checked constantly to make sure she was okay. When they saw on an ultrasound that the baby was growing normally in Maria's uterus, they were thrilled. Their celebration of the pregnancy was more subdued this time, however, until Christopher was born.

Joe says now what many others who have experienced a loss also feel:

> When we think about that time, we realize how young and naive we were. We thought nothing could hurt us. Now we have a much greater appreciation of life, of Christopher, and of each other. We don't take our family for granted anymore.

4

Prenatal Diagnosis and the Unwanted Abortion

"When God made all the decisions, women had no choice but to accept them. If an Act of God gave you a defective child you learned to live with perpetual grief. But there was little guilt or spiritual laceration. Now, however, that science and technology tell mothers they do not have to accept that fate, the Act of God is transformed into an act of her own. The decisions she may have to make can be harrowing."

Jessie Bernard,
The Future of Motherhood

In the past, if a husband and wife were aware of a genetic problem in the family, they often avoided having any children at all. The fear of having an abnormal baby outweighed their desire for children, and they suffered the sorrow of not raising the family they wanted. If a couple gave birth to a deformed child, they accepted him or her as best they could.

Yet in the past two decades the technological capability for prenatal diagnosis has developed at an extremely rapid rate, and, since 1973, legal abortion during the first part of a pregnancy has become available to most women. A diagnosis of abnormalities can thus be followed by an abortion (referred to as a selective abortion). As a result, a whole new set of options, experiences, decisions, and controversies has arisen in recent years.

In addition to the many practical and financial problems involved in prenatal diagnosis, parents suffer the emotional stress of considering whether they will abort if a wanted child is diagnosed as having problems. If they go through with an abortion, they must deal with the same feelings of grief experienced by other parents who lose a child, compounded by the feelings of guilt for their participation in the infant's death. This is another—and increasingly frequent—tragic ending of pregnancy.

The first decision for many parents is whether to have prenatal testing. The pressures on women to undergo testing are increasing. Sociologist Barbara Katz Rothman points out that there is a growing emphasis on "quality control" in the production of babies, with less and less tolerance for imperfections. Prenatal diagnosis is presented as a choice and an advantage, but for many women it turns a normal pregnancy into a time of great trauma and uncertainty.

There are many reasons why a woman might have prenatal tests. The most common is her age, since women have a greater chance of bearing abnormal children as they get older. Legal decisions have determined that physicians must advise women thirty-five and older of the risks of childbearing and of the possibility of prenatal tests.

There are other situations that might lead a physician to advise parents to consider prenatal testing. A previous pregnancy that produced an abnormal child, a history of genetic disease in the family, the experience of three or more miscarriages, or the presence of male relatives with such sex-linked diseases as hemophilia are all reasons for suggesting prenatal diagnosis.

A couple in any of these situations may want to consult a genetic counselor even before beginning a pregnancy, especially if they are undecided as to whether or not to conceive. Usually the counselor reviews the health of the couple, including any known diseases or disorders, and takes a detailed family history. Explanations regarding the possible causes of previous problems are provided when known. Blood and skin tests may be done. If the woman is already pregnant and prenatal testing is recommended, the counselor can suggest how to obtain it and will help a couple to interpret the results and the options available to them.

Two tests which allow a woman to establish the condition of her fetus are chorionic villus sampling and amniocentesis. Chorionic villus sampling (also known as CVS or chorionic biopsy) is a relatively new procedure which makes it possible to examine the chromosomes of a fetus during the first trimester and to determine within two weeks if certain genetic abnormalities are present. A catheter is inserted through the cervix, and a small amount of preplacental tissue is sucked into the catheter and removed for study. Amniocentesis is a procedure usually carried out later in pregnancy that involves the insertion of a hollow needle through the abdominal wall and uterus to obtain amniotic fluid for the determination of many kinds of anomalies.

The decision to have CVS or amniocentesis can be very difficult for a couple to make and often causes anxiety and fear. The procedures themselves, although not usually painful, sound frightening. Women should be aware that there may be risks to themselves or the baby as a result of the procedures, but the overall risks in an experienced center have been reduced to less than one percent. At the age of thirty-five and after, the chances of bearing a deformed child are greater than the risks of prenatal testing.

Other types of tests may be used in prenatal diagnosis. Ultrasound has become very widely used for the detection of a variety of problems and abnormalities. Ultrasound (also known as sonography) is similar to an X ray in that it produces a picture of the fetus in the uterus so that the locations of the fetus and placenta are determined. When used with amniocentesis, it helps the physician place the needle correctly. Ultrasound may also be used without amniocentesis to establish the exact fetal age (by measuring the size of the fetus's head) and to determine multiple births; it can sometimes also detect complicated uterine abnormalities. The absolute safety of ultrasound is yet to be proven, but most physicians believe that it is harmless. A panel of experts convened by the National Institutes of Health recommended that it be used only when necessary because of uncertainty about its effects.

Fetoscopy or placental aspiration is a technique that allows a direct view of the fetus and other contents of the uterus and the extraction of a small fetal blood sample. It has the potential of detecting problems that cannot be uncovered by amniocentesis or ultrasound. This procedure is still in the early stages of research development and is not yet widely available. Risks to the fetus are much greater than they are with amniocentesis; miscarriages result in five to ten percent of these pregnancies, and there may also be some health risks for the mother. Fetal blood sampling is also being performed now by the insertion of a needle into the umbilical cord.

A blood test called Maternal Serum Alpha Fetoprotein (MSAFP) is being used increasingly to screen pregnant women for the presence of neural tube defects such as anencephaly or spina bifida and for Down's syndrome. This test has the advantage of needing only a blood sample, but many physicians are reluctant to use it because of the large proportion of "false positives." Most women whose tests show extra high or low alpha fetoprotein levels do not usually have an abnormal baby, yet they must endure further testing and great anxiety.

Waiting for the results of the amniocentesis is a time of considerable anxiety. Nancy B., a twenty-eight-year-old mother whose first baby had Down's syndrome, told of her experience after having amniocentesis during her second pregnancy:

> They told me that the results would take three weeks. I had a friend who got the results in two weeks, so when two weeks passed I waited by the phone. By the third week to the day no one called. Every time the phone would ring my heart was in my mouth, I was going crazy. I finally decided near the end of that day to call them.

Nancy's anxiety is typical of the parents' feelings while awaiting test results. Her subsequent experience is less typical, but it suggests that the feelings of parents in this situation are not always realized:

> I reached the social worker and she said, "Mrs. B., we were going to call you tonight." Right away I knew that something was wrong. I said, "Is it Down's syndrome?" and she said, "No,

something else." I asked her what and she said she could not discuss it over the phone and asked if we could come down the next day at one o'clock. I said yes. I hung up the phone, and I was hysterical when I called my husband. We both could not believe that we would have to wait until one o'clock the next day. He came home and called back, but only a laboratory assistant was in. She knew the results but also said that she could not tell me. I asked him to ask her, "Is it spina bifida?" She said no. I didn't know what else to ask. The two of us were going out of our minds. We thought, What a way to treat people. It turned out the cells didn't grow and we had to do a test over again.

In less than five percent of fetuses tested through amniocentesis, the existence of an abnormality is revealed. How couples are told about this unfavorable result is very important. It is equally important that the physician advise the couple of their options and provide all information regarding the problems directly, openly, and compassionately. It is very difficult to be told such shocking news, absorb all the medical information, and then make a decision in a short period of time. A couple should be encouraged to request information or explanations in subsequent conversations with the physician. Unfortunately, there is not a great deal of time to spare if an abortion is being considered.

Most couples receive the news either from an obstetrician or from a genetic counselor. They are professionals who usually try to remain impartial about the decision to have an abortion, yet each has his or her own biases that stem from personal and religious backgrounds. Families need to realize that the way this person presents the facts—what is stressed, what is told first, which options are discussed and how—might influence their decision. If they are unsure about the advice, a second opinion can be helpful.

The quality of genetic counseling varies greatly throughout the United States. Even in the best centers, personal contacts are limited to the moments of decision-making, although the time between the test and the report of results and the period following an abortion are when couples experience the greatest stress. This is the very time they receive the least support.

Some couples may have reason to seek advice about aborting

a wanted baby without having prenatal tests. For instance, a woman who contracts German measles (rubella) early in her pregnancy is likely to give birth to a deformed child. Exposure to occupational or environmental hazards—radiation or certain toxic chemicals—or the ingestion of certain medications during pregnancy are reasons to suspect that the health of the fetus may be endangered.

For some women, the danger of any pregnancy to their own health may lead them to consider abortion. The therapeutic abortion, as this situation is called, has long been considered a major reason for termination of pregnancy and is least likely to be opposed on religious or moral grounds. It may occur at any time during the pregnancy and therefore is an experience that varies enormously from one woman to another. Fortunately, medical technology has advanced to the point where therapeutic abortion is not necessary as often as it was in the past.

By the time most couples are faced with a decision about abortion, the baby usually has started to kick and the movements become a dramatic reminder that he or she is alive. In addition, friends and relatives have noticed or been informed of the pregnancy and have given their congratulations. At that point, if the parents choose abortion, their private pain becomes public knowledge.

According to a report issued by the National Institutes of Health, ninety-five percent of the women who learn through amniocentesis that the fetus is abnormal choose to have an abortion. The decision is easier for some couples to make than for others. Some ask genetic counselors what they would do; others have their minds made up even before the results are available. Background and religious feelings may play a role in the decision. Just as waiting for results of tests is very difficult, the time between deciding to abort and completing the procedure is filled with frustration and apprehension. Ordinarily a couple tries to schedule the abortion as quickly as possible in order to shorten this terrible period.

Having an abortion after the twelfth week of pregnancy is usually a very different experience from having one in the first three months. The risks are greater, the procedure is entirely different, and the woman is often very surprised to find herself in the labor and delivery rooms of a hospital. In normal deliveries, if there is preparation for labor, including breathing exercises, the woman is more relaxed and better able to cope with the pain of delivery. But the anxiety that accompanies a selective abortion is often compounded by a lack of this kind of physical and psychological preparation—often the woman is never told it would be similar to a normal delivery. Therefore, her labor pains may be more intense than they would have been for a full-term baby.

Karen's account illustrates what many women experience during a selective abortion. She had noticed a rash one day during her third month of pregnancy. Although her doctor assured her that rashes are common in pregnancy, Karen worked with children and recognized her symptoms as German measles. After some resistance, her obstetrician referred her to a dermatologist, who, in turn, sent her to a pediatrician. Feeling frustrated and angry at not getting definite answers, she sought out a rubella specialist on her own. The specialist confirmed a severe case of primary rubella. By this time, almost a month had passed since the rash first appeared. She recalls:

> From the moment we knew it was definite that I had the measles, my husband and I knew that we would have an abortion. I wanted the abortion as soon as possible. I couldn't bear to walk around a day longer. I was showing and everybody knew I was pregnant. The baby had been kicking. They said that they could schedule me a week later. I screamed that it was not possible for me to go around being pregnant. I told him, "I have already made my decision, I am carrying this deformed baby around, I do not want it, I cannot look at myself, I'll kill myself if you make me wait until next week." I knew this was very dramatic, but this was how I felt. But they still couldn't admit me for another week. I cried more during that week than I cried in a lifetime. You have this idea that you have a baby but you don't. The idea of trying to realize it's happening, to understand why. The waiting was unbearable.
>
> One week later, at eight o'clock in the morning, they checked me into my room on the maternity floor. I felt terrible—that I was killing this child. I was also totally unprepared for what would happen, even though I had been told the technical details.

They told me the experience would feel somewhere between menstrual cramps and easy labor. Was that ever a joke! I went into a labor room and first they drew some fluid out of my abdomen. I was scared, but it was not painful. Then they put the hormone in. At that point they asked permission if they could have the fetus afterward to study and I said yes. It made me feel good to know that maybe I was doing some good.

Karen's abortion was carried out with the use of a hormone called prostaglandin, which is considered by many physicians to be the fastest and safest method for inducing delivery. It is now usually given in the form of a suppository. Saline abortion, which used to be more common, is now sometimes used for abortions carried out after the twentieth week of pregnancy. With this method, a salt solution is injected into the uterus to replace amniotic fluid. This causes the placenta to separate from the womb, leading to the death of the fetus. These methods may have uncomfortable side effects, such as nausea, fever, and diarrhea.

For a second trimester abortion, a dilation and evacuation (D & E) is the procedure that has the fewest side effects and is completed in the shortest amount of time. In a D & E, the cervix is dilated and suction is used to remove the fetus. Because of delays in obtaining the results of amniocentesis, many selective abortions occur after the twentieth week when the D & E— and abortions generally—are often unavailable because of questions about safety and because of the reluctance of hospital staffs to perform abortions so late in a pregnancy.

Except with a D & E, a late abortion can take several days to be completed, as in Karen's case:

Nothing happened that day. I had no idea it would take so long to deliver. That night I could not sleep. At four o'clock in the morning I went into hard labor. The contractions were horrible. I couldn't believe how out of control I was. I was in the labor room and a woman came in and started to put the fetal heart monitor on me. I told her I didn't think she should be putting that on, and she said it was a common procedure. I said I wanted it off—if the baby is alive, I don't want to know about it. I couldn't bear to hear its heartbeat. I demanded to see the supervisor; she came in, saw it on me, and took a scissors and snipped it off. She was very apologetic. I just wasn't able to tell the first nurse, who didn't seem to know why I was there, that I was having an abortion.

From that moment, one nurse stayed with me. Suddenly I felt like pushing and I knew something was happening. I was on my back and couldn't see anything. I went from intense pain to euphoria. The thing that went through my head the whole time was that it would soon be over and then it would be a memory.

They let me go home the next day. I felt very depressed and sorry for myself. The next few months after that were very difficult. I didn't quite understand how bad I felt. I found those months to be as difficult as the whole experience. I was very much alone. I still find it hard to believe that this really happened to me.

In cases of selective abortion, there is grief for a wanted child, questions about the characteristics of the baby—not usually seen by the parents—worries about future pregnancies, ambivalence about abortion itself, and guilt—terrible guilt.

Guilt may be particularly strong when the condition of the fetus is not definitely known. For instance, when a woman knows she is a carrier of a sex-linked disorder, such as hemophilia, it can be predicted that on the average, half of all her male children will be afflicted with that disorder. Amniocentesis can reveal the sex of the infant, but not the presence of that disease. Some parents make the difficult decision to abort a male fetus because of the chance that he might be affected. Fortunately, new techniques of prenatal detection for hemophilia are gradually erasing the need for making that agonizing choice.

Many parents are upset and frustrated by the lack of information they are given and feel unable to make a well-considered decision in such a short period of time. Their frustration is intensified by the controversy surrounding abortion. Poor women in particular have been deprived of choice because of the unwillingness of Congress to allow Medicaid funding for abortions after the diagnosis of a defect. Only in a few states are public monies available to pay for abortions for the poor. In some areas it may be very difficult to find a physician who will agree to perform a late abortion.

Most people who may need abortions for medical reasons resent being put in the same category as those who use abortion as a means of birth control. They are also angry at pressure groups seeking to eliminate the possibility of legal abortion.

Supporters of genetic counseling and diagnosis point out that ninety-five percent of fetuses are found to be normal. Because of tests such as ultrasound and amniocentesis, parents who might otherwise have avoided pregnancy or automatically have had an abortion are now able to have healthy children. As one report stated, the "Russian roulette atmosphere" for couples who fear birth defects can now be eliminated.

Although parents who do have an abortion believe that it was the right decision, they are shocked and overwhelmed by the experience. They may have a very difficult time talking out their feelings with others and making the event real for themselves. They may feel that they will be criticized rather than supported, that no one will understand or sympathize with their grief. As one woman said:

> It was very hard to talk to anyone about it. When I did tell someone, it seemed they were either shocked or else they tried to tell me it was all for the best. No one understands that I miss that baby. He was so much a part of me.

The feelings expressed by this woman will be experienced by a growing number of couples as the practice of prenatal diagnosis increases. Yet limitations on the accessibility of abortion services are likely to augment the frustrations of families who desperately want to have a healthy child. As the dilemmas surrounding the creation, the ending, and the quality of life continue to be subjects for public debate, they will also continue to be sources of personal anguish for many families.

5

Stillbirth

"To everything there is a season, and a time to every purpose under the heaven. A time to be born and a time to die." These well-known words from the Bible affirm the expected order of life. Between birth and death there is a time to live, "a time to sow and a time to reap ... a time to weep and a time to laugh." But when the time to be born is also the time to die, when the beginning of life is the same as its end, when the time to love never comes, then this order is violated. The cry of the longed-for baby becomes a sob of bereavement from the family; the anticipated baptism becomes a dreaded funeral. This is a stillbirth.

> They hung a bright yellow butterfly from the ceiling and declared the baby's room ready. He had labored for weeks on sanding and painting the crib. The drawers were filled with tiny undershirts and night clothes, the changing table stocked with pins and lotion. Together they wound up the mobile over the crib and once again listened to the music of "Winnie the Pooh." The baby would love this room, so full of colorful things. Satisfied with their work, impatient for the last few weeks of waiting to be over, they went to bed. As he had done every night for months, John leaned over and whispered into Glenda's navel, "Good night, Robert or Elizabeth."

Glenda and John's experience illustrates some of the feelings and events that can occur in the case of a stillbirth. They had been married four years and felt they were ready to start a family. In the eighth month of her pregnancy Glenda quit her teaching job. John, although worried a little about losing the income from Glenda's teaching, looked forward to their first son or daughter. Like most women, Glenda remembered almost every detail as she recounted her experience five years after the events:

Time seemed to stop as my due date approached. The big day came and passed and still there was no sign of labor. I was so large and uncomfortable that I rarely went out of the house. I was not used to staying home and now I was very impatient. Two weeks passed and I went into the hospital for a stress test because of the risk that a baby more than two weeks overdue might not be getting enough oxygen and nutrition through the umbilical cord. The test results showed no problems, and John and I went back home to wait. The doctor said he did not want to induce labor or perform a Caesarean because of the risks involved, and we agreed. We were looking forward to having a natural childbirth experience. The pillows and the bag of items that the Lamaze instructor had suggested were already in the car, and the suitcase was packed. But we became increasingly nervous as each day slowly passed. Finally I went into labor.

I was very excited but calm—I was really doing it! The contractions were five minutes apart; I watched some television and called John to tell him to come home. Then I ate a little bit of Jell-O, like I was supposed to. The contractions were about three minutes apart. John came running home after closing his store and we went to the emergency room at the hospital as planned. My labor was going fine but then, when the nurse checked the baby's heartbeat, she didn't hear anything. She was very calm and said, "Just a minute, I have to get another instrument to check this further." And then she left the room. I was not worried. Sometimes my doctor, during previous prenatal exams, had had trouble finding the heartbeat.

The nurse came back with the doctor, who was as white as a ghost. I asked him why he was so white, and he remarked that he had not been in the sun lately. He examined me and said I was almost ready to give birth. They rushed me to the labor room and attached another fetal heart monitor. There was still no sign of a heartbeat! All the nurses were rushing around. They tossed my Lamaze bag on a counter and threw my pillows away. I knew something was wrong. I found the courage to say to the doctor,

"If there is anything wrong you have to tell me, because we are going to have to deal with it and I have to know." He said sadly. "We are expecting the worst."

John and I looked at each other—neither of us could say a word. It was as if we were paralyzed. I kept thinking, How am I going to tell my mom? I wasn't crying at first. I couldn't quite believe it and was hanging on that slight chance that the baby was all right. I was not given any anesthesia because the doctor thought that there was a small possibility of the baby's being alive and believed it was best that I go ahead with a natural delivery.

The labor was long and painful, and although the doctor was not there very much, the nurses were really helpful and understanding. John said I carried on terribly, that I was crying and saying things like "This is for nothing." I felt pretty bad, and I was just waiting for it to be over; it was just a useless formality that had to be gone through. Finally, the baby was delivered, and from the reaction of the doctor and nurses I knew it was dead. John told me the baby was a boy.

I wanted to see my baby after he was delivered, but John wasn't so sure that I should. When the nurse suggested that it would be good for us to see and hold him, John agreed. We waited as the baby was washed, dressed, and wrapped in a blanket. I was extremely anxious while we waited. The nurse talked with us then and told us that because he was overdue his skin would be peeling.

Finally they brought the baby in. He was all wrapped up in a blanket and the nurse gave him to me to hold. I wanted to see him without the blanket to see if he was really all right. I asked if I could look at his feet and the nurse unfolded the blanket a little so I could see them. I really wanted to see him completely without the blanket but I was too embarrassed to ask. He looked just like he was sleeping.

The nurse stayed with us the entire time that we held our baby. Although she was very nice and helpful, I wish she had left and given us some time to be alone with our baby. Of course, we never thought to ask her.

We looked carefully at all of his features—he had John's nose and my mouth and chin. Then we returned him quickly to the nurse. We felt so awkward and unsure about what we were supposed to do. But I'll always remember how he looked. He was a perfect baby—just beautiful.

Until the past few years, stillborn babies were kept hidden from their parents, and the experience Glenda and John had in seeing their son would have been unusual. Even during normal birth, fathers were not allowed in the delivery room, and mothers were either under anesthesia or covered with a drape to hide from them any view of the baby as he or she was being born. In addition, it was generally believed that seeing a dead infant would leave an imprint on the parents' minds that could cause even more grief. And it was easier for members of the medical staff not to face their own anxieties concerning stillbirth. Recently, however, many medical professionals have found that seeing and holding the baby helps the parents face the reality of what has happened and begin the normal mourning process.

Dr. Emanuel Lewis, a psychiatrist at Charing Cross Hospital in London, has been one of the most active proponents of this approach. He criticizes what he refers to as the "normal 'rugby pass' management of stillbirth ... the catching of a stillbirth after delivery. The quick accurate back-pass through the labor room door to someone who catches the baby and rapidly covers it and hides it from the parents and everyone." He emphasizes the importance of the parents spending time with the baby, examining the features, giving him or her a name, keeping a memento, and having a funeral so that they will have memories of the infant. It is easier, according to Dr. Lewis, to mourn and to resolve one's grief when there is a known person, not just a fantasy.

Often, when parents do not see their dead infant, they imagine him or her as being terribly deformed or ugly. Seeing the baby is a relief for many. If the baby is deformed, it is helpful to have the nurse explain to the parents what the defects are so they will know what to expect. As Dr. Lewis says, "What is imagined about the horror of a deformity is usually worse than the reality." Most parents focus on the positive features, even when the baby does not look normal. They tend to remember characteristics that resemble family members and to think of the baby as unusually beautiful.

The desire to see the dead infant is not universal. Some parents feel that it is easier to deal with the tragedy and their feelings if they don't see the baby; later some may regret this decision, yet others are sure they made the right choice. Alan

Swinton, a chaplain who works at the Aberdeen Maternity Hospital in Scotland, is one person who challenges Dr. Lewis's position. He feels that the decision to see the baby should be left up to the parents and that the staff should support whatever decision they make.

In some American hospitals, parents who at first do not want to see their baby are asked again later in the day, and some then agree. If they still refuse, a picture is taken for the infant's file, because months later the parents may ask what their baby looked like; the doctor can then offer to give them a picture.

Glenda and John felt they made the right decision about seeing their baby. Glenda said that she still remembers what the baby looked like and hopes she always will. "I just wish I had taken some pictures. It sounds so odd, but that's really one regret I have."

As soon as they left the delivery room, the nurse asked if she could talk to John alone. She wanted to know who his undertaker was. John was stunned and angry:

> My baby had just died, and here they were asking about a funeral director. I felt like rather than bringing a baby into the world who everyone thinks is cute and cuddly, it was like I had defecated in the nursery and they wanted me to clean it up as quickly as possible and dispose of the garbage. I didn't know of any undertakers—Why would I?—so they said for $50.00 they would take care of everything. My gut response was that this was my baby and I would take care of finding someone.
>
> Then the nurse asked me to sign a death certificate. She explained that there is no birth certificate unless the baby is alive at birth. I noticed that she had written in Baby Boy in place of a first name. I told her that the baby had a name but she said we should save that name for the next child. All I could think was, Well that's *his* name—Robert. Later I regretted not having insisted on changing the certificate. I felt nobody should ever go without a name. For nine months that child was alive whether or not it was born dead. So I just keep the name in my mind.

So many decisions to be made and no time to think. How can one make rational choices at a time of shock and disbelief? It is almost inevitable that there will be regrets later—why didn't I think to do it some other way? More time would help parents reflect and even change their minds. But most of them do remarkably well in handling this difficult situation.

The numbing effects of the shock Glenda and John experienced when they learned the baby was probably dead helped them through the labor and delivery. Not until after the infant emerged did they begin to recognize the full impact of their loss and experience the emotions of grief. In many other cases, however, the parents are aware of the infant's death in advance of delivery since, in most stillbirths, the death occurs before the onset of labor. The parents are torn by anxiety, trying to accept the reality and at the same time hoping that somehow they and the doctor are wrong.

Bruce and Melissa are one such couple. Both thirty years old, they already had two children and wanted one more. Since the previous births had been uneventful, they were quite relaxed during the third pregnancy. But when the ninth month began, Melissa noticed that the baby's movements had stopped. The familiar kicking seemed less vigorous, and then it disappeared altogether:

> I totally panicked. I kept telling myself that the baby was just resting up before delivery or that she was using all her energy for the final growth spurt. But I knew deep down that something was wrong. When I called the doctor, she told me to come in immediately. I've never been so nervous in my life as when I got on that table.
>
> The doctor tried everything but there just wasn't any heartbeat. She seemed to feel very sorry—she was an old friend who had delivered both my boys. She told me it would be best to go through with delivery and just to go home and wait a couple of weeks to see if labor would start on its own. I pleaded with her to take the baby immediately. I couldn't imagine walking around with a big stomach containing a dead baby. She then explained that there are risks with the induction of labor or with a Caesarean operation and that it would be better to deliver naturally unless complications developed.

The recent development of prostaglandin suppositories has made induction of labor a safer procedure than in the past, and a growing proportion of doctors are advising women such as Melissa to proceed quickly to delivery. However, the prostaglandin can have side effects such as severe nausea, and some women prefer to wait for natural labor to occur. The waiting time can give the family a chance to start to get used to the terrible reality of the baby's death. It is also a painful time of endurance, as Melissa discovered.

Walking out through that waiting room, with all the pregnant women looking so calm, was a real trial. I tried not to cry so I wouldn't upset them, and I guess I was pretty out of it anyway. It wasn't until I got home and called Bruce that it began to hit me that there really wouldn't be a baby. I just couldn't believe it; I kept thinking there must be a mistake. How could this happen?

The next two weeks were like a nightmare. Since Bruce didn't feel the kicking stop like I did, he refused to believe the baby was gone. He kept trying to tell me everything would be okay, even though he really knew that it wouldn't. And the boys were so confused. They couldn't understand why their little sister—we were sure it was going to be a girl—wasn't coming. I hardly went out because I was afraid to face people. Once I went shopping and I ran into an acquaintance who greeted me all excited: "Congratulations! When is your baby due?" I didn't want to explain the whole situation, so I just said, "I'm not going to have this baby." She looked confused, but I said no more and walked away.

Labor finally began and I called the doctor and went to the hospital. Since this was my third pregnancy, I knew what to expect. However, this time I was given a lot of sedatives, and my labor and delivery seemed completely unreal. I can remember the nurses saying in unison, 'Push! Push!' But I just couldn't. I really didn't want my baby to come out. I did not want her to leave me so soon.

They told me it was a little baby girl, just what we had wanted. The nurses took her away all wrapped up. I was too afraid to see her, since she had been dead for two weeks and I was sure she'd look horrible. They just wheeled me out to a room on the maternity floor. I feel guilty saying this, but at the time my strongest feeling was relief. I was really glad it was over with. And I was so drained that all I wanted to do was sleep.

When I woke up a few hours later, the nurse asked if there was anything I wanted. I asked to see a priest, not because I am very religious, but I wanted to know where the baby was in terms of the Catholic Church. Was she born? Was she a U.S. citizen? I had always heard that if a baby was not baptized he went to Limbo, a place neither in heaven nor hell. Where was my baby now? Nobody thinks she existed, yet I carried her for nine months. I lived with her and I knew her.

The nurse called the hospital's Catholic chaplain, who came immediately to talk to me. He said that he believed that God would always accept a baby into His Kingdom and that he would baptize the baby. I felt a little reassured about that.

After the priest left, I was full of questions and tried to make sense of what had happened to me. I was numb. I was always the strong person in my family and I felt I had to stay in control. But I wanted to talk to someone who knew what I was going through and could answer my questions.

My major concern was getting information about the baby. What had been wrong with the baby? Why did she die? A few hours later my doctor came in and seemed uncomfortable. She told me how sorry she was and then explained that the baby died because of lack of oxygen, but that she did not know why this occurred. Somehow I was not satisfied. I wanted her to explain in more detail.

Many parents want more medical information about the causes of the stillbirth than they receive. For example, Dr. Ann Cartwright of the Institute for Social Studies in Medical Care in London interviewed 196 mothers of stillborns three to five months after the tragedy and found that eighty percent were dissatisfied with the information they had been given.

Yet sometimes there simply is no satisfactory information available. In up to half of all fetal deaths, the cause of death is never determined. There are, however, a number of possible reasons that are known. Anoxia, or the lack of oxygen, is one of the most common causes. The fetus depends on a continued supply of oxygen and nourishment from the mother's body by way of the placenta and umbilical cord. If either of these does not function properly, the baby's life is endangered.

In many cases doctors believe that the umbilical cord functioned properly but may have been temporarily compressed before or during the delivery. This is often hard to prove. Sometimes the cord drops before the baby does (prolapsed cord) and is pressed by the baby as he or she is emerging. It is also possible that the cord may be wrapped tightly around the baby's neck.

All of these can cut off the oxygen supply to an otherwise healthy baby.

There are also a number of ways in which the placenta may be the cause of the baby's death. This spongy structure attached to the uterus sometimes separates prematurely from the uterus (abruptio placentae). If it is implanted too low in the uterus (placenta previa), it can shear off late in pregnancy and hemorrhage results. In addition, a baby who is postmature—more than two weeks overdue—may be deprived of necessary nourishment from the placenta.

There are other reasons besides problems with the cord or placenta that may cause the baby's death. Maternal conditions such as toxemia, high blood pressure, or diabetes can affect the proper flow of nourishment to the fetus. A mother who has Rh negative blood creates antibodies to an Rh positive baby, and unless treated, these antibodies may attack the red blood cells of a subsequent fetus and cause severe anemia and even death. If the mother's water breaks prematurely, the infant can be threatened by infections. Or there may be serious abnormalities in the infant that cause death to occur before birth. And sometimes it is labor itself that is so abnormally stressful that a healthy infant cannot survive.

It has been said that the passage through the birth canal is the most dangerous journey in a child's life. Many conditions can intervene to make this journey an unsucceful one. With all the medical knowledge now available, the reasons may still be impossible to discover.

Doctors usually want an autopsy performed to see if any factors related to the death can be determined. Some parents refuse permission for an autopsy because they consider it an unnecessary violation of the child or because they are opposed on religious grounds. Other parents find great reassurance in knowing that the baby was perfectly formed even when the cause of death cannot be determined.

Melissa and Bruce agreed to an autopsy. They wanted to know as much as possible about the condition of their baby. They felt it would help them in planning for a future child. It would also alleviate their feelings of uncertainty and guilt.

The first night in the hospital after the birth was very difficult for Melissa. She said:

> Even though a double set of doors separated my room from the corridor, I could hear the babies crying in the nursery. I turned the television on very loud to drown out the sound, but it didn't help much. I needed to talk to someone, but it was late at night and I did not dare call anyone. I wished Bruce were there. It would have been easy to put in a cot so that he could have stayed with me. This was a time when I really needed to be with him and I think the hospital could have been more flexible with their rules. Of course, I never thought to ask at the time, but then again no one from the hospital staff suggested it.
>
> The next day my doctor came in and said that I could be discharged from the hospital the following day, since I was recovering well. I wanted to go home so badly, and I jumped at the chance. But leaving the hospital was more difficult than I expected. In the elevator there was another woman going home with her baby, and I didn't know how I was going to get through it. I felt so empty walking out of the hospital.
>
> I thought that having two other children at home would fill this void. But when I arrived home I realized that I could not replace one child with another. My children were so happy to see me, but I dreaded talking to them about what had happened to the baby. Somehow I didn't feel up to talking about it just yet. So I said nothing.
>
> The worst time was when my milk came in. The doctor did not want to give me a shot, so I knew I would just have to wait until the milk dried up. I felt like my body was one big wound with fluids coming out in every direction. I was bleeding quite a bit, I couldn't sit down because of the episiotomy, and here the milk I had so looked forward to nourishing my baby with was dripping uselessly from my breasts. I was just so miserable. It seemed totally unfair to have to go through all this. Since I still looked pregnant, I was worried that people might ask me when I was expecting my baby; for a long time, I didn't want to leave the house. I didn't even go to the baby's funeral.

Bruce had begun to make the funeral arrangements while Melissa was still in the hospital. The funeral director helped find a plot and asked a priest to preside. He also suggested that they bury the baby in clothes, and Bruce went out to buy a dress for her:

It was the hardest thing I have ever done in my life. I went to a children's store nearby, and there was a big sale on. The place was busy with pregnant women and new mothers. I picked out the smallest size dress and the woman said, "Oh, I have this in a larger size on sale. She'll outgrow this one, why don't you buy the bigger one?" I didn't tell her anything and kept the smaller dress. Tears came into my eyes as I paid for it, and then I broke down when I got into the car.

I had never been to a funeral before and was glad that the priest kept the service simple and brief. Afterward, Melissa was sorry that she had not gone. The next day she asked me to take her to the cemetery. She told me that she had to know where the baby was. I drove her into the cemetery, but I couldn't remember exactly where they buried her. Melissa cried and I knew I couldn't rest until we found her. Finally, I saw the flowers that we had bought for her grave. It was as if God was watching over us. We stopped and she took a rose from the flowers and put it on top of the grave.

When we returned home, we went into the room we had prepared for the baby. I dismantled the crib while she took the clothes from the drawers and packed them in a box. It was very sad. We stored everything in a room in the basement and told each other we would use them again.

I think I got over my grief more quickly than Melissa did. I was so relieved that she was recovering physically, and I consoled myself by thinking that, if the baby had survived, she might be retarded or chronically ill. I thought Melissa was feeling better, but she still fantasized that the baby was alive somewhere. When she went in the basement, she avoided the room where the baby things were stored because she imagined that the baby lived in that room. When she finally told me about this, I took her into the room and showed her that there was no one there. Then we drove to the cemetery to visit the grave.

With Bruce's help, Melissa was eventually able to accept the reality of the baby's death and begin to redirect her thoughts into new activities with her other children. She is not depressed anymore, she says, but neither has she forgotten her dead baby.

The experiences of Glenda and John and Bruce and Melissa suggest some of the differences in reaction to a stillbirth. Since Glenda and John discovered the tragic news suddenly but still hoped for a miracle, they were mostly numb during labor and delivery. Glenda remembers how inappropriate her first thoughts seemed to her at the time—worrying about her mother's reaction, wondering how the nurses felt. Her own emotions had been repressed, only to be released at a later time.

Bruce and Melissa had a longer time to adjust to the certainty that their baby would not be born alive. Although they did not accept the facts to the extent of announcing the death or beginning funeral arrangements, they did stop their planning for the infant's arrival. They closed the baby's room, canceled their plans for a party, and tried to prepare their children. By the time they went to the hospital, the initial shock was beginning to wear off and they faced delivery with feelings of depression and anger mixed with resignation.

These two couples are from different backgrounds and had different reasons for wanting a child, yet each faced similar problems in the hospital and felt similar emotions in response to their baby's death. Each of the husbands was asked to sign a death certificate and to make immediate decisions about autopsy and funeral arrangements. Neither was prepared for such startling requests. Each felt that he had to provide strength for his wife and that he had no one to lean on for some much-needed support in such a difficult situation. Both wives faced the anxiety and loneliness of remaining in a hospital near new mothers and their babies. Each wanted to have her husband close to her and to leave for home as soon as possible. And each experienced the sadness and pain of feeling her breasts swell with useless milk. All four grieved, each in his or her own way.

But the desire to understand what had happened—and perhaps more important why it had happened to them—was never satisfied for either couple. This left them anxious and uncertain about future children. Glenda and John are still trying to decide about their future. But Bruce and Melissa, who nervously planned for another child, are now enjoying their new daughter, Jessica.

Dr. Lewis has described stillbirth as an "empty tragedy": "After a stillbirth there is a double sense of loss for the bereaved mother, who now has a void where there was so evidently a fullness. Even with a live birth the mother feels a sense of loss, but the consolation of a surviving 'outside baby' helps the mother to overcome her puzzling and bewildering sadness at losing her 'inside baby.' With a stillbirth, the mother has to cope with an outer as well as an inner void."

The void left by stillbirth affects other members of the family as well as the mother. They must all find a way to come to terms with the mysterious paradox of stillbirth—that delivery is an ending, that death precedes birth, that the baby who moved for months while inside is now outside—and still.

6

Infant Death

". . . I watched her breathe every precious breath on the respirator. I saw her covered with wires and tubes. I kept watch. She was special to me and I would tell her over and over, 'Daddy is here. Daddy loves you.' The three days she lived were hell—not knowing if she would make it, uncertain about what plans we should make. Somehow I thought she would live; I was hopeful. When she died, at least I was there with her. The grief was unbearable. But there was also a sense of relief. The uncertainty, the waiting were finally over."

The baby who is alive at birth but critically ill, whether he or she lives a few hours, days, weeks, or even months, creates for parents a painful time of waiting. They are tormented by the uncertainty, the hopes and the fears of the outcome.

One of the most difficult feelings for parents to deal with in a situation like this is the uncertainty of not knowing if the baby will live and be healthy. Yet they have other worries too. At a time when the mother is physically weakened by the birth (particularly if she has had a Caesarean), she is anxious about wanting to spend time with the infant and also wanting to care for her other children at home. If the baby is transferred to a distant medical center, there are additional complications of traveling there and staying in a strange city and having to rely on unfamiliar doctors. The often exorbitant costs of travel and of care for the baby also trouble the parents.

For many, there is the added dilemma of not knowing how to

relate to this new baby. How attached should they become to a baby who may be dying? Should they have a baptism or naming ceremony as they had planned? Should they send out the announcement cards? What should they do with the clothes and toys they have already received as gifts?

Some cases are complicated by the birth of a baby with such severe physical or mental abnormalities that a decision about whether to treat the baby becomes an issue. This situation thrusts the parents into an area of considerable medical, legal, and ethical controversy, but also, more important, one of severe personal anguish.

Until recently, parents were excluded from the hospital nursery and suffered all the more from being unable to do anything for their babies. But new developments in research have both dispelled worries about infection when proper precautions are taken and demonstrated the value of parental contact with their babies. Now, many hospitals encourage parents to visit, to feed, and to care for their baby.

A variety of conditions are responsible for early infant death. The most common are premature birth, brain damage occurring before or during the birth due to a lack of oxygen, and congenital abnormalities. A rapidly growing cause of newborn death is the passage of the AIDS virus from an infected mother. In other cases a baby appears to be healthy at the time of birth, but then a life-threatening condition (such as a defective heart or liver) becomes evident after several days or weeks.

Prematurity and low birth weight (below 2500 grams) are still the leading causes of neonatal death. There is no known reason why some babies arrive early, and there are as yet few ways to prevent this from happening. Many of these babies, with the aid of intensive medical care, live healthy normal lives, yet other babies die or will be chronically ill. Parents whose baby has a premature birth are caught off guard, and the ideal natural birth becomes a frantic and frightening experience. They are not prepared to be parents so soon.

Sally and Ken's response to the birth of their second child ten weeks early typifies some of the feelings that many parents have. Sally, a nursery school teacher, had planned to have the baby after the school term was over. She was totally surprised and unprepared when she went into premature labor one morning just as she was getting ready to go to work.

We were all sitting at the breakfast table—my husband, our son, and myself—and suddenly I felt like I was sitting in a puddle. My water had broken. I was astonished to realize that I was in active labor. I went upstairs quickly so that my son wouldn't see me in such a state. Ken called for an ambulance, and because there wasn't enough time to get to my obstetrician in the city, I was taken to the emergency room of a local hospital where a resident delivered the baby. Everything was so chaotic. I just couldn't believe I was really having a baby already. Then I heard her crying faintly. I had only a quick glance of a tiny baby before she was rushed away.

She was transferred immediately to another hospital that had the equipment and special care for her needs. My husband went with her. I asked if I could be transferred to the same hospital that she was in, but was told that they did not have enough bed space. So I just lay in my bed feeling more alone and empty than I'd ever felt in my life, wondering if it were all a dream.

I thought I was being punished, that I had caused her to be born early because I had a cold and was constantly coughing. I felt totally useless and unneeded and convinced that I was a terrible mother.

I couldn't do anything to help my baby. I didn't even know what was happening to her. I was so isolated. And I worried about my son, who must have been scared and confused. I was a total failure and felt very sorry for myself.

It helped a lot when Ken came that night and brought a Polaroid picture of the baby. What a surprise. I was glad at least to have that picture, because my fear was that I would never see her again. We had decided if it were a girl we would call her Rebecca. Even though we weren't sure whether she would make it, we felt at least she should have a name. So the little baby in the picture was now Rebecca.

She died the day I left the hospital. I never even had a chance to hold my baby. I'll never stop regretting that.

In most cases a premature birth is an emergency situation. Many women do not recognize the first signs of labor, thinking the contractions to be gas pains. By the time the pains are recognized as labor, delivery may be imminent. It is a frightening time for the couple.

If the baby must be transferred to another hospital, the father has a special role, very different from the one that he had expected. Suddenly his responsibilities are enormous, and he is the one who at first has the most contact with the baby. Ken was amazed at his own reaction:

> I went to the medical center when Rebecca was transferred there, and all I could think about was how scared I was. I was scared for Sally and hated leaving her behind, and I was scared for the baby, that she might die. When I went into the intensive care unit, a nurse asked if I wanted to touch Rebecca. That really petrified me. She was so tiny, I was sure I would hurt her and then never be able to forgive myself. But the staff was very helpful, and over those next few horrible days I developed a special relationship with that baby. I felt that I was responsible for her, and I struggled with her as she fought to live. I was devastated when she died.

The survival rate among premature infants has been greatly improved by new medical techniques and by the organization of regional intensive care units for newborns. But all too often the physical problems presented by these tiny infants, particularly their inability to retain heat and the poor development of their lungs, cannot be solved. Frequently appropriate medical care is not available. Some forms of prematurity continue to be a mystery to obstetricians. If the numbers of infant deaths can be dramatically reduced in the future, thousands of families will be spared the grief that Ken and Sally experienced.

One of the risky conditions that may lead to premature delivery is a multiple birth. When two or more infants are born together, the chances of death are increased. Parents then grieve for several children at once. When one twin is dying and the other survives, parents must face the almost impossible task of caring for and grieving for one child while rejoicing over the other's survival. There is resentment toward the sick baby for requiring so much energy and attention and toward the healthy baby for being so well and expecting all the loving care any new baby needs. Added to anger is the feeling of guilt for not being able to give enough attention to either of them.

Whether a baby is in trouble because of prematurity or because of some other cause, parents wonder what was wrong with their own bodies that caused the tragedy. If there is a possibility of genetically caused deformities, the crisis of self-doubt can affect grandparents and other family members as well.

When an infant's death is due to brain damage resulting from a break in the oxygen supply around the time of birth, a common feeling is one of anger toward the doctor. The baby was healthy; the doctor should have been aware of distress, should have prevented it somehow. In some cases this anger is justified, but often it is simply a natural response to the frustration of not being able to control every aspect of birth and guarantee a normal outcome.

Physicians also experience this frustration, and in response some may avoid the parents whose infant represents a failure to them, even if nothing they could have done would have made any difference. This is especially unfortunate at a time when parents are seeking to understand as much as possible about their child's condition.

For example, when Janet and Ed's son, Joshua, was born with a condition called spina bifida, they were very concerned to know just what this meant. They were fortunate to be in a hospital where a medical team was accustomed to working with infants who have this condition and with their parents. Having six weeks with Joshua gave Ed and Janet a chance to know him, to feel at ease with the nursery and staff, and to begin to prepare themselves for their new son's death.

When Janet went into labor and arrived at the hospital it was decided that, because the baby was in a breech position, a Caesarean would be performed. Janet was awake during the birth, and so she was aware that something was wrong:

> At the moment the baby was born, I heard him cry. Everybody was working hard around my feet, and no one said anything. I asked, "What is wrong?" The doctor didn't say anything. As they

moved the baby to an isolette I could see a sac on his back. I asked, "What is that on his back?" and the doctor quietly said, "Let's talk about it later." My heart was pounding and I said, "No, what is that?" I had to know. He said the baby had a little problem and that we would not know more until he talked to the neonatologist. I had no choice but to wait. The nightmare had just started.

I was in the recovery room for four hours, still not knowing what was wrong and how serious the baby's condition was. I was very uncomfortable and in a lot of pain. I was angry at that baby for causing me so much pain and then for not being perfect.

Later, when I was in my room, the doctor came in with a specialist. They told Ed and me that it was spina bifida—I had never heard of that condition. They explained that it was a serious birth defect resulting from the abnormal formation of the spine, and that in Joshua's case, there were other problems as well. They presented a very bleak outlook. They thought that he would not live through the night. I was too weak to go up to the nursery that night, but the next day, when they told me he was alive, I was determined to go and see him.

I knew that the baby had abnormalities, but I had no idea what to expect. It was a very strange feeling, waiting to see my baby, wondering how I'd react to him. I felt self-conscious and embarrassed, sure that everyone knew that I was the one who had the deformed baby.

The nurse helped me to scrub and then wheeled me into a quiet spare room in the nursery area. She prepared me a little by saying what Joshua would look like and what kinds of equipment were used in the newborn unit. When he was brought to me, I thought, "Is this my baby?" I felt uncomfortable as the nurse watched, but she left and then I was able to look more closely at him. I was surprised that he looked just like a baby, not a monster.

I was exhausted after the Caesarean and couldn't stay long. The nurses let me know that I could call or come any time, day or night. They would answer any question I had about his treatment. They always talked about little Josh, and they asked how my husband and I were doing. Their attitude was fantastic. It was the best thing that happened to me since I entered the hospital.

The staff members in many neonatal intensive care units throughout the United States are not only skilled at providing for the baby's care, but they are also increasingly sensitive to the emotional needs of the parents. Working in teams, they are specially trained to recognize the importance of involving parents in every possible way. The nursery, with all its machinery, wires, tubes, and fragile babies, may seem ominous to the outsider, but for the parents who have a baby in the unit it becomes a special place—their baby's home.

The staff in these nurseries work hard to create this homelike environment for the baby. They decorate the walls, encourage parents to bring in toys, music, and mobiles, and attempt to stimulate the infants' senses in as many ways as possible. In some places tapes of the parents' voices are often played.

When several families have infants in a special care nursery at the same time, they can sometimes provide one another with encouragement and consolation. Even though they are strangers, they recognize the common bond that helps them understand each other's feelings better than anyone else can. In some medical centers, formal groups have been organized so that parents have the opportunity to meet and talk with each other and with a staff person, who can answer the many questions that always arise.

One way that mothers can become more involved in the care of their babies is by nursing. On her second visit to the nursery, Janet was asked if she wanted to try to nurse her baby. She recalled:

> I jumped at the chance. I had no idea they would let me. I had felt so inadequate compared to the nurses—it seemed that they were more his mother than I was. Now that I had a special, important function, it made me feel useful. The baby did not suck very well and I was tired after the Caesarean, but I used a pump most of the time and the nurses were very encouraging. I finally began to feel like I was really his mother.

For many parents who know that the baby is sure to die, the decision to nurse can be difficult. But many mothers are not even aware that it is possible to nurse their baby. If the baby is on a respirator, they can use a breast pump and the baby will be fed the milk through a tube. When a hospital does not have a pump, a member of La Leche League can be helpful to a mother who wishes to nurse.

Janet was fortunate to be in the same hospital as the baby so that she could visit him often. It was also easier for Ed. He did not have to run back and forth between two hospitals, visiting his wife in one and the baby in another. They had easier access to the information they needed and could share in decisions concerning the baby's care.

Sally and Ken did not have such an advantage. Sally had a very difficult stay in the hospital because her baby was transferred to another hospital. Had she been able to move too, she would have had a chance to see her baby and her feelings of isolation would have been avoided. Although there are often valid reasons why a mother cannot be moved with her child, such as lack of bed space, the woman's condition, or the doctor's reluctance either to refer a patient or travel to see her, both hospitals should make every effort to allow a couple the possibility of being with their baby.

When the hospital with the intensive care nursery is very distant from the woman's family or when the transfer would create a great financial burden, some families prefer not to move the mother. If she does not go with the baby—for whatever reason—the possibility of calling the second hospital at any time to talk about the baby's condition is crucial. It has also become the practice in many hospitals to bring a baby to the mother to hold or at least touch before he or she is transferred. If this had been done for Sally, she would not have to regret so strongly the lack of any contact with her baby.

Cost is a factor for most parents in this situation. They worry about the bills for the specialists and the operations, and the expense of the intensive care nursery, which in many places is well over $1000 per day. They rarely talk about finance at the time because their main concern is the life and health of the baby, yet they wonder how they are going to be able to pay for everything.

After the baby has died and the bills begin to arrive, some parents feel very bitter. As one parent said, "Don't you think watching the suffering and death of our baby was punishment enough? Then to get a $50,000 bill to pay on top of that. It's so unfair." Some doctors reduce their charges when a baby dies, but the total cost is usually still enormous.

When Ed began to recover from the initial shock of his son Joshua's diagnosis and realized that the baby would live for many more days or even weeks, he started to worry about finances. Since he was embarrassed to ask anyone about cost, fearing he would be thought heartless, he was very relieved when the social worker working in the newborn unit raised the issue. She helped him review his insurance coverage and fill out the necessary forms for financial assistance. With this taken care of, he could concentrate more completely on his son's health.

Ed and Janet worried a great deal about how to behave toward the baby. Aside from fearing that they might harm him by any wrong move, they were afraid of becoming too attached to him. As Ed recalled:

> I wanted to love that baby, to cuddle him and kiss him just like every other parent with a normal child. But I needed to protect myself too. I worried that every day I spent with him would make it harder to lose him. We grew to love him in spite of ourselves—he looked so cute and helpless. We wanted him to live and come home with us, but we also knew that if he survived, our lives would be totally overwhelmed by the care of a very sick child. We felt that he could never live a happy life. I was torn apart by all these different emotions.
>
> As the days went on, I was getting used to the fact that he would die, and I found myself letting go and wanting to go see him less and less. I felt guilty about that, and I felt self-conscious about how people expected me to be acting. The social worker helped by just reassuring us that whatever we felt comfortable doing or whatever we were feeling was okay. Now I look back at the time I spent with him as being very special.

One of the worst dilemmas for parents arises when there is a question about whether their baby should be allowed to die. Because of advances in medical technology during the past decades, doctors are able to keep many gravely ill infants alive. However, the medical profession and the public have become concerned with the "quality of life"; the question of whether every infant should be treated with heroic measures, no matter what its condition, has been hotly debated.

Newborn euthanasia is never voluntary. A decision is made for the baby, and the baby cannot state his or her feelings. Part of the problem is determining who should make the decision. Who will be the baby's advocate? How does one define the "quality of life"? Is it legal to let a baby die?

Several well-publicized "Baby Doe" cases focused public attention on these questions in the early 1980s. An Indiana infant born in 1982 with Down's syndrome died from a condition which could have been surgically corrected after his parents refused surgery and obtained court approval of their decision. This case prompted a response from the Reagan administration, requiring that all handicapped infants be treated. Hospitals risked losing federal funding if they did not comply, and notices were posted in hospitals giving a toll-free hotline for people to call with anonymous reports of violations. "Baby Doe squads" were assigned to enforce these rules.

Objections from professional groups such as the American Academy of Pediatrics and several court rulings led to some modification of the rules, allowing very limited circumstances for withholding care—essentially, when the treatment would not prevent the death of the infant. The posted notices, the hot line and the "Baby Doe squads" were eliminated. The revised regulations also recommended the establishment of Infant Care Review Committees for discussion of complicated situations. These strict criteria for withholding treatment were overturned in court, but further regulations have led to continued restrictions in some states.

The controversy and publicity which surrounded the Baby Doe rules have reduced the possibility, which once existed for parents and physicians, to choose not to keep a severely deformed baby alive. Such choices were made with great pain, but with an awareness of the likelihood of very negative effects of further treatment on both the infant and the family.

Parents usually need and want the opportunity to be included in the decision, to have all the information shared with them. This requires considerable effort and patience on the part of the physicians, since it is difficult for parents who are upset and still in shock to comprehend all the facts and opinions.

Dr. Raymond S. Duff and Dr. A.G.M. Campbell, who have written about the ethics of the intensive care nursery, explain the way cases are treated at Yale–New Haven Hospital:

> As a given problem may require, some or all of several persons (including families, nurses, social workers, physicians, chaplains, and others) may convene to exchange information and reach decisions. Thus, staff and parents function more or less as a small community in which a concerted attempt is made to ensure that each member may participate and know the family will not have to bear that heavy burden alone.

This sounds ideal. However, because many physicians have a difficult time dealing with these situations or want to spare parents from the heavy burden of making a decision or because of hospital practices, this "community participation" does not always occur. Many hospitals have created ethics committees to review individual cases where there are special problems to be discussed. But most often the physician makes a decision, and it is carried out without further discussion or consultation.

Generally, parents accept the physician's advice. If there is a disagreement, however, this adds to their frustration. For instance, parents may feel that life with a retarded or deformed child will be intolerable and ask that treatment be discontinued. In some hospitals they are treated as if they are criminals committing murder. Some doctors insist on taking every possible measure to save a baby's life. As one doctor said, "I was trained to cure, to heal, not to let die." Many physicians believe that they must be the baby's advocate, defending every effort to save life. The physicians may take the parents to court to obtain a decision. In extreme cases, if the court decides against them, the parents may give up custody of their infant.

In a reverse case, parents may urge the physician to take every possible measure to keep their baby alive when the prognosis is hopeless or when the physician believes that the parents do not comprehend the consequences of doing so. The physician in these cases will continue treatment but may also continue to advise the parents about the situation, allowing them time to reconsider.

To make any decision under such circumstances is horrendous for everyone, but to avoid the issue altogether is worse. As Duff and Campbell wrote, ". . . pretending there is no decision to be made is an arbitrary and potentially devastating decision of default. Since families and patients must live with the problem one way or another in any case, the physician's failure to face the issues may constitute a victimizing abandonment of patients and their families in times of greatest needs."

Whichever option is taken, the parents suffer the consequences of wondering if they made the right decision and what their lives would be like if they had made a different choice. If the decision is made to let the baby die, the torment for the parents continues. Watching their son or daughter die is devastating, and living with the choice takes courage.

Peg and Rick's experience illustrates some of the feelings and confusions that surround parents when they must decide whether or not to preserve the life of their child. They had been married eight years and had been trying to have a family since they were married. They desperately wanted children and were ecstatic when Peg was pregnant. Then their daughter was born with a severe abnormality that was diagnosed soon after birth. Peg recounts their ordeal:

> I can't tell you how happy we were when Kim was born. Although the doctor had noticed at the delivery that two of her fingers were webbed, he left on an optimistic note, and we were very proud and confident of our new little daughter. Later that day, another doctor noticed that one ear was set lower than the other, and we were told that there was a good possibility that there were other abnormalities. We panicked. We could tell by the way they told us that it was very serious.
>
> The next day they noticed other problems with her heart, and the neonatologist who was called in expressed his concern that it was adding up to a syndrome. We thought he meant Down's syndrome, since that is really all we knew about. He explained that they thought it was something called trisomy 18. The picture he drew of our little girl was grim—severe mental retardation, major heart problems, and many other abnormalities. He called for a second opinion and they were ninety percent sure it was this syndrome, but they could not be absolutely certain without chromosome studies.

Then they asked us if they should continue rigorous treatment. I was astounded—first that they should ask that question and second of all I thought that there was a ten percent chance that everything was not as bad as they thought. In the back of my mind was the fact that I was a miracle baby. I was an Rh baby and it was thought with certainty that I would not be alive. Knowing this, I would grab onto any golden thread about her condition. I couldn't make this decision without knowing for certain.

Other doctors were called in—a geneticist, another neonatologist—names of specialists I had never even heard of. It all happened quickly and I was confused and numbed by the experience. I thought that period of time was the most difficult in my life. My whole body was affected—I couldn't eat or sleep. It was hard to digest all the information from all the different doctors.

After the tests confirmed that what they had said was certain, my husband and I agreed with the medical staff that all heroics should be stopped. As much as we desperately wanted a child, we felt that it was not fair to bring a child into this world who would live only with such pain.

We never shared the decision we had to make with most of our friends and relatives. I guess we were afraid how we might look to them and that they would not understand. During the time the baby lived, people would try to be encouraging about her survival. This may sound terrible, but I would go to the hospital every day and pray that she die. People didn't understand that; they were praying that she live and I was praying that she die. I don't understand it all myself.

The nurses showed me how to feed Kim and change her. I would dress her in cute clothes. She was a good baby. As time went on, it became harder to visit her. I knew she was going to die and felt guilty if I did not go. I wanted to be with her, especially when she died, but it was also so hard to be there.

Kim lived three and a half weeks. She died at 2 o'clock in the morning. We went back that day and they let us see her. I dressed her and held her and then said good-bye.

After she died, I felt temporary relief, and then the grief started all over again. But soon after I kept thinking to myself over and over, what have I done? What if we had continued treatment? Did I make the right decision? Even though I knew that I was not alone in making the decision and the doctors had encouraged it, I felt responsible. I was her mother. I had a veto. It took many months of hashing it out and talking it over with the few people whom I did tell. Eventually I felt resolved with the facts and believed that the decision was for the best.

Rick was also very upset by the events:

> I saw Kim every day, but after a week I could no longer visit her—I felt I was torturing myself watching her die. I came one last time and said good-bye. I am sorry it all happened and that we had such an ordeal to go through. However, I would still make the same decision and I am still convinced that it was the best thing for the baby.

The majority of infant deaths occur despite every effort to preserve life, and the question of discontinuing treatment does not arise regularly. But it does happen often enough to be an issue for many parents.

All these parents, except Sally, had an opportunity to be with their infants. This gave them vivid memories to cherish, even though they were of a brief and trying time. All of them remember the painful day when they buried the baby. They selected simple markers with the baby's name and dates of birth and death. One family chose a plot next to the grave of the beloved grandmother for whom the baby had been named. Another couple decided to cremate their child and bury him in a beautiful countryside setting under a cherry tree. They wrote their own simple memorial service to say their farewell.

All the parents mentioned their depression, their constant pre-occupation with the events surrounding the baby's birth and death. As one mother said: "It takes a long time before these feelings are no longer a part of every day or even every hour. I always picture in my mind that tiny baby, crying in the nursery, fighting to live. But I can think of her now without so much pain and feel glad that she was part of our family at least for a little while."

THE LOST CHILDREN

the ones we never speak of—
miscarried, stillborn,
removed by decree,
taken too soon, crossed over.
They slip red mittens in our hands,
smell of warm wet wool,
are always out of sight.
We glimpse them on escalators,
over the shoulders of dark-haired women;
they return to us in dreams.
We hold them, as they evanesce;
we never speak their names.
How many children do you have?
Two, we answer, thinking three,
or three, we answer, thinking four;
they are always with us.

The lost children
come to us
at night
and whisper
in the shells
of our ears.
They are waving good-bye
on school buses,
they are separated from us
in stadiums,
they are lost in shopping malls
with unspeakable pools,
they disappear on beaches,
they shine at night in the stars.

                                   Barbara Crooker

III
PERSONAL NETWORKS

7

The Couple
Impact on the Relationship

"From the time you are very little, you have a fantasy—you'll find Prince Charming, get married, have perfect children and live together happily ever after. For a while it seemed to be coming true. I got married and my husband and I were very happy together. But when our first child died, the bubble burst. Afterward we realized that life was not so simple and that a marriage has its struggles too."

Whatever a couple's relationship is like before the loss of a child, afterward it is likely to undergo change. Parents may assume that since they have shared such a great tragedy together, helping each other to recover will draw them together. In many cases this does happen. With some parents there is no obvious change, but with others already existing problems are made worse or new ones are created.

Grieving is a lonely process. Sometimes even the closest of couples find that they can provide each other with only limited support when they lose a baby. As much as they might wish to, a man and woman cannot "make it go away" for each other. Their feelings can also never be exactly the same; each one grieves at a different pace and in a different way.

In trying to cope with their own individual pain, parents have less strength for each other. As Schiff wrote in *The Bereaved Parent*, "In the back of each of their minds, they believed they could lean on each other as they mourned. But you cannot lean on something bent double from its own burden." This realization comes slowly to couples and, at a time when they expect the greatest closeness, it may lead to resentment and disappointment.

The woman who is still depressed over the death of her infant, for example, cannot understand how her husband could think about going out for a good time or about making love. Is he so unfeeling? The man, on the other hand, may be frustrated by the failure of his efforts to distract his wife. Will she always be like this? One father discussed the difficulties he and his wife experienced after their premature baby died:

> I think to some degree it put a wall between us because she reacted very differently to the baby's death than I did. It's become an area that to some extent is off limits for us to talk about. She couldn't accept that I didn't act as upset as she was. And I felt so helpless. You go to bed at night and your wife is lying next to you crying and it is very difficult. What can you say? It's not like you had a fight and can roll over and kiss and make up. Some nights I didn't even want to come home because I knew I'd find her crying. It was easier to try to avoid the subject. I think it helped when we finally understood that it's okay to feel grief differently.

The failure to communicate is the most serious obstacle to resolving the tensions that frequently arise from the loss of an infant. Researchers who have interviewed parents after their infant died observed that for some couples the interview was the first time they had talked to each other about their loss. That inability to talk about feelings can be very frustrating, as one man whose wife had suffered a miscarriage remembered:

> I was feeling really lousy, but I thought if I showed how upset I was, it would just make things worse for her. So I tried to be cheerful to make her feel better. I got tired of trying so hard, since nothing I did seemed to make her any happier. Finally I exploded and told her how I felt. I was amazed to find out that she had been mad at me for making jokes and acting like it hadn't bothered me at all! What a relief—I didn't have to act anymore.

Fortunately, most couples discover ways to begin to communicate, and the tragedy may ultimately draw them together and strengthen their relationship. One woman explained how a stillbirth affected her marriage and how she and her husband were able to help each other:

> After the tragedy hit us, we couldn't have made it without each other. I had someone to lash out at. I could shout at him, and he understood. I could say, "Why did this have to happen to us?" I encouraged Ed to show his feelings and we were able to cry a lot together. We have become much closer because of it.

Sometimes one partner does not want to talk about the tragedy as much as the other one does. In this situation, some grieving parents find it helpful to set aside a specific and limited time each day to talk over their feelings. This encourages them to communicate about the tragedy without the fear that grief will become an all-consuming preoccupation.

When a man and a woman talk to each other at these times, they share something special and unique. In addition to expressing their personal feelings, they can talk about their dreams of what the baby would have become or about the events surrounding his or her death. Since their child either never lived outside the mother's womb or survived only a short time, the parents do not have many concrete memories, but talking about what their child would have been like ("Oh, she would have been tall like her father and become a lawyer") creates a legacy for their baby, a way of sharing the loss.

Sometimes talking is not necessary, as one man found in comforting his partner:

> When I sensed she was depressed, I would hold on to her and let her know that I was there. She would cry and I would hold her tighter—that was all I could do. Although I felt inadequate, I sensed that she wanted me to be there.

A young couple may never have been through a major crisis before. They may not as yet have developed the communication patterns necessary for helping each other in a time of trouble. If their relationship is strong, the basis for acquiring these skills is already there and they can weather the tensions and the loneliness.

Sometimes the man cannot be present during the tragedy. He

may be in the military or away on business. The woman in this situation finds herself alone, upset, and angry that her partner cannot be with her. The man who is far away is frustrated by his helplessness and feels isolated because no one around him seems to understand his feelings and predicament.

When a relationship is already weak, the couple is likely to have greater difficulties in resisting the stresses created by the loss. They may not be as willing to make the effort, or they may already have established barriers to communication that are hard to remove.

In some cases, the stress of bereavement may intensify existing weaknesses in a marriage to the point that a couple considers divorce. One woman gave such an example:

> My miscarriage was the last straw that broke up my marriage. If the baby had lived, I'm sure I would still be married. But my husband just didn't care about what was happening, and he couldn't understand how I felt. It made me see him as he really is, and later I decided to leave him.

Sometimes the fear of divorce is so great that it becomes a possibility despite the desires or intentions of either partner:

> I was sure that John must hate me for not being able to have a child like other women. No matter what he said, I was convinced that he would want a divorce. I pounced on every ambiguous comment, every time he turned his head the wrong way or came home five minutes late—everything was proof that our marriage was over. And I guess I started acting cold toward him, withdrawing into myself as protection. We finally had it out one night. When I told him what I felt, he was shocked. He said he was distant because he was feeling bad about the baby and didn't know how to talk to me about it. Once we started to talk, I realized my worry about divorce had been only in my own mind.

If a relationship is already in trouble and the pregnancy was planned to save it or as an incentive for marriage, the death of that child creates the potential for especially troubling problems. If one person did not really want a child but agreed in order to please the other, there is bound to be some animosity or bitterness. And certainly if a couple agreed reluctantly to get married because of a pregnancy and then there is no child, the resentment and feelings of being trapped can be severe.

A couple may also disagree on important decisions regarding the pregnancy or the baby's treatment. If one of them, for example, feels strongly that a finding of abnormalities should lead to abortion and the other opposes abortion, there can be serious strain on the relationship. When they disagree about whether to operate on or resuscitate an infant, the potential for anger and blaming is tremendous. Other members of the family may add pressure to the dispute, creating a major power struggle. Recovery from this sort of situation requires a great deal of effort from both parents. It is at such times of decision-making that the medical professionals can be aware of the possibility of trouble and help the family to sort through all of the information and their feelings about what should be done.

Even when there are no obvious disagreements, there is the potential for a man and woman to blame each other for their loss. In these cases the anger can be overwhelming. He thinks that perhaps she was not careful enough during her pregnancy and shouldn't have worked; she blames him for urging her to make love or for arguing and upsetting her. One of them may bring up previous affairs or an earlier abortion. None of these are likely to be related to the baby's death. Sometimes the tragedy becomes an excuse for bringing up issues that had already been sources—perhaps hidden—of tension in a relationship.

Anger, guilt, and blaming are unavoidable responses to the tragic loss. The parents seek in every possible way to make sense of what has happened, to find some reason to hold on to. A reason gives meaning to the event and focus to their feelings. But so often there is no logical explanation, and then the person who is closest bears the brunt of this search for unknowable clues. When the death of a child is due to an abnormality that can be linked to one parent by genetic studies, the couple must work even harder to keep guilt and blame from being disruptive.

When individuals are feeling angry at each other or depressed, when they are having trouble communicating, it is hardly surprising that their desire and ability to relate sexually may temporarily stop. It is hard to give love and affection when one feels drained physically and emotionally and wants to be nurtured.

Sexual problems may go beyond the couple's feelings about their loss and about each other. The act of making love has its own meaning to each individual. Because lovemaking is pleasurable, grieving parents may reject it as inappropriate. "I don't feel like it" becomes "How could we?" or, worse, "How could you want to?" This can interfere with a couple's ability to resume their normal sexual relationship.

Sexual relations also create a painful reminder of a joyful—or careless—time months earlier, when the baby's short life began. The act created the child; the child's death removes from many any desire to repeat the act.

The connection between sexuality and tragedy can also create fear of another pregnancy. For one woman, this association made it impossible to consider sexual relations: "I wouldn't let Tom get near me for months after the miscarriage. I guess I was just afraid that I might have to go through that horrible experience again." A man expressed a similar sentiment: "I just couldn't put her through that again."

Some couples have an opposite response. Instead of losing interest in sex they rush to try to replace the lost baby. And for some, sexual intimacy helps to provide the comfort they seek.

Because husband and wife may respond differently to their loss, it is likely that one will want sexual relations more than the other. David Hendin and Joan Marks, in *The Genetic Connection*, point out how sad it is when a man and woman find it difficult to relate intimately after bereavement:

> A vicious and obstructive cycle may ensue: two sensitive, hurting individuals who now more than ever need the closeness of a strong relationship and an expression of physical love, find instead that their separate pain draws them apart to the point where they can no longer express that love.

Fortunately, these problems are usually short-lived, although at the time it may be hard to imagine that they will diminish. Many couples find that they can be close and loving, giving strength to each other, without the strains that intercourse represents at first. They can talk about their reluctance and fears, reassuring each other that this difficult time will not last forever. When the effort is successful, the reestablishment of intimacy can help both partners feel better about themselves and about their relationship.

Financial problems can be another potential source of troubles. If the baby was in a neonatal intensive care unit, parents may owe the hospital and the doctor a great deal of money. Medical insurance does not always cover the total expenses of the special care nursery. There may be a loss of income if work must be interrupted. If a baby has been transferred to a faraway medical center, the unexpected cost of travel and lodging can add up quickly. The burden of such financial problems with nothing to show for it creates bitterness and long-term stress. When a couple is in trouble, the worries about money create one more problem.

"We had nothing—no baby and now no money," one woman complained. "The arguments about money became endless." Professional financial advice may be needed to solve serious money difficulties.

It is common for couples to find it very difficult to help each other. They may be afraid to express their anger and their fears, embarrassed to show tears. They withdraw from each other, or they quarrel about unrelated issues. If the tensions persist, a professional family therapist may be needed to assist the couple in solving this crisis or in understanding what underlying tensions may have been brought to the surface by the tragedy.

Although many couples experience tensions, these usually fade eventually. The positive effects on their relationship stand out most sharply for some people. Often they gain increased respect and admiration for each other. One woman described such an effect from her miscarriage:

> I was really impressed by how helpful he was. He seemed to know just how to handle everything at the hospital and he was very sensitive to my feelings. I sensed that he also respected me even more because I was able to deal with the situation and didn't completely fall apart.

A man may experience a strong feeling of relief that the woman he loves is recovering physically. Seeing her lying in a hospital, bloodied, sedated, and in distress can be very frightening for him. He may have feared for her life and is thankful to have her safely back home.

A man and woman's greater appreciation for each other and their efforts to be comforting may prompt them to spend more time together than they had before, to make a special effort to go out and start new activities together. Just being around each other more, giving extra little gifts, going on a trip, and generally pampering each other are all ways that the expression of caring creates a stronger bond between the two people.

Many couples discover through their struggle a new appreciation of how valuable they are to each other. They try to put aside their differences and cherish each other more. They may spend more time together enjoying the children they already have or planning for others to come. These couples understand very well Schiff's urging in *The Bereaved Parent:* "Value that marriage. You lost enough."

8

Single Women
Teenagers and Adults

For many women whose pregnancies end in failure, there is no husband or partner to share in the decisions and to give the needed support through the delivery and the months of grief that follow. The woman in this situation may be a young teenager barely emerging from childhood, or she may be thirty-five years old and well established in a career. She may have carefully planned the pregnancy or have conceived accidentally. She may already have other children or this may be her first. She may be recently divorced or widowed. Whatever the situation and whatever the reasons for her becoming pregnant, she has unique problems in dealing with a tragic outcome and is likely to need special support and understanding.

Not very long ago, American society did not accept the woman who bore a child out of wedlock. If an unmarried woman became pregnant, she was expected to get married and have the child. The alternative was to leave town, pretending to visit a relative, and go to a maternity home; then she was urged to give up the baby for adoption and return home as if nothing had happened. In either case she was forced to leave her school or job. The only other option was to resort to the dangers of an illegal abortionist. In most cases, the woman who did not hide her pregnancy was ridiculed and ostracized, and the child was called "illegitimate," a "bastard."

Now a woman has more choices: she can usually obtain a

safe and legal abortion, she can give up the child for adoption, or she can decide to keep the baby. In all of these situations, she can usually remain in school or at her job. As more and more single women are choosing to bear and raise their children, the popular attitudes are changing.

Even with greater social acceptance, however, the unmarried pregnant woman is still the exception. Knowing this, and aware that she is violating the norms still held by many people, the woman who chooses to have a child alone must be very committed to her decision and prepared for criticism and lack of support.

Although the single woman may have a strong desire to have a child, she is nevertheless affected by the same ambivalence all future parents experience in contemplating this major change in their lives. There are other worries as well: Will there be enough money? Will she have to depend on her parents? What kind of work will she be able to find? What will happen to her social life? What kind of future will the baby have without a father? She is likely, however, to feel that doubts must be suppressed in the attempt to convince herself and others that having the baby is the right thing to do. Then, if after all her turmoil and fears, her pregnancy ends abruptly in tragedy, she finds herself grieving alone, with little compassion from those around her in many cases.

Unfortunately, the younger the girl the higher the risk of danger for the baby as well as for the mother. Adolescents have a four to five times higher rate of serious complications than women in their twenties due to a greater likelihood of poor prenatal care and nutrition, venereal disease, and drug problems. These factors contribute to toxemia in the mother and to increased rates of prematurity, low birth weight, neurological defects, and mental retardation in the baby. With all of these complications, it is not surprising that fetal and infant mortality rates are higher for adolescents.

Since the rate of complications is so high, special attention should be given to the problems of teenagers, especially those who are single, when their pregnancies end tragically. There has been considerable research on the reasons for teenage pregnancy but very little as yet on the impact of the loss of a child on these young mothers.

The adolescent years are a time of physical and emotional maturation and the establishment of a separate individual identity. There are rapid hormonal changes and strong concerns about body image and sexuality. This time is usually marked by confusion, intense emotions, and loneliness. Adolescents often feel that others do not understand their feelings; they themselves sometimes do not even understand what they are feeling. If they become pregnant and then lose the baby, whether early by miscarriage or after weeks of watching the infant die, the teenagers are particularly vulnerable and less able to cope with the experience than older women.

Studies of pregnant teenagers suggest that their motivations are often connected with the difficulties and turmoil of adolescence. Certainly not all teenagers who conceive want to do so, and some become pregnant through rape or incest. But even more than women in their twenties and thirties, adolescent girls may consciously or unconsciously want to become pregnant as a way of resolving emotional and family tensions. Many times a young girl who feels unloved and unwanted may wish for a baby so that she will have someone to love her and someone for her to love. Wanting approval and attention from friends, the teenager may feel she will gain some special distinction from being a mother. Her sexual activity may have been a way to become close to someone, to rid herself of her isolation. Her plan to keep the baby may also be motivated by a desire to keep her lover, to create a permanent bond between them.

Yet under ordinary circumstances, when the pregnancy proceeds normally, these efforts may not be successful. Her boyfriend may leave her, her parents may be angry with her, her friends may exclude her from their social events. If, after all of this, the pregnancy ends in tragedy, her isolation usually becomes even more intense. Since no one seems to understand her loss, she is more alone than ever.

Feelings of worthlessness and self-doubt are sometimes underlying reasons for a pregnancy. When the outcome is failure, a girl's feelings about herself are even more diminished—her failure is complete. One woman recalled how she had felt as a teenager:

> When the baby was born dead, I hated myself. I felt at that time that I would never amount to anything, and this just showed everybody what a nothing I really was.

In trying to create her individual identity as an adult, a girl may feel anger and hostility toward her parents or other authorities. By becoming pregnant, she wants to show that she too is an adult and can assume responsibility. She may be trying to hurt her parents by defying their authority. But when her pregnancy ends without a baby, she may feel that she has lost her bid for independence and that she must return to the role of a child.

Adolescence is a time of separation from parents, which often creates a great sense of loss. The pregnancy may have been a way to compensate, and if the baby dies, the emptiness that results can lead to severe depression.

When a pregnancy ends in tragedy, the love and support of others are especially needed. Yet if the teenager is already alienated from her family and if the boyfriend is uncaring, she has no one to turn to. Even without such alienation, what is a tragedy to her may be seen by her parents and her boyfriend as a welcome solution to the problem of her being pregnant. The adolescent may feel that others are unsympathetic and insensitive to her grief. As one seventeen-year-old girl described her experience:

> I wanted the baby and told my parents that I was going to have it and take care of it myself, even if I had to quit school. My parents wanted me to have an abortion and continue school. I was an embarrassment to them. When the baby died two days after birth, I was very upset and depressed. But my parents seemed really happy. They thought that this was the answer to their prayers. They never even came to the hospital to see the baby. I'll never be able to forgive them for what they said to me. I can't wait to leave home.

The girl herself may feel relief at the end of what may have been an unwanted pregnancy or because the responsibilities of parenthood can be postponed. This relief can cause guilt and confusion, and it may be very difficult for her to discuss the conflicting emotions she feels. The guilt may be particularly acute if she considered having an abortion or tried to get one but was unable to for financial or other reasons.

The obstetrician can play an important role in counseling the patient. Too often, however, the young girl does not have one doctor responsible for her care since she has gone to a clinic where there are many different physicians. Even if she has a physician, she is likely to be uncomfortable talking with him or her. As one sixteen-year-old said:

> I couldn't help but feel that he disapproved of me for being pregnant. And he seemed so hurried, I was afraid to ask him anything. I never found out what really happened to the baby.

As concern has increased nationally over the numbers of pregnant teenagers, public money has become available for counseling programs in hospitals. Many private programs are also available to help the adolescent through pregnancy and delivery. The girl whose baby is stillborn or dies shortly after birth may therefore already have been in contact with a social worker, whose presence and help now become crucial. If she miscarries, these services are not likely to be accessible.

Many teenagers are reluctant to take advantage of the counseling that is available, either because they are convinced that they do not need help or because they do not trust organized services. They may also fear that those persons whom they know—school guidance counselors and clergy—will look upon them with disapproval.

Isolated and uncertain, the teenager must deal with a mixture of intense emotions that accompanies the loss of a baby. Some may feel that outward expressions of feelings such as crying are childish, that they must behave like adults, not realizing that crying and talking are healthy releases of sadness.

Nancy Horowitz, a social worker who provided services to pregnant adolescents in Chicago, found that many teenagers whose pregnancies end tragically try to relieve their feelings of mourning and depression by getting pregnant again very quickly. According to one fifteen-year-old girl:

I don't even think about how I feel about losing the baby, and I
don't want to talk about it. I just know I want to get pregnant
again and have another baby.

Horowitz also found that many teenagers are extremely worried about the failure of their bodies to function properly and
feel a need to become pregnant again to prove they are normal.
If they do become pregnant right away without working through
the grief for the first baby, it will be difficult for them to
complete the mourning process and reach a state of resolution.

In spite of all the problems, the loss of a child can become a
catalyst for new development, maturity, and growth. Counseling
can help the teenager understand her feelings, her needs, and
herself and realize that there will be a time in the future to have
a baby when she is older and better able to take care of one. The
crisis may open a dialogue between the girl and her parents,
creating new bonds of love and trust.

The many poor single women, no longer teenagers but still
without the means to assure good nutrition and medical care,
are also prone to serious complications. If they are on welfare,
perhaps supporting other children, their reception by the medical and social services is sometimes less than sympathetic during
pregnancy and delivery. They may be unfortunate to encounter
those insensitive officials who accept the myth that another child
is desired only for an increase in the welfare check and who
cannot understand the overwhelming grief that is felt if the baby
dies. If the women are from very rural areas and uneducated or
if they are members of minority groups, the prejudices of white
middle-class professionals may only serve to intensify their feelings of alienation and powerlessness.

Although there has been very little research on the specific
problems of these women after a birth tragedy, what there is
suggests that their bereavement is very similar to that of married
and more affluent women. It is the lack of resources, both
financial and social, that contributes to making their situation so
difficult.

The woman who was married at the time of conception and is

then divorced or widowed during the pregnancy is also in a difficult situation. The divorced woman's marriage may already have been in serious trouble and the pregnancy either unwanted or planned as a way to save the marriage. When she is left alone and pregnant, she may feel considerable anger as well as anxiety about the expected child. The widow, on the other hand, may think of the expected baby as a reminder of the love that has been destroyed by death. She may fear the added burden of a baby but look forward to raising the living legacy of her mourned husband.

In both of these situations, there is a great deal of ambivalence mixed with grief and anger during the time the baby is anticipated. When the pregnancy ends in failure, the woman is likely to be overwhelmed by many intense emotions—by relief, despair, and renewed grief for the loss she has so recently experienced.

A new and growing category of single women who become pregnant are those who are educated, may be established in a career, and want children but feel they can no longer wait to find someone to marry first. They are in their late twenties or thirties and strongly wish to be mothers, even if doing so means raising a child alone. They may have conceived accidentally but then decided that the time is right to have a baby. Or they may go to great lengths to meet the man whom they would like a child to resemble, perhaps not even telling him when pregnancy occurs. A growing number of single women, both lesbian and heterosexual, are using artificial insemination. When they become pregnant, they are often nervous but at the same time eager to have the baby.

Although these single women may be sure they have made the right choice, they are still sensitive to the hurtful and thoughtless remarks they sometimes hear from friends, relatives, and even strangers: "Why don't you have an abortion?" "You're hurting the baby by not giving him a father." "How are you going to handle it?" "How selfish can you be!"

Having gone through the uncomfortable task of telling their parents and dealing with their objections, women are often alone when they feel the infant's first kicks and when they experience the joys of planning and waiting for the baby's arrival. Setting up baby sitters or child care, making job arrangements, working out finances, going to childbirth classes alone, reorganizing the apartment for the baby, perhaps moving back home—the troubles as well as the pleasures are solitary. When all of this is for naught because the fetus or baby dies, the normal grieving can be intensified by anger and despair. As one twenty-nine-year-old woman recalled:

> The nights were especially hard, lying there with no one next to me to feel the baby move, to talk with about how the room should be decorated or what names to choose. It was also difficult as I got closer to term and I began to resent the things I had to do, like lugging the garbage out to the street, that other women wouldn't have to do. I guess I was envious of the married women I saw who were pregnant.
>   Then when the baby died just before birth, I was beside myself. All that I had been through, and now nothing to show for it! I wanted that baby so much!

Added to the many emotions involved in grief may be an extra sense of guilt for having tried to do what so many people disapproved of. The bereaved mother may feel she is being especially singled out for punishment.

Many of these single women, like many teenagers, are fortunate to have supportive families and friends who share their plans and help in the preparations for childbirth. Their presence becomes essential when the tragedy occurs:

> I was very lucky to meet a Lamaze teacher who practiced with me beforehand and stayed with me during delivery. When the baby was born in serious condition, it was a good thing she was there. She was very helpful during those three horrible days and again when I had to make decisions about an autopsy and funeral. I don't know what I would have done without her.

The single woman who has carefully planned for her baby may feel that she is proving her independence and her ability to be responsible. When a tragedy occurs, her confidence is often shattered. For many women, the effort of becoming pregnant and planning for a baby is too great, and they are determined never to go through such a trauma again. Having become very aware during the pregnancy of the difficulties of single parenthood, the woman may feel some relief that it is all over. But for women who very much wanted a child and can no longer look forward to having one, there is a deep frustration in addition to the grief for the baby who was so loved.

For many adult single women, as for many married women, the tragedy may convince them all the more of their desire for children. Knowing now that she is able to conceive and having prepared herself to cope with all the difficulties of single parenthood, the woman may be more determined than ever to have a baby. With good medical attention and emotional support from others, the chances are excellent that she can have a satisfying and successful pregnancy.

9

Children at Home
Understanding Their Needs

"He stood outside my hospital room window and stretched up to see me. I knew he was disappointed, but all he said was, 'It's okay, Mom. Come home soon and we'll play together.' When I got home, he gave me his favorite toy along with a big hug and did a lot to help me around the house. I loved him more than ever then."

It is terribly difficult to explain the loss of a child to one's other children, especially when they are very young. But talking with those who are so close, whose love and concern for their parents is so complete, and helping them understand and accept what has happened can be beneficial for the parents, and the presence of these children can be wonderfully comforting. They seem all the more precious when another child has died, and their efforts to reassure grieving parents are often moving.

Every member of the family, including the children, is affected by a birth tragedy. Psychiatrist Cain noted this in writing about miscarriage: "Miscarriages do not occur in a uterus, but in a woman; and miscarriages do not occur solely in a woman, but in a family." One seven-year-old boy's response shows this impact. When his teacher said she was sorry to hear that his mom's baby had died, his reaction was, "It's OUR baby who died!"

Birth and death together. It's confusing and frightening enough for adults, but how are young children to understand it? For them the baby never really existed, or lived only briefly. What

106

does this mean for them? Why are the parents so distraught? Too often, children's feelings about these issues are ignored or misunderstood. When parents are struggling to deal with their own feelings, they find it even harder to respond to the emotional needs of their other children.

For some parents, the dual task of trying to make sense of what has happened to them and also helping their other children may be so overwhelming that they decide to tackle only one aspect. They ignore the children or send them to stay with others until they themselves feel better, or they attend to the children's needs so completely that their own feelings are repressed. Either of these strategies may shortchange both adults and children in their need to face and respond to reality. This is why involving children and explaining to them what is happening is crucial for the parents as well as for the children. Understanding some of the possible reactions of children to infant loss can allow parents to anticipate their children's concerns and to reassure them.

Under the best of circumstances, when everything about a pregnancy and birth goes well, other children in the family have difficulty dealing with the separation from Mother when she enters the hospital, the confusion about birth and hospitals, the shift of everyone else's attention to a new child. These are "normal" problems. But if the new baby is seriously ill or has died, there are many additional problems that children may experience: confusion about what happened, the guilt of believing they might have caused the baby's death, isolation from their grieving parents, and fears for their own lives and security. They too, like their parents, are bereaved; they may be saddened, disappointed, and angry about not having the baby they expected.

During the pregnancy, the children's parents had been talking to them about birth and life, preparing them for a new sibling. It is unlikely that the possibility of a death will have been considered or mentioned. It is no wonder that children are shocked and confused when the parents tell them that the new baby will not be coming home, that he or she has died, or that the pregnancy ended in miscarriage.

Children's emotions are sometimes revealed by the explanations they give for the baby's death. When Zoë Smialek, a nurse, asked siblings why their baby brother or sister had died, they responded, "God wanted him," "I hit him," "He was bad and wouldn't stop crying," "Mommy dropped him on his head." Like their parents, children also seek explanations and try to make sense out of what has happened.

They may, as their parents do, look to their own thoughts and behavior to find a cause, feeling guilty even though there is no way they could have been responsible. Many children view the world in a very self-centered way, so they naturally see everything as somehow related to themselves. They feel alternately extremely powerful and totally helpless, and it is the feeling of powerfulness that allows and encourages the child to feel responsible.

Young children are convinced that a wish can cause something to happen, and when a death occurs they might remember wishing—perhaps unconsciously—that the baby would not arrive. Every young child watches Mother's growing abdomen with ambivalence. A new baby will be a playmate, a potential ally against parents or other siblings, a friend. On the other hand, the infant will also be the center of attention, a rival for the parents' affection and time. It is not surprising then that a child would have negative thoughts during Mother's pregnancy and, because of these thoughts, blame himself or herself for the baby's death.

A child can focus not only on his or her wishes but also on specific actions—bumping into Mother's belly, demanding to be picked up, or making too much noise and upsetting Mother. Although parents also feel guilty about their own thoughts and activities, they at least have the intellectual ability to tell themselves that the guilt is irrational. Children cannot always make such distinctions.

In some cases, children may blame their parents for what has happened to the infant and become disappointed and angry. Mother and Father had promised a cute little brother or sister and failed to produce one. One mother remembered vividly her five-year-old daughter's furious outbursts after a second miscarriage: "You're always promising me a baby and then it doesn't come! Other people have babies. Why don't we have one?"

The death of a baby is very frightening to a young child. After all, he or she was carried and delivered by the same mother whose pregnancy, this time, ended in tragedy. What is to prevent a similar fate from attacking him or her as well?

If a child has seen Mother bleeding and in severe pain, there may be fear for her safety. The images of Mother suffering physically and of both parents anxious and depressed can be frightening to the young child who thinks of adults as all-powerful.

Fear of abandonment by the mother appears to be a predominant feeling in children less than five years old when confronted by death. They are likely to be particularly frightened when the mother is in the hospital and cannot be seen. As one mother whose infant died during childbirth recalled:

> My son, who was three at the time, was sure that I had died. Even though everyone told him I was okay, he saw that I was gone and that the relatives were upset. There was no phone at home, so I couldn't call. Until I actually left the hospital and saw him, he was convinced that I was dead.

The introduction of sibling visitation in many hospital maternity services for families who have had a healthy baby has helped to lessen children's fears of abandonment. When a baby is ill or has died, these fears are intensified by the awareness that something is wrong, and it becomes especially important for a child to have the chance to visit the mother in the hospital.

Scared, remorseful, and confused by the unexpected tragedy, a child can easily wonder if he or she is still loved. If the parents are so upset, they must not be satisfied with the children they already have. Parental support and reassurance are essential at this time.

Sometimes children do not express their feelings of guilt, fear, or insecurity but keep them hidden. Professionals who have studied children's reactions advise parents to raise the issues even if a child has not said anything. They suggest that it is important to remind children how normal it is for them to wonder if they are responsible for what happened, but that in no way are they to blame. The parents must emphasize that they will be there to love their children and that the baby's death does not mean that Mother and Father will die too.

Just when they need special attention and care, children are often isolated from their parents. Mother is in the hospital or hiding in her bedroom. Father is distraught and overwhelmed, trying to help Mother, take care of house and kids, make funeral or other arrangements, and also keep up with his work.

The need to be with, talk to, and constantly reassure other children is often too much for a parent to handle. As Helen Arnstein writes,

> When a child has died, it may be an almost unsurmountable burden for grief-stricken parents, struggling with their own shock and depression, anger and guilt, to give comfort and reassurance to their other child or children. It is almost cruel to ask a parent not to withdraw his attention and love from the surviving child or children who may be needing emotional support more than ever due to their own distraught feelings about the tragedy.

She assures parents that it is common for them to withdraw or for the child to be unreceptive at first and that they should not let such reactions make them feel worse than they already do. This is a time when close friends and relatives with whom a child feels comfortable can be helpful; they can spend time with him or her until parent and child are ready to reconnect.

The children may feel particularly cut off when the baby is still alive and struggling for survival in a hospital. Parents spend much of their free time going to a medical center, possibly far away and perhaps excluding children. The focus of parents' energy and concerns is necessarily on the baby, and the assistance of relatives and neighbors is crucial for the care of other children.

Siblings do not have to be excluded from this vigil, however, and may be enormously reassured when they are made a part of the family's efforts. Some sisters and brothers make pictures or select toys for the baby. When there is a long ride to a medical center, parents who bring their children have the extra hours of the trip for the family to be together. A family friend can keep children company in the waiting room. In a few hospitals, the children are allowed to see the baby through the nursery window, an important step in making the infant who is the center of so much concern a real person to them.

When there was never a visible baby—in the case of most miscarriages or ectopic pregnancies—it may be difficult for parents to know what to tell their children. The task is especially troubling for parents who choose to abort a deformed fetus. For all parents, it is hard to know how to tell a young child that the expected baby will never be there. As one parent said, "You can't even explain it to yourself; I don't know how you can explain it to the children."

Because it is so difficult to find the right thing to say, there is a temptation, especially with miscarriage, not to say anything at all. As one mother who had a two-and-a-half-year-old son at the time of her miscarriage said, "I didn't say anything to Tommy because I didn't even think he was fully aware that I was pregnant, even though I had told him we were going to have a baby." Even children under five react to the actions and feelings of their parents. Although a child may not have known for certain that his or her mother was pregnant, he or she most likely senses that something happened to upset the parents and thus becomes upset by that.

Sometimes parents, in their own confusion and shock, tell the children something that is not true and have to change their story later. This was the case for one woman who gave birth to a severely deformed infant who was expected to die almost immediately:

> When you have two others at home, you don't know what to say to them. They were all very little and waiting at home for their new baby. At first I told them the baby died. I just didn't know what to tell them. I couldn't believe this was happening to me. My youngest child was four years old—how do you go about trying to explain? Then the baby didn't die right away. The kids could tell I was upset. People were coming over and whispering. The phones were ringing. The hospital kept calling. A social worker came to talk about whether we would institutionalize him. Finally, I had to sit down and tell them that the baby was still alive but would never come home.

Just as in the case of Tommy, the two-and-a-half-year-old whose mother miscarried, these two children were certainly aware of their parents' moods and of the changes in their environment. Children cannot be deceived easily nor can they be protected from tragedy. A child who is misled or told nothing may later on wonder whether other important matters are being discussed honestly.

Death has been a taboo subject in American society, and children especially have been protected from it. They rarely see people dying because this usually occurs in hospitals. Funerals have been deemphasized and grieving is often suppressed. Even so, children are aware of death and need to understand it when it happens.

Rabbi Earl Grollman, the editor of *Explaining Death to Children,* acknowledges that it is easier to advise parents on what not to say about death. No one formula exists that is always appropriate. Grollman suggests introducing the idea and the reality of death to children at an early age, using examples of animals and flowers, so that a family crisis is not their first exposure to death. The best that grieving parents can be expected to do is present the facts simply and clearly, taking into account the child's age and experience.

The thought of dying occurs at a very young age. Most school-age children have thought about death a great deal, and although they may not mention it, it is a part of their fantasies and play. At all ages, children have misconceptions about death. For example, one three-year-old was about to visit her aunt's new baby a few months after her own mother's stillbirth. The three-year-old said, "Mommy, let's go visit the baby now before he dies." She thought that all babies die.

Children's reactions vary considerably according to age. Very young children may be most concerned about the disturbance in their routine and fear they will not be taken care of. A very common reaction in somewhat older children is a change in behavior, such as increased aggressiveness, playing dead, or breaking toys. It is more difficult for an older child to express grief directly if he or she has been told that crying is a sign of childishness.

The efforts of adults to protect children from the reality of death often add to their confusion. For instance, saying that a dead person has gone on a trip or is asleep may lead a child to be afraid that he or she will die while traveling or sleeping. Even explaining simply that the baby was sick and therefore died, without distinguishing a life-threatening disorder from ordinary diseases, may result in tremendous anxiety in a child when minor illness occurs.

A very common source of confusion for a young child is not understanding what happens to a person after death. Told that the baby is in heaven, a child may be confused by a grave in the ground or may look for the infant whenever he or she is in a high place. One child was afraid of going in an elevator because he connected it in his mind to the baby going up to heaven. Even saying that God wanted the baby to be with Him may lead the child to be angry at God and afraid that he or she will be chosen next. The lesson that God loves good children may frighten a child into thinking it is better to be bad and survive. The familiar phrase "We lost our baby" may also be confusing to a young child, since many children interpret what they hear literally. This can be seen in the account cited by Dr. Roberta Times in *Living with an Empty Chair:*

> At age three or four while shopping with my mother I overheard a conversation with a neighbor—"It's a shame she lost her mother—she was so young." I envisioned a girl my age walking out of a store, noticing her mother wasn't following, and not being able to find her. . . . For years I couldn't understand why the girl had stopped looking for her mother, and how it was possible for them to never find each other.

It is essential that both younger and older children express their feelings, fears, and questions. Yet discussions are unlikely to occur all at once, as children usually resent being forced to talk about their feelings. In many cases, however, when there is no release for emotions, symptoms of disturbance may appear at a later time. Dr. Cain and his associates found some cases of long-term psychological problems, such as fears of marriage and childbearing, rooted in a mother's miscarriage. These might be prevented if the child is encouraged to ask what happened and feels reassured by parents. Sometimes professional counseling for the parents and/or child may be required.

One child's temporarily disturbed reaction is cited by Eda LeShan, in *Learning to Say Good-by*. She tells the story of a seven-year-old whose parents had a premature baby who died shortly after birth. The baby was cremated and there was no funeral. The boy wanted to know where the baby was but didn't ask. Instead, he imagined the baby was in the house. As a result, he would not open closets or drawers because he was afraid of coming upon a dead baby. When his parents finally understood the reason for their son's behavior, they were able to assist him in overcoming his fears, with the help of counseling.

Having a funeral is a healthy way for the family to start to share the mourning process together and to avoid the kinds of problems this seven-year-old experienced. Some parents choose to protect their children by keeping them away from the funeral and from the other aspects of mourning. Most professionals believe that a child around seven or older should be encouraged—but not forced—to attend the funeral in order to recognize the reality of death and feel included in an important family event. An explanation in advance about what will happen can lessen the anxiety and confusion a child may have. If the child is with someone he or she feels close to and is given a chance to ask questions, the funeral can be beneficial and provide a basis for talking about the baby with parents later.

Often children seem to understand, change the subject quickly, and act as if it is forgotten. But questions frequently arise later as they continue to seek an understanding of what happened. It is not unusual for children's concerns to emerge in forms that may not be obviously related to the loss—in their games, in their drawings, in their dreams—providing parents the opportunity to discuss the events and their feelings with the children again.

Talking with their children about the dead infant, even years afterward, can be helpful to parents and children. One woman told of her son's reaction to her six miscarriages:

> My son complains sometimes that he is an only child. I tell him that there might have been six others and look at all the fights

you'd be having now. We sit down and talk about what their names might have been. He would say, "Oh, you wouldn't call them this or that name." It is a good relationship, and talking with him about something that is so important to both of us brings us closer. We're very open with each other, and I always try to answer his questions.

Parents are sometimes shocked when children bring up the tragedy some years later and use it as a convenient vehicle to express their anger or insecurity. One mother of an eight-year-old whose twin had died in infancy had such an experience when she scolded her daughter. The child responded, "I'll bet you wish my sister were here instead of me, that it was me who died instead." The mother was able to remain firm in her scolding while still reassuring the daughter of her love.

The SHARE organization (see Appendix) has published a book for children called *Thumpy's Story* about a bunny rabbit whose sibling dies. In a simple and straightforward way it conveys to a child the emotions he or she may feel in this situation. The child can use a Thumpy workbook to write down his or her own feelings. Books like these can give parents a way of opening the discussion with their children.

Having experienced one tragedy, parents may be tempted to spoil their children, those they already have and the ones who come later. They are also certain to be extra fearful for their well-being. These normal fears may lead to overprotectiveness and anxiety in relations with the children.

Carolyn Szybist writes about what happened to her soon after the tragic death of her son:

> I became the perfect, overprotective, smothering, all-consuming parent to my young daughter. I was afraid to let her from my sight but also afraid to accept the responsibility for her care. It was a time of decisionless decisions. I was her constant companion and playmate. I needed others to help with her care but resented their helpfulness.

The difficult task of explaining arises again when the parents have children later on. Some parents prefer to hide the tragedy until the children are grown, but a child who becomes aware of a dead sibling at an early age will not be shocked by hearing the information secondhand or as an adult. It is important that parents who have borne a defective child speak with other children as they get older about the possible implications for their own offspring. They might seek genetic counseling together to obtain clearer answers.

Since the parents are deeply affected by their tragedy, it is impossible for the children to be shielded from it. Yet parents who find ways of coping well with their own grief are providing the best possible atmosphere in which their children can also come to accept and grow from the experience. More important perhaps than the specific words they say to a child are the love and security they provide and the impressions they give of being able to express and deal with their own feelings—this in itself is reassuring.

There are as yet few studies of the impact of birth tragedies on other children in a family. Surely their lives are touched by these events, some in subtle ways, others more profoundly. Because so little is known about the effects of infant death on children, parents are left to their own resources and to the help of those around them in assisting their children. Yet children are unusually resilient, often more so than adults. And it is the other children who are also remarkable resources for their parents—the source of caring, distraction, and comfort.

10

Grandparents
A Special Grief

"It has been my dream to have a grandchild—to watch my daughter's child grow. When my daughter became pregnant, I was so happy and proud. What should I be called—Grandma—Nana? Then when my son-in-law called and told us that the baby had died at birth, I was totally devastated. How could this terrible thing have happened to my little girl? And my grandchild—the one I loved so much already. At the hospital I found it unbearable to see my daughter and her husband crying, knowing that there was nothing I could do."

For grandparents, the death of a child is a double blow: the disappointment of their expectations for a grandchild and the pain of seeing their own children suffering.

They had shared with their children the anticipation of a child, the excitement of the growing belly, the planning of the birth. Most likely they had told all their friends about the expected grandchild, imagined how the child would look, and planned visits and gifts. Even if they never saw the baby, they still feel grief for a person who was very special to them.

Grandparents bear the added burden of knowing their own children are grieving. They wish they could protect them from the hurt as they had tried to protect them as young children many years earlier. But the young children are grown up now, and their parents can only help. They cannot take away the pain, and they are saddened by their own helplessness.

If there are no other grandchildren in the family, grandparents must go through a wrenching process of readjustment. They had gradually become accustomed to the idea of a new life stage, to their new identity as grandparents, with all the joy and ambivalence about aging which that change entails. Now they must accept a new reality. One woman described herself as a "grandmother not-to-be," and this phrase captures well the difficult shifts in identity.

Psychiatrist Robert Jay Lifton writes about the feelings of "survivor guilt" experienced by people who have lived through a holocaust that killed many others around them. They cannot understand why the others are gone and they are still there, and they feel terribly guilty for having escaped the fate of their friends and relatives. The parent, and especially the grandparent, of an infant who dies often has a similar sensation—it makes no sense that they have survived an infant. The world is in disorder, turned upside down. One grandfather said:

> I'll never forget having to bury my grandchild. I felt it should have been me in that grave, not him. The children and grandchildren are supposed to bury the old people, not the other way around.

Some grandparents—grandmothers in particular—expect to have a major share in raising the baby. Their daughters may be young and unmarried, still living at home, or they may be married but planning to return to work quickly, and Grandma had planned to take care of the baby. For some grandmothers, this new role may have been unwelcome, and their sadness is mixed with relief, but for those who looked forward to the presence of a new baby in their homes there is an extra sense of personal loss.

Whatever feelings of grief the grandparents may have, most bereaved parents acknowledge that they were the most helpful and supportive people in the difficult first few days and weeks. They offered consolation, physical care, distraction, and, most important, their love. One woman remembered:

> My parents were just terrific. They came immediately and took care of everything—the cooking, the cleaning, screening phone

calls, entertaining visitors. It was just what I needed those first few days—to be totally pampered and not have to worry about a thing. And there were some special moments—my mother gave me a bath, just as if I was a little girl again. And my father helped me start walking around again. Every day he took me for a beautiful walk in the park, walking slowly with me as I regained my strength.

For grandparents who live far away from their children, there are special frustrations. They want to help their children but may not have the money or time to travel. They can help by talking on the phone or writing, but they wish they could do more. Those who do visit may feel they do not want to invade their children's privacy by staying with them for an extended period of time, so their visit is brief.

Some grandparents, on the other hand, may try to control the situation more than their children want. They seek to protect the bereaved parents, making decisions for them about the funeral or about care of the grandchildren at home. This may be appreciated as helpful, but sometimes it is seen as interfering. The bereaved parent may not understand that such actions are often an effort to cope with the loss.

The grandparents' grief may be expressed in a variety of ways. Often they are extremely angry—at the doctor, at the son-in-law or daughter-in-law, and even at the baby. As they watch their children's pain, they sometimes cannot help feeling angry at its source. If the baby survives for a while, in some hospitals grandparents may visit and participate, even if briefly, in the infant's care. In this way they share more fully in the parents' love for the tiny patient.

Many grandparents also feel guilt, just as the parents do. If the baby had a genetic problem that led to the miscarriage, abortion, stillbirth, or infant death, the grandparents may feel responsible. "What if it was my genes that were passed to the child and caused this? I wonder if they blame me for what happened?" one grandmother feared. Yet the genetic process is complicated, and often abnormalities appear that are not hereditary.

If the grandparents are quite sure, based on tests or family history, that they have transmitted a genetic problem, they must make an effort to accept that this is in no way their "fault." In talking with their children they may learn that their children do not blame them in the least. A skillful genetic counselor may also help to dispel many of the anxieties surrounding hereditary illness.

Sometimes there is a history of reproductive problems or infant loss in the grandparents' generation. The grandmother especially may wonder if she has passed along to her daughter a propensity for tragic pregnancies. This predicament has become especially acute with discoveries of the effects of the drug DES (diethylstilbestrol) on the daughters of women who took it to prevent miscarriage. These daughters are now known to experience higher-than-average fetal death. Since the drug was prescribed by physicians to assist in the creation of life, how could any of these mothers have known its potential dangers?

The tragedies of pregnancy and birth are still mysterious, and everyone involved looks for reasons to help make sense of what is so frustratingly incomprehensible. This search for explanation most often creates unnecessary suffering when it results in excessive self-blame.

One grandfather found relief from his guilt after talking it over with his daughter. He had worried that she hadn't really wanted to get pregnant and did so only in response to subtle pressure from him. When she miscarried, he felt responsible for her grief:

> I was getting old and I really wanted a grandchild before I died. My daughter sensed this, and I was afraid she probably wouldn't have become pregnant as soon as she did. After talking to her one day about this feeling, she told me that she and her husband also desperately wanted children. It was a great relief.

Denial is another type of response. One man, for instance, tried to block out the existence of his dying grandchild. Finally his wife talked him into realizing that there was a baby alive and that he had to acknowledge this. He had visited his daughter at the hospital, but now he asked her to accompany him to the nursery to see the baby.

Some grandparents express their grief very openly. For example, Smialek found in her study of reactions to infant death that "in many families it has been the grandmother rather than the mother who shows the more pronounced grief reaction. In some instances it becomes apparent that the grandmother is . . . deeply grieving over the loss of a significant loved one in her past." She describes one grandmother who had herself lost an infant and felt the painful revival of her own bereavement with the death of her grandchild.

A similar example appears in another grandmother's comment:

> I think I felt worse when my daughter's baby died than I did when my own died. I know how painful such an experience is and was terribly upset that my own daughter should have to face such suffering.

Grandparents should share their feelings with the parents as an important part of the recovery process for the whole family. Many grandparents feel, however, that they must conceal their pain in order to provide much-needed physical and emotional support to the bereaved couple, as well as to avoid upsetting them further. In many cases when grandparents act this way, the couple misinterprets their response. That was one mother's experience after her baby died:

> My in-laws came to stay with us for two days afterward. They were helpful in preparing meals and taking care of other physical needs, but I don't remember their crying or saying anything about the baby. Afterward I wondered if they had felt any grief.

Grandparents may cover their feelings so as to reassure the grieving couple that someone in the family is in control and will take care of the household without needing to be taken care of themselves. Showing their grief, however, will probably give the bereaved the feeling of understanding and sharing.

As one grandfather of a stillborn child wrote in a letter to the *British Medical Journal:*

> It may be worth mentioning that grandparents, too, can feel bereaved. My wife and I were, I think, surprised at the depth of

our own sense of loss. The main point here, of course, is that if this is ignored or repressed it can lead to family resentments . . . but if it is faced and shared, it can provide strength to both parents and grandparents and can . . . deepen relationships within the family.

11

Friends and Relatives
Helping the Bereaved

In a Baoulé village in West Africa a death has occurred. Relatives and friends gather quickly from surrounding villages, and as they arrive they all greet the bereaved family with the word Nyako. The word is repeated many times by the visitors, and the family responds, "Nyako." The men gather in a circle, and individuals rise to recite words of comfort, beginning and ending with Nyako. The mourners again respond, "Nyako."

In contrast to the Baoulé and many other cultures, Americans have no prescribed words to express their sympathy after a death occurs. Even when there are set rituals—a funeral, a wake—most Americans are uncomfortable with people who have experienced a death. We have no phrases to convey the feelings of solidarity and compassion in the face of loss. And yet it is the support of others, family and friends, that eases the isolation and anguish of bereavement.

Dr. Glenn Vernon, author of *Sociology of Death*, asked 1,500 college students what they would do if they met someone who had recently lost a loved one. Only twenty-five percent said they would mention the death. Forty percent said they would rather the other person brought up the subject. And another twenty-five percent preferred that the death not be mentioned at all. The remainder had no idea what they would do.

This study showed the feeling in a clearly defined bereavement situation. But when a pregnancy ends in tragedy, friends and relatives are even more uncertain about what to do. Too often, therefore, they say the wrong thing or nothing at all. The whole situation is confusing. Is it or is it not a tragedy? Should the parents be treated as though they had "lost a loved one"? What others often do not realize is that a major tragedy has occurred—probably the worst so far in the life of a young adult.

In other mourning situations, the bereaved often help their friends who are uncomfortable by directing the conversation. But in this case even the parents themselves are not really sure how to act. How do you grieve for someone who existed mostly in mental images and perhaps in internal movements? Their experience is filled with contradictions and ambiguities. For instance, if it was the first pregnancy, they wonder: are they parents or aren't they?

Parents who are mourning for their infant receive a strong message from society that their loss is not significant. Sad, yes—but not really a tragedy. "At least you have other children," people say. Or "Well, you can always have another one." The comments of others may make a bereaved parent begin to question his or her own feelings and then try to tailor them to the perceived expectations of others. As one mother said after her child was stillborn:

> Sometimes I felt proud of myself for seeming strong and being able to talk about it without breaking down. I didn't want people to pity me. And then I would worry about whether people would think I was callous. And when I did cry, I worried that I seemed overly emotional.

It is not easy for the bereaved to discover for themselves what their genuine feelings are rather than what they are supposed to feel. But they know that their tragedy is real, that they are in pain.

At times it seems hard to communicate this pain because there is simply no appropriate language with which to describe the tragedy. For parents of a stillborn child, for example, to speak about "the day our baby died" is terribly difficult when it was also "the day our baby was born." The cause of so much anguish is thus reduced to "it"—"the day *it* happened."

The baby is also often referred to as "it." Even when parents have given a name to the dead infant, they rarely use the name in conversation. Was the infant a person or only an "it"? When there is no name, when the child's sex is not even known—most likely with a miscarriage or ectopic pregnancy and sometimes with selective abortion—it is even harder for parents to verbalize their sense of having lost a baby.

Referring to the infant by name, when there was a name, helps the bereaved parents acknowledge the reality of their loss. Some parents are surprised at how helpful this is:

> A friend asked if we had named our stillborn baby. After telling her the name, we both began referring to the baby by her name, Sarah. It felt so good to call her a name.

> When we chose the name Jonathan before the birth of our son, I thought I wouldn't use the shorter versions of the name. However, in the hospital, people referred to him by nicknames. They always talked about Jonny, or asked me how Jon was. I was pleased to hear these names. He sounded like a real person even though he had so many problems and was dying.

Problems in communicating with others about the tragedy arise almost immediately after the event. How is one going to break the news? There was anticipation of a joyful announcement; instead there is now an unexpected report of tragedy. Carefully prepared announcement cards become useless. Instead there is awkwardness, embarrassment, sadness, and anger:

> I knew my parents were waiting eagerly for the news of the birth of their first grandchild. I waited more than a day before I had the courage to call and tell them that she was born but would probably not survive.

> People called and asked, "Have you had your baby yet?" I would always hesitate, I didn't know what to answer. Usually I'd say, "Yes and no." Yes because we had the baby and no because we didn't. One friend who lived in another town called a month later, bubbling with cheerfulness. Her first words were, "What kind of baby did you have?" I couldn't help feeling mad, even though she had no way to know. All I could think to say was, "A dead one."

In many situations, friends are not even aware there was a pregnancy. If a woman miscarries early or if the expectant parents live at a distance from relatives and friends, they wonder how to convey two pieces of news at once. Can others understand the importance of the loss of a baby whose existence was unknown to them?

The mother who carries a baby, knowing she will soon have an abortion because she has learned of deformities or knowing that the infant is already dead, faces an excruciating few days or weeks. Every time she leaves her home, people congratulate her and ask when the child is due. Friends also ask the father about the progress of the expected infant. Every question about the baby is painful for the bereaved. Should they tell the truth?

Some parents find it easier if someone else informs others for them:

> I found it such a relief that my neighbors who knew I was expecting a baby were told about the death right away by someone else. Then I didn't have to worry about calling people to let them know. By the time I came home, they were all prepared with food and flowers for me.

While this is very helpful for some parents, others prefer to tell friends themselves. Breaking the news is a way the bereaved parents can begin to talk about their feelings to others and make the event "real" to themselves. This may explain the resentment felt by one father after his baby died:

> I returned to work soon after our son was stillborn and realized that the whole office knew. I discovered my mother had called my secretary to tell her. I was furious—I felt she was doing something behind my back that I would have preferred to do myself.

Although it can be hard to speak to others about the event, communication is an essential part of the healing process. Whether the news is conveyed initially by the parents or by someone else, it is the continuation of the dialogue over the months and even the years that follow which is most important.

Maintaining the dialogue is difficult for both the parents and their friends and relatives:

> I felt that when I talked about our experience people were very threatened by it, so I stopped mentioning it even though I really wanted to talk.

> With someone I knew well, I was anxious to talk about it, but the pain was so deep that it was very difficult. So I had mixed feelings about it, and no one encouraged me to talk.

A very strained situation may occur when good friends of the bereaved parents are expecting a baby or already have young children, especially one around the same age theirs would have been. Parents react in different ways to this. Some isolate themselves, afraid they will be thought of as a jinx. Some, however, try very hard to preserve their friendship but find difficulties:

> My best friend was reluctant to visit me when she knew she would have to bring her baby. I wanted her to visit and feel comfortable, so I tried to act like it didn't bother me. I took pictures of the baby and asked about his progress. After a while she began to relax about it and then really got into talking about him a lot. This was very painful for me. I felt like she had forgotten what happened to me, but I didn't know how to tell her. It wasn't until after my next child was born that we finally talked about it. It would have been better if we had cleared the air sooner.

The bereaved parents' need for the comfort and support of others is enormous. But all too often they feel they must isolate themselves or hide their feelings.

The father's feelings are especially likely to be misunderstood. Some people assume that the tragedy happened only to the mother. Friends and family may forget that the man is not just the partner of a grieving mother, he is also a bereaved parent. One father expressed resentment at being excluded:

> All during childbirth classes and labor and delivery, husbands are secondary. So it wasn't surprising that I was ignored when something went wrong. People asked, "How is your wife?" They never thought to ask how I was.

The father may feel that he must act in control and concentrate on cheering up his wife. He may find it difficult to express his emotions openly to others, and they in turn often find it awkward to ask him how he is feeling.

Mother and father both need to feel that others are sensitive to their anguish and share the sense of loss. They need to be able to discuss their feelings, to express the anger, the guilt, the sense of failure. They need to be reassured that their feelings are legitimate, that they are going through a normal grieving process. They need to repeat conversations, to be constantly reassured, to have someone who will listen to the same details again and again.

There are times when they need to talk about other things, to feel, even for a brief time, that life goes on normally and that they are just like everyone else. And there are times when the smallest gestures are the most appreciated—a call, a note, an invitation to lunch, a jigsaw puzzle for distraction, an offer to help with cleaning or care of other children.

Some parents mentioned a particular incident that touched them:

> When Joan came to visit I mentioned that the doctor was worried that I hadn't had a bowel movement yet. Not long after she left, the doorbell rang, and there she was with a huge jar of stewed prunes. That was my first laugh. It was such a thoughtful idea.

As helpful as they may try to be, friends and relatives who are unfamiliar with the experience of bereavement may simply not be able to comprehend what the parents are feeling. Many bereaved parents, therefore, seek out people who have had experiences like their own. Family and friends may help by offering to put them in touch with other bereaved parents or with organized support groups such as those listed in the Appendix of this book.

A difficult dilemma for friends and relatives arises when they are asked for their opinion or when, unasked, they believe the parents need some advice. This situation may arise, for example, when a baby's condition is uncertain and a second medical opinion could be helpful or when a couple must decide whether to terminate a pregnancy after learning that their baby will not be normal. If parents are trying to decide about a funeral or are thinking of suing the physician, they may seek advice. Or a friend may believe that a parent having great difficulty in recovering from the event needs professional counseling.

Even when family and friends are aware of a need for help, their own fears of dealing with grief and dying may make it difficult for them to be of assistance. Some rationalize their inaction by saying, "We are not needed. . . . They want to be alone. . . . This is not our business. . . ." Some do not want to become involved, or don't know how, and some are afraid of the consequences if they do.

It is especially difficult when decisions that may affect the parents for the rest of their lives have to be made quickly. One man reflected on the conflict he felt when his sister asked for advice about having an abortion after she had just learned her baby would never be normal:

> It was too big a decision for me to make. I had nothing to lose in the situation since I was a third party and not responding from the viewpoint of having to be the parent of this child. Clearly if she decided not to have the abortion because of the advice I had given, and the baby turned out to be an incredible burden on her, she would have resented me for the rest of her life. I did not say anything because I did not want to hurt her.

At the time of critical decision-making, parents may not be aware of all the options available to them. Sometimes others can be most helpful simply by gathering the information necessary for making the best possible decision and by reviewing with the family all the positive and negative aspects of each option.

The efforts of others to be comforting may occasionally have a negative effect. Those who hope to erase the pain by minimizing the loss, for instance, are usually unsuccessful:

> A friend came to see me at the hospital. She said, "Well, I'm very sorry, but after all it's for the best, since you wouldn't want the baby to grow up and be sick and then die. It's better that it

happens now and not later." It was a very heartless thing for her to say, and it upset me more than anything anybody else had said.

The temptation to try to find something positive in the tragic event, while understandable, is rarely appreciated. The woman who is told that she will be a better mother for having had this experience, for example, can only wonder how that is possible, as she is likely to feel that she will be a more anxious mother.

The comments from people who seem to have forgotten, even momentarily, often hurt the most. As time goes by, others may seem to forget the experience altogether, and thoughtless remarks may increase:

> About six months after our baby died, I was talking with my cousin about a friend's response to her new baby. She said, "When you have your first child, you'll understand." I thought to myself, "What do you think I had?" She caught herself and tried to correct her comment, but clearly she had forgotten for the moment.

Even immediately after the tragedy occurs, there are people who say nothing at all, who act as if nothing happened. Studies of parents after newborn loss find that this "conspiracy of silence" is typical and that it is upsetting to most parents. The parents' grief is therefore frequently compounded by hurt feelings and anger toward those they care about:

> A number of friends never called or mentioned our tragedy. Even some who came to see us managed to avoid mentioning the subject completely. When I returned to work, many people said nothing to me about the baby, as if nothing had happened. And some of these were people with whom I had talked a lot about my pregnancy. If I said anything about what had happened, I felt it made people uncomfortable. My disappointment and anger at others was at times even greater than my grief. I found that I was reevaluating my friendships based on how well people came through for me.

Negative encounters often damage relationships with one's family and friends, with the result that grief over the loss may be made worse by a growing isolation from others. The pain of bereavement is severe enough without the added burden of anger and strained relationships.

Sometimes family members and friends who do not respond feel they are being helpful by doing nothing. Perhaps they are told by someone, or they tell others, to refrain from calling the bereaved parents so as not to upset them. But the parents may wonder why no one seems to care. Other family members or friends fear that any mention of the tragedy may revive the pain and that talking about other subjects would be a helpful distraction. One woman remembers:

> When I had my miscarriage, I told a good friend about it, and he quickly changed the subject. I was hurt and disappointed until his wife told me later that he had been upset but thought I wouldn't want to talk about it.

The parents may, in fact, be ambivalent about discussing a subject so laden with sadness and therefore may unconsciously give others an unspoken message that they do not want to dwell on it. They may expect some discomfort and deliberately lead conversations in other directions; then, afterward, they wonder why the friend had not talked about their grief. Understanding one's own needs and then communicating them to others can facilitate the recovery process for the bereaved and also help others to provide the most appropriate support.

Bereaved parents who confront the friends who disappointed them are relieved when they understand what the friends' intentions were. They begin to realize how difficult it is for other people to face and discuss grief and that silence does not necessarily mean a lack of caring and concern. Discussion also helps by reminding the parents of the awkwardness they themselves probably felt in the past when responding to the grief of others.

Friends and relatives who listen and react with understanding, who console and distract, are cherished by bereaved parents. Existing relationships may be strengthened when there is a deepened appreciation of others' affection and helpfulness. New friendships may develop with people who were not previously close but who provided a special word or action at the right moment. And those who realize that the need for support lasts a long time, and who are there to offer it, are the ones who help make it possible to go on.

IV
PUBLIC ISSUES

12

Medical Care
The Families' Needs and Experiences

Death in obstetrics just does not seem to fit. Doctors enter the field to help create life. The nurses want to work in maternity so they can rejoice with the parents of new babies and enjoy the contact with cuddly newborns. Few people are prepared to deal with death and bereavement in such a setting.

It is easier to ignore death than to confront it, easier to act as if nothing has happened and send the parents home quickly with little or no explanation, support, or encouragement. Dr. S. Bourne of London agrees. When he surveyed the physicians who had presided at one hundred stillbirths and one hundred live births, he found that

> the doctor whose patient has had a stillbirth does not want to know, he does not want to notice and he does not want to remember anything about it. This must mean doctors under strain and a group of patients in danger of neglect.

This attitude can be found not only among physicians but other hospital personnel as well. It may seem callous but it is usually due to the staff's lack of understanding and feelings of inadequacy in helping the bereaved parents.

Hospital staff members are the first people present when a death occurs. It is in their power, through their reactions and the quality of care they provide, to make an enormous difference in the experience of the parents. The staff can help make the tragedy more bearable and avoid making it worse by insensitivity, error, or inattention to need.

In far too many hospitals, staff members are untrained in ways of helping parents. They restrict contact between family and baby, dispose quickly of the infant who has died, unthinkingly place a bereaved mother in a room with the mother of a healthy new baby, and generally ignore the needs of the distraught couple. These hospitals have either not established policies for responding to tragic birth events or they fall back on restrictive policies that make the experience even more traumatic.

In some hospitals, the staff is trained to meet the special needs of bereaved parents. In these cases the parents benefit greatly, as does the staff, by having something to offer. What the staff can offer that parents appreciate most is a completeness of information and an understanding of the parents' emotional needs. When doctors and nurses meet these needs, with or without a conscious policy, parents remember them gratefully as "terrific, sympathetic, just like family."

Many parents, however, do not benefit from a prepared hospital staff. Sometimes, especially with a miscarriage, the hospital stay is very brief, or they do not go to the hospital at all.

The responsibility of medical personnel, however, begins early in the pregnancy and extends to follow-up visits. It is during these outpatient visits to the doctor and in preparation classes that parents can begin to air their fears and gather the information that will help them if problems develop.

Expectant couples often do not want to know that it is possible for something to go wrong. "It won't happen to me," they reassure themselves, blocking out any hints that not all pregnancies are successful. For many, "doctor knows best" and parents prefer not to raise questions; if they just trust the physician completely, then everything will be all right. Some physicians encourage this attitude and frown on patients who ask questions, even belittling their worries. Yet even when a physician or childbirth educator responds to all the fears and explains the possibility of problems, some parents may not pay attention or will become annoyed at being alarmed.

If these parents do face a complication, they are completely shocked and unprepared. Although no amount of advance information can fully equip a person at the time of tragedy and too much warning can create unnecessary anxiety, many parents wish afterward that they had had some idea of what to expect and what they had the right to ask for. Physicians and childbirth educators can provide this for parents—the reassurance that in all likelihood their baby will be fine and the knowledge that if he or she dies or is very ill they should have time with the baby and call upon people who will be able to help.

Some physicians believe it important to tell newly pregnant women at least about the possibility of miscarriage, since it is so common, and advise them what to do in case they have some spotting. Women who discover they are bleeding are therefore not taken totally by surprise.

During prenatal visits, doctors also discuss genetic tests with those women for whom it may be appropriate. If a deformity is found, the physician can help tremendously in deciding whether to abort and in explaining to parents what an abortion is like. Too often parents go through this experience with very little support from medical people.

When doctors and nurses are unprepared and frightened to approach someone who is distraught, a parent may interpret their response as a sign that he or she is an outcast, someone terrible to be ignored and isolated. As one mother of a stillborn boy recounted:

> I felt my doctor had deserted me. He never called or came to look and see how I was doing. I called his office and it was days before he even returned my call. Didn't he even care?

In a study of middle-class parents whose babies were stillborn, sixty percent expressed dissatisfaction with their physicians, finding them unsupportive, uncaring. In our own interviews, two-thirds cited dissatisfaction with some aspect of the care they received. This does not mean the doctors do not care, but many do not show their feelings. Many agonize over whether they could have done something to prevent the tragedy. They are uncomfortable with death and with the necessity of facing a family they feel they have failed. So, feeling inadequate and, at the same time, being wary of the parents' emotions, a doctor may try to avoid the situation altogether. As Dr. Abraham Bergman writes, "Our ethos is cure rather than care, and death, after all, represents failure. We quickly turn back to tasks where the tools we possess can be applied."

In many cases, there is no physician whom parents know and to whom they can turn for help. The many poor women who rely on public hospitals or clinics often see a different physician or resident on every visit and several unknown medical students and doctors when they enter the hospital. Many middle-class women have a physician who is part of a group and who may not be present when they deliver. This situation can be particularly hard, as one woman felt when her baby died a few hours after birth:

> I went into labor on a weekend and my doctor was out of town. His partner was called in and was there during the crisis. But I had only met him once and never liked him very much. That just made everything harder on us when we needed someone who knew us to talk to.

In some settings, the nurse-midwife is playing an increasingly important role in assuring continuity of care. In large group practices or clinics, a mother can feel more secure knowing that there is this one knowledgeable person whom she will see at every stage of pregnancy and delivery. Many parents are more comfortable with the midwife; they feel she is less hurried and more sympathetic and responsive to their questions.

What parents want most from the medical staff is information. A father whose son died shortly after birth complained about how difficult it was to obtain an explanation:

> I needed to talk to the doctor, to find out what happened. But I never really got any answers. I didn't expect to know every last technical detail, but at least some explanation so we could make sense of it and figure out where to go from there. Had we done something to cause this? Should we have another baby? But the more we asked, the more defensive he seemed, as if we were

accusing him of having done something wrong. All we wanted
was to know, not to blame him.

Since anger is common after a death and malpractice suits are
becoming more prevalent, a doctor may interpret persistent questioning as an attack. Sometimes it is. But the physician who
avoids all questions succeeds only in promoting mistrust and
suspicion. The physician who can accept anger as a normal
reaction, who makes direct, honest, and immediate statements
about what is happening, "without any word games" as one
father noted, without trying to "protect" parents from harsh
reality, is the most appreciated.

Providing an explanation is not a simple task. Sometimes
there is none. And even if there is, at a time of shock people
cannot assimilate a great deal of technical information; they may
hear only part of the explanation or misunderstand it. For
example, two people may hear very different messages in the
same statement. One mother whose child was born with grave
deformities requiring medical intervention mentioned this problem:

> It is interesting that through the whole process my husband and I
> read everything differently in what the doctor said. My husband
> would pick up all the negative facts and made his decision not to
> treat the baby very quickly, and I would hold on to a positive fact
> and wouldn't give up so fast.

To counteract these difficulties, it is usually necessary for the
doctor to explain what has happened several times and to be
available for questions that may arise later. He or she may also
ask the parents to feed back what they have heard in order to
know how much they have understood. Parents at first may
focus on one aspect of the experience; later they will begin to
wonder about another aspect. The physician cannot completely
answer all their questions in a single session shortly after the
event. For this reason, some doctors meet several times with
couples during the weeks following their loss. Some write down
important facts and instructions so that parents can review them
in a less hurried setting.

Even before parents leave the hospital, there are many ways

in which an aware and sensitive medical staff can help them. Perhaps most important is encouraging the parents to see and hold their baby. This opportunity, even after a late miscarriage, is being advocated increasingly by nurses and physicians. They are responding to studies reflecting the damage caused by not seeing the baby and parents' comments, such as: "If only I could have seen her. I have nothing to hold on to, nothing at all" and "I still remember what he looked like, a perfect baby. I treasure that image in my mind."

Too often a physician may feel that the father's viewing of the baby is sufficient. But the mother needs the opportunity just as much. Members of a medical staff are especially reluctant to show parents a badly deformed infant or one who has been dead for a time before birth for fear that parents will be emotionally harmed by this sight.

Nancy O'Donohue is one of the growing number of people who feel differently. As nursing supervisor at Kings County Hospital in Brooklyn, she became convinced from her own experience with over four hundred families that seeing the baby is best:

> We never once had a mother who saw her baby that was deformed and regretted it. I have seen a mother who had a stillborn baby that was perfectly formed but chose not to see him and then came back later wanting to know if he was human.
>
> We always describe what the baby looks like. Sometimes if the baby is very severely deformed and even the nurses can't bear to see it, we still offer the mother the possibility of seeing the baby but secretly hope she'll say no. Many do accept the offer, and the result is always positive. In one case, for instance, the mother said, "I want to see him anyway." A month later, when she was asked what the baby looked like, she talked about his perfect ears—parents always find some positive aspect to focus on.

Initially, parents may refuse to see an infant but regret this decision the next day. They may think it is too late to change their minds or be afraid to ask. For these reasons, O'Donohue gives the parents a second opportunity after they have had a chance to think about their decision. She has even retrieved infants from the morgue and wrapped them in warm blankets to show them to the parents.

In a growing number of hospitals, a staff member takes pictures which are available to parents. Some decline at first but return weeks later asking for the photo. Photographs are especially helpful to the parent who never saw the baby but later seeks reassurance that he or she was real and not a monster. For some people a picture is not only a cherished memento but also tangible evidence to others that there really was a baby.

The pictures should be taken soon after the delivery or death, with the baby dressed and presented to look as good as possible. Because seeing the photograph for the first time can be painful, it is important to give it to the parents in a supportive environment. Unusual features of the baby can be explained first, so that the parent who never saw his or her infant will not be shocked by anomalies or physical changes.

When the family lives at a great distance from the hospital, the pictures may have to be sent by mail. A phone call before the photos are mailed can help prepare the parents. Sister Jane Marie Lamb of the SHARE support organization suggests that a warning on the envelope would be helpful, alerting the parents that they may not want to open the package if they're alone.

If the baby is alive at birth and moved to an intensive care unit, the staff can provide other important services. They can allow parents not only to see their baby but to participate actively in the infant's care. One way is for the mother to breast-feed the infant, even with a breast pump. The possibility of calling or visiting at any time and having easy access to information about the baby makes the parents feel more comfortable in the nursery. Some parents may want to stay close to their baby, and they can do so in those hospitals that provide a special room near the nursery in which parents can sleep. A tour of the unit and an explanation of all its equipment will help prevent misconceptions about what is happening. One mother regretted that no one did this for her:

There are things that happen that, if they were explained, would ease a lot of pain. For example, I thought the baby was having a difficult time breathing on the respirator; that every breath was an effort for him. When I mentioned this later, I was told that the baby was not working hard, that it was the respirator that was working to force the air into him.

In some hospitals, when an infant is dying, the physician encourages the parents' relatives and friends to visit the baby. This opportunity helps the parents later in their grief, because the child has been established as a real person to those around them.

If the baby must be transferred to a different hospital, it is especially important to involve the parents. Dr. Gary Benfield and his associates at the Children's Hospital in Akron, Ohio, to which many infants are brought from other hospitals, describe how the parents are engaged in the transfer from the initial stages. They are shown the baby and given a chance to ask questions; they are provided with the necessary phone numbers for contacting the Children's Hospital and furnished a map that shows them how to get there. Most important, they are encouraged to visit the hospital at any time. Once the baby has arrived at the intensive care unit, a picture is taken and shown to the mother who has remained in the other hospital.

For parents who have experienced a miscarriage or ectopic pregnancy, seeing the fetus is not generally as important an issue. Some feel that seeing the remains of the pregnancy or knowing what happened to them can only be harmful. What they do express a strong desire for is information about the cause of their loss and about the grieving process itself.

A major issue for any mother whose infant has died or is very ill is the location of her hospital room. Most mothers express their desire to be as far away as possible from healthy babies and their excited parents. The experience of hearing babies crying in the nursery or seeing them being fed by their mothers can be excruciating. Not only does the mother feel especially miserable around the constant reminders of her own emptiness and failure, but she also feels awkward and worries about making other mothers uncomfortable. She needs to face the reality of her own baby's illness or death, but it is cruel to force her to witness other people's joy.

Some women prefer to remain on the maternity floor, usually in a private room, either because of more liberal family visiting hours or because they do not want to feel isolated for their failure to have a healthy child. Maternity nurses who are trained to help bereaved parents may find it easier to keep the mothers on their floor, although they should have the option of visiting them elsewhere in the hospital if the mother chooses to move. Offering parents a choice of floor can be a positive way of giving them some control over what is happening to them when everything else seems out of their control.

The terrible loneliness felt by the disappointed mother becomes worse if hospital policy restricts her family's visiting. Hospitals have reasons for rules, but strict adherence to them is not always appropriate. One grandfather mentioned his distress when he was not allowed to see his daughter and his new grandson immediately:

> As soon as we heard the news I raced to the hospital. I ran in the door—I wanted to see my daughter and my first grandson before he died. But I was stopped at the entrance by a security man telling me I would have to wait two hours for the correct visiting time. I pleaded but was told this was a strict rule that he could not break. I was so frustrated that I broke down and cried. Finally he let me in.

Many hospitals do not allow a father to stay overnight in the room with the mother even though this could ease her feelings of emptiness. Having her other children visit can also be reassuring to her as well as to the children themselves. Early discharge is sometimes the best solution, and unless there are serious complications most women can leave the hospital soon after delivery.

Many bereaved parents feel out of place on the maternity floor. Because their situations are unusual, the routine nursing strategies do not apply and sometimes mistakes are made. One mother of a stillborn child complained that by error a nurse came into her room and asked cheerfully, "How is the little baby doing today?" The mother responded, "The baby is dead!" In some hospitals, an unobtrusive symbol such as a teardrop is placed on the door of a patient who has had a loss. In that way all staff members can be alerted to try to avoid such mistakes.

Hurtful comments are one reason for parents' anger at the doctors, the nurses, and the hospital. Parents are also angry at the possibility of some medical error having caused their grief. They are angry when they receive bills for services they thought were poor or insensitive. They are angry at being given evasive answers. They are angry because they feel misunderstood and because their grief was dismissed as trivial.

The general impression of insensitivity arises from comments that some staff members make in an effort to be comforting. As one woman said:

> I knew something was wrong just by the way everyone was scurrying around in the delivery room and by that terrible silence. Then we knew the baby was dead. The doctor's only comment was, "It must be congenital," as if to say it certainly must be my fault, not his. Then a nurse said, "It would be worse if you had a five-year-old that died." I suppose she was right, but it certainly didn't make me feel any better. Later, the doctor said, "You're young; you'll have lots more kids." I was appalled—I was thirty-three already. Where do they learn all these stupid comments?

Another source of anger is the way parents are approached for permission to perform an autopsy. This request occurs quickly after a death and comes as a jolt to the parents, who are not yet prepared to make such a decision.

Parents often have strong feelings or fears about an autopsy. They may be eager for such an examination to learn all they can about the baby's condition. They are especially concerned about the implications of the cause of death for future children or even others they already have. Some parents oppose an autopsy as a violation of their infant's tiny body. As one parent said, "He's been through enough. I don't want him to suffer any more probing by doctors." Others may have religious objections or worry needlessly that the body cannot be properly displayed at the funeral.

If parents are approached cautiously and with an understanding of their feelings, the initial request for an autopsy can be the beginning of discussions about what happened to the baby. Autopsy results can form the basis for further discussion during a follow-up interview. Many times results are not reported automatically and parents have to ask for them. Even if it is unlikely that an autopsy will reveal new knowledge, parents may want to eliminate any possibility that unknown problems exist. Sometimes when no autopsy is performed, parents later regret not having information that might have been revealed. The doctor should give them a chance to think over their decision and change their minds without pressure.

It is important for the medical staff to discuss funeral and burial arrangements with parents. Presenting the available options and recommending a chaplain to assist them is very helpful. Many parents, especially after a miscarriage or stillbirth, may want the hospital to take care of the body or think that this is their only option. These parents may wonder later exactly what the hospital did with the baby and fear it is somewhere in a jar on a shelf. A staff member might mention that many wonder about this and then, if the parents wish, explain what the hospital's practice is. This can be comforting to those who are afraid to ask.

Too often parents are pressured into making a decision about the disposal of the body and become angry at the insensitive way this matter is handled. Once again, they need some time to think about such an important question and to discuss it with others so that they will not make a decision in haste and shock and be sorry about it later.

Various members of the staff—doctors, nurses, social workers, midwives, chaplains—can assist parents in beginning the process of grieving by telling them that grief is normal and to be expected and by describing the many emotions they will feel over the weeks and months to come. The practice of heavily sedating the grieving mother while she is in the hospital works against her own efforts to recover.

Some professionals try to prepare parents for the thoughtless comments they are likely to hear from people trying to be helpful and forearm them with appropriate responses. A social worker who works with parents of dying infants explained her approach:

> I try to give them ammunition for dealing with insensitive people. There are comments they'll hear and be angry about, and sometimes it helps to hear them in advance. I tell them people will try to help them, saying: "You really didn't know that baby!" They can answer that their relationship with the baby started way back with the first thought of being pregnant, that even if he lived only a day he was part of their lives for much longer than that. Or people will say: "It is for the best!" Well, it's never for the best, it's a terrible situation!

Often the nurse, the social worker, or the chaplain is the one who is most in touch with parents and who can provide many crucial insights. Since these professionals often do not seem as distant or hurried as the doctor, they can act as advocates and interpreters, translating parents' and physicians' concerns to each other. Parents may feel more comfortable in expressing fears and questions to them.

Unfortunately, many newly bereaved parents are not sure how to pose questions. They are confused about how to act and wonder what others expect from them. The nurse or social worker, attuned to their situation, can relieve much of their anxiety by telling them that their feelings are common—that whatever they feel comfortable doing is normal—and by helping them to formulate their questions. They also can be sensitive to the parents who are afraid to ask the doctor anything, either because they do not want to hear unwelcome answers or because they do not want to anger and alienate the physician. Parents whose baby is still alive can be reassured that raising questions will not cause the doctor to neglect their infant. It may even be necessary to interpret a physician's mood to parents, since they may take every word or facial movement as a reflection on their own situation.

Health professionals around the country have made tremendous progress in the last few years in their efforts to insure that parents benefit from the best possible emotional support. Many hospitals have established "perinatal bereavement teams" and policies to make sure that every family with a loss is referred to the team member on call. The team is usually comprised of social workers, chaplains, and nurses who are trained to understand bereavement and to help families with both immediate and longer-term needs. They are the ones who make sure that families have all of the mementoes, information, and options that can be offered them.

Unfortunately most programs do not include families who have suffered a miscarriage or ectopic pregnancy. The numbers are large and the woman usually does not stay in the hospital very long. But increasingly, perinatal bereavement teams are trying to help these families as well. One unusual hospital in Pennsylvania, Lancaster Osteopathic, bought a small section of a cemetery for burial of miscarried fetuses and gives every family a photograph of the cemetery marker and an engraved memorial certificate with the date of their loss.

Follow-up meetings and support groups are often included in these programs, giving parents the feeling that their relationship with the hospital staff has not ended with the baby's death. Follow-up is time-consuming and often parents do not want it or are afraid to take advantage of it. Returning to a hospital or an office that evokes painful memories may be too difficult. Occasionally a parent will say it is not necessary to talk, that it's better to try to forget rather than get upset again by talking about what happened. But those who do take advantage of this follow-up are grateful and very often reassured by the information and advice they receive. Many parents later express regret that there had been no such follow-up.

Although many obstetricians do ask mothers to come in for the standard four- or six-week physical checkup, they too rarely use this visit as a time for both parents to air their worries and concerns. Some neonatologists attempt to follow up with the parents whose infants were under their care. One described his approach to these interviews:

> The most important thing initially is to listen, to ask what questions they have. If you start first with reviewing the case, then they might never mention their questions. They'll think that since

the doctor hasn't mentioned the particular point, then it must be irrelevant, so they won't bring it up.

Once these concerns have been reviewed, this physician asks the parents how they are doing emotionally, how their family is handling the tragedy, how others in the community are responding to them.

A social worker may also be involved in a follow-up. One mentioned that she used the approach of asking each parent to describe how the other was doing. This usually succeeded in opening up areas of possible concern that a person might have been reluctant to raise on his or her own.

If a woman becomes pregnant again, she may look for a different doctor, either because of dissatisfaction or simply to make the next pregnancy as different as possible from the one that ended so badly. The next time parents may have a clearer idea of what they want from a physician and a hospital—more empathy, more experience, more progressive policies—and will shop around carefully. Some, however, are very impressed by their original doctor's helpfulness and cannot imagine going to anyone else.

During the next pregnancy, the parents look for encouragement from the physicians and office nurses and for understanding of their anxieties. One woman who did not get this understanding remembers:

> My doctor told me I was foolish to worry and that I would just be hurting the baby if I were too anxious. He made me feel worse. Couldn't he understand what I had been through? If it had happened to him, I'm sure he would worry just as much!

When the physician is sensitive to the parents' concern, he or she can help alleviate the anxiety—for instance, by amplifying the fetal heartbeat more often than usual for the parents to hear, and in general by understanding the reason for their fears.

A growing number of professional conferences and in-service training sessions include discussions of the psychological care of grieving parents. Research on family reactions is also growing and has led to more awareness by the hospital staff of the problems that are bound to arise.

One benefit of these sessions is that they can give staff members the opportunity to talk with each other about their own feelings of grief when a baby dies. One doctor remarked that every baby's death is painful to him. "It's always upsetting," he said. "I've never been able to get used to it." These feelings are rarely visible to the parents. A maternity nursing supervisor observed:

> People think the doctors have no feelings. But I've seen them telling parents their baby has died and then a few minutes later I find them around the corner or in the staff lounge crying. This affects all of us more than people know.

Doctors and nurses may have been taught that it is "unprofessional" to become emotionally involved with patients, but the most helpful professionals are often those who can honestly share the parents' grief. A physician described his view on the importance of this openness:

> One of the things that is important is to take a minute to back off and objectively assess what steps need to be taken. Keep those things in mind, and then don't be objective. Parents need people around them to act like people, not to be cool and professional. It's all right to cry.

The staff member's grief is especially acute when he or she has had the chance to take care of a baby in the nursery. Sometimes an infant may survive for months in the hospital, and the nurses begin to bring in toys and may even think of the baby, somehow, as their own. The whole staff strongly feels the death of such a baby. For some nurses, it is particularly difficult to care for an infant after treatment has been withdrawn. When staff members provide necessary emotional support for each other, they make it easier to continue working in a very stressful setting.

Parents rarely see this side of the professionals they come into contact with. To the person who has just been through a tragic event, the doctors can appear to be powerful, arrogant, and uncaring, the hospital a depressing prison. But the concept of a

professional, as psychiatrist Robert J. Lifton points out, origi-
nated with the idea that one advocates (or "professes") on
behalf of the client's total needs. When the people in medical
positions do understand and respond to the needs of parents,
they make it easier to cope with a very troubling experience.

As one nurse described the role of medical staff: "If we can
reach parents while they are still here, and if decisions and
problems are handled well from the start, then we can help
parents avoid long-term problems. What we're doing is really a
form of preventive medicine."

13

Religion
Baptism, Funerals,
and the Role of the Clergy

"It had been an hour since we came out of the delivery room, leaving our dead baby behind. The nurse approached us with forms to sign and the startling question, 'Who is your undertaker?' We were totally at a loss. We were young and had just moved into the area, so we were astonished at the thought that we should have an undertaker just as one would have a doctor. We were angry that the hospital staff needed to know how to dispose of our baby so quickly. But it forced us to realize that our baby was really dead and that some action needed to be taken to bury her.

"We never thought for a minute that instead of a crib we'd need a casket. Instead of reading our books on child rearing, we would be reading prayers and sympathy cards. We were young, our kids were young—who thinks about cemetery plots and undertakers?"

Almost immediately after their baby's death, parents are faced with the awful necessity of deciding something they usually know nothing about. As a young couple, they are unlikely to know an undertaker or even to have attended many funerals. They are bewildered—to whom can they turn for guidance?

The hospital staff may try to make it easier for a family— particularly after a miscarriage or stillbirth—by offering to relieve them of any planning; they offer to "take care of it" for the parents. At first this may be a relief to the parents, but later they may wonder whether they could have had a service for the baby and regret that they did not.

The funeral service is one of the rituals that traditionally

151

accompany major turning points in people's lives. At birth and at death especially, the community joins with a family in religious rites either of celebration or of mourning. Even without formal religious ceremonies, such significant events as a birth or a death are still announced and marked in some public fashion.

Yet when these two events occur together, there is seldom any ritual. Even if an infant lives for several days or weeks, the ceremonies are brief or nonexistent. There is not enough coming together of family and community in a way that offers hope and comfort. The psychological and social benefits of birth and death rituals are withheld from the family; once more they are given the message, in yet another way, that their loss isn't very important, that their baby wasn't a real person. But it is precisely at such a time that a family may find religious beliefs and practices and the assistance of clergy and funeral directors to be of greatest help.

One of the first questions that parents may have regarding religious practice is whether a baby should be named or baptized. When a baby is born and is well, there are a variety of practices to celebrate his or her arrival. Catholics and some Protestants baptize an infant, either as a welcome into the Christian community or to ensure entrance into heaven. Other Protestant churches have a dedication service or a christening for naming a newborn. Jews have a naming ceremony for girls and a service for the circumcision and naming of boys.

When an infant dies before birth, there is usually no baptism or other ceremony. The major exception is the Catholic church, in which a dead fetus is almost always baptized. In traditional Catholic belief, an unbaptized infant cannot get into heaven and therefore goes to Limbo. Because of fear for the infant's fate, doctors and nurses, especially in Catholic hospitals, are often prepared to baptize a dead fetus rapidly in the case of a miscarriage or stillbirth.

Recently some Catholic theologians have disputed the idea of Limbo. They claim that the origins of baptism emphasize the initiation into the community, and it is therefore not essential for a dead infant. According to one Catholic scholar, a younger priest would be more likely to disregard the idea of Limbo and instead would say, "We really don't know what the fate of people is. We should stop talking as if we had a hot line to Heaven. If God is merciful, He'll take care of it."

But "just to be sure," and since anyone can administer the rite of baptism in Catholic practice, it is carried out automatically by a parent or by hospital personnel. For instance, a mother who miscarries at home may baptize the expelled embryo. If she is Protestant, however, this is not necessary, since Protestants consider baptism to be a ritual for the living, having no effect on the fate of the child's soul. Some Protestant parents choose to baptize a stillborn fetus anyway, a procedure that is ordinarily not forbidden.

If the baby is alive at birth but gravely ill, the decision about baptism depends on the usual practice of the family's church in regard to all babies. On occasion, parents request the ceremony for a dying child even if their church ordinarily opposes infant baptism. The ministers who comply do so because they consider the parents' needs to be more important than a strict interpretation of church tradition.

One minister described his approach to baptism of dying infants:

> I try to make the baptism as elaborate as if we were in a church, even if it is in an intensive care unit. I try to find out first what the ceremony means to the parents and what their concerns are. For example, if a parent is feeling guilty about the child's condition, I would say in the service that we wonder what we might have done, and how it could have been different, and ask God to grant relief from these feelings. The minister should be a family's spokesman to God, and too often we miss the opportunity to build ritual that reflects the needs of the situation.

This minister's view suggests one of the ways in which a ritual can be helpful to parents.

Another ceremony that some members of the clergy offer is a farewell service once an infant has died. This may replace a funeral service, as in the experience of one rabbi who tries to perform the service while the family and the baby are present in the hospital. During it he speaks of their hopes and dreams for the baby. A minister described a different kind of farewell in which he places his hands on the child's forehead, inviting the parents to do the same if they choose, and blesses the baby. In Catholic practice, where there is the sacrament of anointing the sick, the dead or dying child is dabbed with oil that has been blessed by the bishop and special prayers are said. Such ceremonies give the family the chance to say good-bye to their precious baby with the help of a supportive pastor.

Much too quickly after the death, the family must consider what to do about a funeral. But a parent in shock from the sudden unexpected loss of an infant is not likely to know what he or she wants or to be able to express it. One father recalled his state of mind after his wife's miscarriage:

> At that point you are kind of led around like a sheep. I had enough problems to worry about that I just didn't care what was done about the burial.

Because of the parents' bewilderment and the lack of any clear direction from most religious denominations, the majority of miscarried and stillborn infants are buried or cremated by the hospital. Later, parents may wonder what was done with their baby but are afraid to ask. If they do ask a hospital representative, they may discover that the laws of their state require that every dead fetus be buried in an individual grave.

The parents may also later regret not having had the chance to bury their own baby and to have a ceremony performed at the burial. Such an example is this account of a mother whose child was stillborn:

> We contacted the rabbi, who said that he would take care of everything. He told us that, according to Jewish tradition, there are no rituals for a stillborn. We had no funeral, no mourning period, no opportunity to say the prayers for the dead. The baby was buried by the rabbi, and I don't even know exactly where she is. I don't like the fact that she's buried in a corner of the cemetery as if she had done something wrong and been ostracized from the community. At first I was relieved not to have to face a public ritual which I knew would have been very difficult, but now I feel that it would have been more helpful to have the usual practices. It was like we were illegitimate mourners.

This family followed their religious practice but sorely felt the lack of any ceremony. Judaism is just one of many religious traditions throughout the world that have not historically had a formal funeral for a fetus or young infant. These practices appear to arise from a situation where fetal and infant death were so common that a child was not considered to be part of the community unless there was an indication that he or she would survive. Increasingly rabbis as well as other clergy are having religious services for babies in accordance with the families' wishes.

It seems ironic that religious laws do not require the full funeral service for an infant even when they define the fetus as a person from the time of conception for other purposes. For instance, the Catholic antiabortion stand is based on the belief that the fetus has the same status as a person, and Jewish law states that if a woman has miscarried, her next child does not need the ceremony that is usually performed for a firstborn.

The explanation generally given for not performing the usual funeral rites is that a fetus or infant does not "need" them. The funeral is, in some traditions, a rite of purification to insure the deceased's return to God. The infant, being already in a state of purity, does not require these ceremonies.

Funerals are not so much a benefit to the deceased as they are a source of psychological aid for the family. They help promote a healthy recovery from grief by bringing family and community together to provide support for the bereaved and to give mourners a chance to express their overwhelming feelings of anger, guilt, and sorrow. Funerals help make the fact of death a reality. They also offer a spiritual context in which to help explain the meaning of the terrible event. And they give the bereaved something concrete to do in a time of bewilderment.

Despite these benefits, there are many reasons, other than the lack of usual religious practice, why a family would not have a funeral for an infant. One reason is that the mother who is still hospitalized would not be able to attend. One way to lessen this problem is for the minister to tape the service and then visit the mother to play the tape for her right after the burial. In some hospitals a service is arranged in the chapel. Even when the hospital takes charge of arrangements, it is possible in some cases for the parents to dress the baby in preparation for burial.

If the parents are young and possibly newly settled in a community or considering moving somewhere else later, they are often unaffiliated with a church. For any of these reasons, the young couple may not own or wish to purchase a burial plot. One man who decided to buy a plot for his stillborn daughter reflected on the strange feeling this purchase evoked:

> We picked an area that we thought was pretty where there was a cemetery. It was weird, though; we had to buy four gravesites, because in our community, you can only get them in fours. It really brought home to us that we were making a decision that this was where *we* wanted to be buried too.

To avoid such a permanent commitment, to simplify the decisions, and to protect themselves from pain, many parents agree to have a funeral director place the baby in a corner of the local cemetery. A mother whose daughter died after four days is glad that she had no ceremony:

> My husband took care of everything. At first I was upset because I wanted to know where she was buried, but he wouldn't tell me. I realized later that it was for the best. There's more of a break that way. If I did know where she was, there would be more of a chance of my brooding over the death.

Every parent has different needs; the most difficult problem is determining what they are. Most parents prefer the usual practice of a brief gravesite ceremony that dispenses with most ritual and is limited to the immediate family. If this service lacks the advantages of community support and seems to diminish the sense of importance of loss, it does provide the parents with a known burial site and helps make the death a reality. This practice is more common for the infant who lived a short time, but it is sometimes also done for a stillborn. Rarely is there a funeral in the case of a miscarriage, even though it would be helpful for many parents.

Only Catholic ritual includes a special Mass for an infant

who dies, a celebration of the Eucharist in honor of the angels. Some priests discourage its use, insisting that the child was a human being, not an angel, or because they are worried that the parents will be too distressed by a special service. If the child lives for a short time, there may be a funeral mass. Otherwise there is only a private interment service.

Cremation is an increasingly common practice in the United States for people who die at any age. It is preferred by many people because the ashes can be kept at home or taken to another state without legal complications. It is also simpler and less costly than finding a plot and having a burial. Cremation is a very ancient tradition still practiced in many parts of the world. In the United States, some churches forbid it while others allow it and still have the usual funeral service.

Since in so many cases a funeral is either not required or is greatly abbreviated, the parents must know what they want and then find a sympathetic member of the clergy who will cooperate. In some churches, the parent who requests a service has a great deal of flexibility in planning it. Parents can write their own service or the minister can help to create a ceremony that best responds to the needs and feelings of the family.

Many families prefer to dispense with any formal religious ritual. They may wish, however, to create their own ceremony and to bury the infant's remains in a special place. Jared Massanari writes of the burial of his son Caleb, who died in an intensive care nursery after having been there all of his five and a half months. Jared and his wife, Alice, decided that Caleb should be cremated so that they could take his ashes to a favorite spot in another state. Jared recalls:

> Neither of us wanted to put the ashes in the ground, and in the process lose our last physical contact with Caleb. We didn't want to bury him and say our last good-byes. But the mountain called us. The mountain was where Caleb had to be . . .

Special friends and relatives were invited to participate in the burial. Each spoke about his or her feelings for the baby and for the parents. One read a biblical verse, and they all sang together. Then, Jared wrote,

> . . . I reached for the shovel and shook some dirt over the ashes. Alice followed. Each person proceeded past the grave to cover the ashes with fresh dirt. We lifted the tree into the hole, planting new life where death would always be. Roses were thrown onto the dirt. Then Alice and I started down the hill. The silent procession ended where it had begun.

Parents who choose to have a funeral often do so because it allows them to do something for the baby. Some worry that this opportunity will be taken away from them. One mother who was able to plan a funeral after her miscarriage knew what she wanted only because she had had a previous miscarriage. Both occurred in the fifth month. Both times she delivered a tiny infant at home and then went to the hospital with the baby:

> The first time we had no ceremony at all. By the second time, I had had a chance to think about what I wanted—a funeral and a gravesite that we could visit. People discouraged me but I insisted: "No, this is for me, I don't know why, but I just know I need to do it." We invited people we cared about. My husband spoke and I spoke. We talked about how much we had wanted this child, how we didn't understand why he was taken, that we assumed there was an answer that we just didn't have yet. Later we put a marker on the grave with his name on it.

Parents who have had a miscarriage may have to be very insistent, as this mother was, about having a ceremony, with or without a burial, if that is what they want.

Sympathetic support is especially crucial for the parents who have decided to abort a deformed fetus and wish to have a religious burial. If abortion is forbidden in their religion, finding a member of the clergy who will perform the service is extremely difficult. The religious person who is flexible can be a tremendous aid to these bereaved parents. One mother talked about her relief after the abortion: "The minister was great. He helped us arrange a private service and burial. I felt that was the least we could do for that poor little boy."

Too often the mother is left out of any planning for a service or burial. She may have to insist on participating. For instance, the mother of a stillborn child recalled her concern at the time:

> I was afraid that my husband and the funeral director would take over and do everything. This was my baby, and I wanted to be included in the plans, the flowers, the grave, the payment. I didn't want them to rob me of my child's funeral. I was grateful that the funeral director listened to me and let me do what I wanted.

This mother's desire to pay some amount toward the cost of the funeral is not unusual: it is part of the couple's desire to do something for the baby. Many others, however, resent additional expenses for a child they will never enjoy, especially when a funeral costs hundreds or thousands of dollars. They are appreciative of the many funeral directors who charge parents only for the costs of the casket and opening the grave. It is the undertaker's way of expressing sympathy and of maintaining the good will of the community.

Once the funeral is over, there is no further ritual and no recognition of the continuing grief and depression. Some churches do have an anniversary Mass or mention the recently deceased on All Souls' Day, but only those infants who were alive at birth are included. In Jewish practice there are seven days of mourning (Shiva) during which the family stays at home and is visited regularly by the community, extended periods of more limited mourning, and finally the recitation of the Kaddish prayer on the anniversary of the death. In accordance with Jewish tradition, none of these rituals are required for an infant who did not live thirty days. Nevertheless, some parents draw upon these practices to fill their own needs. One mother whose baby died mentioned her own experience:

> Every year on December 3, no matter what is happening or where I am, I remember what happened that day nine years ago. It is my day of mourning, and so I say Kaddish for the baby.

Baptism, dedication, farewell, funeral, Kaddish. Rarely available and sorely missed. Other practices—the wake, the Shiva mourning period—are all but nonexistent. When they do occur, they provide the family not only with the advantage of ritual and the support of the community, but also with an ongoing contact with sources of potential help—the funeral director, the minister, the priest, the rabbi.

In recent years, funeral directors have become more conscious of the ways in which they can help grieving families. Their national organizations, for instance, have been very active in the sponsorship of conferences on bereavement. In many cases, the family members never speak with a social worker or minister; the funeral director may be the only person they are in contact with who understands the grieving process and can provide counsel. Many are aware, for example, of the therapeutic value to the mother of including her in the decisions and preparations for the service and burial. When researchers in one study asked recently widowed women who was most helpful to them, they mentioned the funeral director more often than any other person.

The clergy can also help the bereaved family deal with their loss and make sense out of their confused feelings of anger, guilt, and sorrow. Members of the clergy who are aware of the process of bereavement can assure people that it is normal and not sinful to be angry at God, that anger is a natural part of the healing process.

The clergy can also help families draw on their own spiritual resources and beliefs in the attempt to reconcile themselves to a tragic and senseless event. Some people may find comfort in thinking that the death was God's will or a test of their faith. They may believe that they have a little angel in heaven watching over them or that death is the beginning of a new life.

For people who do not share these beliefs, however, any effort to comfort them by saying it was God's will may only produce anger. Phrases such as "God needed a little flower for his garden" are often said in kindness but may be resented by parents who wonder why it was *their* little flower that was taken.

Some members of the clergy have not been prepared to counsel the bereaved, especially in cases of infant death. In this they are like most other people; they are uncomfortable with death and rely on the standard forms for responding to it. Even those who are sensitive to the needs of grieving may not understand the significance of the loss of an infant. The lack of a religious tradition seems to reinforce this ignorance. In recent years theological schools and ministerial associations have begun to organize courses and discussions for clergy to provide them with an understanding of the grief process so that they can better help bereaved families. Miscarriage, ectopic pregnancy, stillbirth, selective abortion, and infant death, however, are still left out of most of these discussions.

This lack of understanding can lead to disappointment with the representatives of religion. For many people, the death of an infant also leads them to question their own beliefs, as seen in the following comment:

> Believe me, if there is a heaven above and I go there, the first thing out of my mouth that I am going to ask is why my baby had to die that way, what purpose was there? It doesn't make you a better person. Even if you wanted to punish me, why did you have to punish my whole family? He did nothing wrong, he didn't ask to be born. How could there be a God who would do this?

Even nonbelievers find themselves questioning: Were they being punished? What is the meaning of such a senseless death? It takes a long time for the parents to find peace of mind.

Religion and ritual can help many families in their search for peace of mind. Even those who have no religious affiliations or beliefs can use welcoming and farewell ceremonies to mark the importance of their child's existence.

After the burial, the feelings of grief for the baby are far from over. "What can I do for my baby?" one mother asked. Jared Massanari writes what he did after his son was buried:

> I wanted to make something; what, I wasn't sure. I spotted a small piece of wood and began to saw and chisel and sand it. Soon a car formed itself. . . . Every boy should have a toy car to play with. . . .
>
> Up the mountain to Caleb's tree. Alone I knelt and dug a small hole, placed the toy in the ground, and gently covered it with dirt. I remembered.

In some cases, it may take a long time before a parent finds the right way to memorialize the child. Some people have naming or farewell ceremonies for babies who died ten or twenty years ago. One woman asked her priest to say a Mass for a stillborn daughter, a baby who had been dead for seven years. When he refused, she kept looking until she found a priest who thought it was an excellent idea. The woman mentioned the upcoming Mass to friends in a support group and the word was spread. By the time the Mass was held, dozens of families had come forward to take part, to memorialize their babies, some of whom had died more than thirty years earlier.

Another woman, who was still in the hospital when her husband buried their two-day-old baby, remembers:

> It took me two full years before I could bring myself to visit the cemetery. I guess I was afraid of breaking down there. But I always wished I could have made a service for him. One day I finally decided to go see where he was buried. It was terribly hard the first time. But I was also surprised to see what a beautiful shaded spot he's buried in. It was peaceful there, and I felt glad that at least he was in a pretty location. Now I go about once a year to visit and to bring flowers. At least I have this to hold on to.

14

Law
Considering a Malpractice Suit

"They killed my baby. It was all their fault. I'll never be satisfied until I have my revenge."

Parents are furious when their baby dies. They blame themselves, they blame fate or God, and often they blame the doctor for not having been all-powerful. Sometimes this anger leads them to consider a malpractice suit; it seems to be the only concrete step they can take in response to their frustration.

On some occasions, there is a basis for a suit; negligence on the part of a physician or hospital staff member did cause the infant's death. The parents feel that the trust they placed in their doctor during the months of pregnancy has been violated. Their suspicions of malpractice increase if the doctor responds with evasion or even hostility to their questions. They wonder why information has been withheld, what is being hidden. Disillusioned and angry, some couples seek out a lawyer. A lawsuit can never make up for the loss, but when malpractice has occurred, it is the parents' major means of legal recourse.

Bringing a malpractice suit is very difficult even when there is evidence of blatant misconduct. Families suffer the exhausting emotional trauma of reliving the experience of their baby's death for the years that litigation can take. In many cases, parents cannot find an experienced malpractice lawyer who will agree to represent them. If they do hire a lawyer and if they win the case

or settle out of court, the amount of money they receive is likely
to be small. After all the expenses are paid, there may be little or
nothing left for the family. This is particularly true for a miscarriage, stillbirth, or an early infant death. Large amounts of
money are usually awarded only in the case of damaged children
who survive.

Despite these obstacles, many parents feel that they want to
sue anyway. Theirs is a deep-seated anger toward a presumably
incompetent physician, and they feel that he or she should be
made to pay. The following is a case in point:

> After the baby died, I was willing for a long time to believe that it
> was just a freak accident. My husband and the rest of my family
> were furious at the doctor and believed we should sue so that
> everyone would know how incompetent he is. I didn't think a
> suit could hurt his reputation. But, most of all, I couldn't bear the
> thought of making money from the death of our precious baby.
> And I knew that going to court would mean more grief—I felt I
> had plenty already. Over time, though, as I thought again and
> again about what had happened, and as I talked with other
> doctors who felt the baby had received the wrong treatment, I
> slowly began to realize that my family was right. My baby didn't
> have to die! The thought of suing became an obsession. No
> matter how much it would take of my time and energy, I owed it
> to that baby to make sure that this terrible mistake would never
> happen again. And the doctor owed us something too. We could
> use the money for our other children.

Family members have conflicting emotions and motivations
as they begin litigation. They are rarely prepared, however, for
the difficulties and the frustrations they will face at almost every
stage of the process.

The first difficulty is simply establishing that a baby's death
was actually due to malpractice. The fact that a baby has died or
was seriously impaired does not necessarily mean that anyone is
at fault—no one can guarantee the health of a child. To prove
malpractice, clear evidence must be established to show that the
doctor, nurse, or hospital was negligent and did not provide
the accepted standard of medical care. Simply documenting
that the baby would have survived under a different treatment

program is not sufficient to prove fault. A doctor who makes an error of judgment is not liable, unless the error is so extreme that no reasonable medical professional would have acted in the same way under the same circumstances. Furthermore, it must be proved that negligence directly caused the problem.

The instances in which a family might suspect negligence are varied. For instance, the development of a normal fetus can be harmed by the use of drugs, anesthesia, or X rays. The drug thalidomide, once prescribed for pregnant women, was found to cause severe deformities such as the absence or malformation of limbs. But it was not until many similar cases appeared that a causal connection could be shown between the drug and the defects. Occasionally such situations lead many affected families to act together in bringing class-action suits against drug companies and hospitals as well as physicians.

Another type of suit might be brought if the doctor's actions during delivery have possibly resulted in injury to the baby. Most frequent are the instances where improper treatment leads to a reduction in oxygen to the infant, thereby causing permanent damage. This type of case is very hard to prove because it must be demonstrated that the oxygen deficiency occurred at the time of birth and not earlier and that the doctor could have prevented it from happening. An added difficulty is that doctors often disagree about what steps should be taken if the baby is in distress, as in the controversy over when emergency Caesareans should be performed.

A third kind of case might arise when a physician fails to diagnose an illness in the mother that could damage the child or, having diagnosed it, fails to take the necessary steps to prevent the damage. For example, a mother who exhibits signs of diabetes must be carefully monitored, since her baby is in a very high risk category.

Another basis for suing is the failure of the physician to inform a woman who has a high risk of bearing an abnormal child of this possibility and of the procedures available to detect problems. In one such case, a doctor was taken to court because he failed to warn a thirty-eight-year-old woman that, due to her age, she had a higher-than-average risk of bearing a child with Down's syndrome or to tell her about prenatal diagnosis.

If parents suspect that their child's death or deformity was the result of malpractice, they must decide whether to sue. There is a time limit for filing a suit which varies by state. This "statute of limitations" is usually two to three years, and there is a trend now in a number of states toward shortening the time allowed.

Before contacting a lawyer, a person may first try to see the medical records and make a preliminary evaluation of the facts. Very few states have laws that mandate access to medical records, so this information may not be easy to obtain. Even though a review of the records can often allay suspicions and prevent suits, doctors and hospitals are reluctant to open their files to patients. It may be necessary to hire a lawyer and threaten a lawsuit simply to obtain a copy of the records. One father described his efforts to obtain his wife's records:

> First I called the doctor's office, but I was told that they would send the file only to another physician. I said it was ours, we should have a right to get it directly, but they refused. Then I went to the hospital records office to see about her hospital chart. They said the doctor would have to review it first. I seriously wondered what he might change or take out first. You would think I was a criminal, trying to steal something that wasn't mine! Finally I had to ask a friend who is a lawyer to write a letter in order to get the records. I still wonder if they're complete. After all that, I was upset to get a bill for photocopying— $1.00 a page!

Some attorneys recommend that parents try first to get their own records and that they not mention the possibility of a suit. They worry that a request from a lawyer will scare physicians into removing important documentation. Fortunately, in many states, obtaining records is becoming easier. The American Hospital Association has endorsed this access as one of a patient's rights, and continued consumer pressure is likely to promote it further in the future.

Once the parents have the records, it is not always easy to understand them. Most often they receive forms filled with the scrawled notes of a variety of people. Once these are deciphered, the medical terminology is likely to be meaningless to the average person. It may require extra effort and expense to find a physician who is willing to interpret the records.

Often families choose to go to a lawyer to discuss the case, either before or after getting the records, to find out if the laws in their state make it possible for them to consider a suit. However, finding a qualified malpractice lawyer who will accept the case is surprisingly difficult. While there is an abundance of attorneys, few are knowledgeable in the area of medical malpractice, and even fewer have experience with obstetrics. A lawyer with no experience in the field might do the client a disservice by taking the case, but many times this is the only option available to families.

One of the best ways to find a good lawyer is by referral, either from other attorneys, legal referral services, or the state bar association. The Martindale-Hubbell Law Directory, which can be found in most law school or courthouse libraries, lists attorneys along with their credentials and specialties. Membership in a state or national Association of Trial Lawyers may be one indication of a lawyer's experience in the courtroom.

Finding a lawyer is only the first step. Experienced malpractice lawyers reject more than seventy-five percent of the cases that are brought to them. They know the difficulties of winning such cases and select only those that they consider have a chance of success.

One woman who believed that her child's death was the doctor's fault recounted her agonizing efforts in trying to find a lawyer who would accept her case:

> I was sure I had a good case, but I didn't know where to turn. Friends would recommend this lawyer or that lawyer, but how was I to know if they were any good? I eventually went to three different lawyers. With each one, I would go through hours of describing my situation and filling out forms. One told me fairly soon that the doctor was a friend of his and he wouldn't want to sue him. Another said he was very busy and wasn't sure if I had a good case. The last one was much more thorough and obtained a medical opinion, but finally he said no also. And then he charged

me $500 for the privilege of being turned down! I finally had to give up.

Most attorneys review the medical records and obtain a physician's opinion before deciding whether to accept a case. Some charge the client for this time and for expenses incurred, while others do not; the client should inquire about these possible charges during the first conversation.

If a lawyer rejects the case, it is important to know his or her reason before looking for another lawyer. If the reason for refusing is a personal conflict, or if the attorney accepts only cases with very high monetary claims, another lawyer may be able to provide the help needed. On the other hand, where the evidence, the laws, or case precedents suggest that the family is unlikely to win, it may be necessary to abandon the idea of a suit.

A lawyer may choose not to represent someone in a particular suit if negligence cannot be proved. The major method of proving negligence is through expert testimony of other physicians, yet many doctors are not willing to testify against other doctors. In a survey of Boston physicians, for instance, seventy percent said that they would not testify even against a surgeon who had removed the wrong kidney. Although it has become somewhat easier to find experts to testify since this survey was carried out in the 1960s, expert witnesses are still hard to find and often costly to hire.

Most lawyers agree that medical malpractice cases are not won or lost on the evidence alone. The outcome often depends on the persuasiveness of the expert witness. Both parties present expert witnesses during the trial, and it is not unusual for two experts to contradict each other. The problem with some witnesses was mentioned by one experienced malpractice attorney:

> It is not what happened or what should have happened, but what you can prove happened. You can only do that through a witness, and a very persuasive witness can be lying. However, if the jury believes this person, then that is what happened.

If there is a jury trial, the decision is affected by the biases and backgrounds of individual jurors. Lawyers know that some cases will win in one county but lose in another.

Another major reason lawyers reject most malpractice cases is that the monetary award is not high enough to make their time and effort worthwhile. Many will not accept a case unless they expect the damages to be at least $100,000.

There are two kinds of awards which parents might claim: on their own behalf—for their pain and suffering, or medical expenses; and on behalf of the child—for loss of life and income. The right to recover for any of these reasons varies considerably from one state to another; for instance, in some states there is no way to sue for grief or mental anguish after a wrongful death.

In some states, the courts do not even allow action to be brought on behalf of a child if the death occurred in the mother's womb. The fetus is not considered to have been a person but only a part of the mother. Therefore, in those states, the fetus has no legal existence, and there can be no compensation for the loss of life.

An Illinois case started the trend that has been changing this. The court ruled that a fetus must be seen as a life distinct from the mother when it reaches the stage at which it could survive outside the womb. It found further that it is illogical for the case to depend on whether death occurred just before birth or just after birth. A court in Georgia went further, ruling that a suit may be brought for the loss of an unborn child even if it would not have been able to survive outside the womb, as long as it had shown signs of life by moving in the mother's womb. This decision would cover late miscarriages as well as stillbirth.

Even where parents are entitled to claim damages, the awards are usually very small. Perhaps the parents' grief is not thought to be substantial. The future earnings of a fetus or infant are also difficult to calculate.

It is important for the lawyer who accepts a case to explain to the client what will happen, how long it will take, and what costs will be involved. As one lawyer said:

> I tell people how difficult and long the process is. I want them to understand that everyone is interested in suing in the beginning, but as time goes on, it gets rough, and many people want to quit. If people say yes to me, they are obligating themselves to follow

through. When it is time to go to court, they have to be willing to spend at least two weeks there—they cannot back down at that point.

Before going to trial, a malpractice lawyer spends an average of 400 hours preparing a case. Testimony has to be taken from every member of the hospital staff who had anything to do with the patient during the birth to uncover all the information, some of which may not have been written down in the medical records. This in itself takes days and sometimes weeks. Legal and medical research must be documented, and the proper experts have to be enlisted.

It could take several years from the time a person goes to a lawyer until the case is resolved. In some states it takes over a year simply to get the case on the court calendar. The trial could take anywhere from two days to a month. If the decision is appealed, another eighteen months might pass before there is a final ruling.

In some states, before a case goes to trial, it must be heard by a screening panel, which consists of a lawyer or judge, a physician, and sometimes a layperson. These panels help to determine the merits of a case and serve as a means of weeding out frivolous claims. They can, on the other hand, also discourage a claimant by adding one more step to the process. The proceedings of these panels vary considerably from one state to another. In some states their findings are admitted during the court trial; in others they are not.

Because malpractice suits are long and complicated, the expenses can be enormous. Most such cases are accepted by the lawyer on a contingent-fee basis. This means the lawyer gets a certain percentage of the client's total award as payment for his or her services. This fee, however, does not include the family's expenses for court costs, the services of expert witnesses, examinations by doctors, sheriff's fees, etc., which may run as high as $10,000 to $15,000. Juries are not told how much money a person owes in costs and attorney's fees nor are they supposed to take this into account when they make their decision. Therefore, money awarded for medical bills and for pain and suffering may go instead to pay the lawyer's fee and related expenses.

In many states, the contingent-fee percentage is restricted by law. Some states have a graduated scale which allows a smaller percentage as the award becomes higher. This is intended to encourage lawyers to accept cases with small award potential. Other states allow one standard rate, usually ranging from one-third to one-half of the recovery.

Since very few people could afford to pay a lawyer's hourly rate plus expenses, the contingent-fee system allows more people to sue. It also encourages lawyers to try to get as large amounts for clients as possible. However, the major disadvantage to this method is that lawyers will seldom take cases that are likely to win small monetary awards.

Although the lawyer takes care of getting expert testimony and preparing the case, it is by no means an easy experience for family members involved. The fight is long and bitter. They have to expose their painful birth experience to lawyers, judges, doctors, and perhaps to the public if the case goes to trial. For all that time they have to relive the terrible experience of their baby's death, recalling every feeling and every detail for the many questioners. They have a lot at stake—money, time, and energy—and they feel very vulnerable.

One mother who decided to sue told what happened after she found an experienced attorney:

> I think when we started we were hoping that an out-of-court settlement would be made. The lawyer warned us, however, that we might have to go to trial and should prepare for that possibility. The trial date was set for months away, and all that time I worried constantly. I would go over and over in my mind the events of my pregnancy and the birth. I would think about all the questions the doctor's lawyer might ask. As the time for the trial approached, we discussed with the lawyer what would go on there and what questions we might expect. I would practice questions and answers with my husband. I could hardly do anything else—it was the only thing on my mind.
>
> On the day of the trial the lawyer told us that the doctor's insurance company had offered to settle with us out of court for $7,000. As much as we wanted to avoid a trial, we just couldn't accept so little money—our expenses alone were more than that. We made a counteroffer, which they refused, so we had to go to court.

I was almost paralyzed with fear when the trial started. I knew that I wouldn't be called on the stand the first day, but seeing the doctor in the courtroom was devastating. I couldn't look at him. I looked instead at the jury and thought about how each of them would judge us. When the trial finally started, it moved slowly—there were constant objections and conferences and confusing maneuvers on each side.

The time came for me to testify and I can't even remember now what I said. At times I could hardly speak, and I broke down and cried. It was so humiliating. The doctor's attorney asked me many questions that insinuated that I did something early in my pregnancy that caused the baby's death. He kept asking if I took any medications. Did I have a cold? What did I take for it? Did I smoke? I felt he was trying to trick me. When I finally got out of that chair, my lawyers said I did just fine. I was glad at least that part was over.

The trial lasted three weeks, and then the jury went out. After what seemed an infinite amount of time, they came back and awarded us damages of $20,000. We were disappointed. We knew we owed the lawyer a third of that and that our expenses were $8,000. We were left with a little over $5,000 for our pain and suffering.

It was so long and hard, and we didn't win very much, but we felt that we were vindicated. Even though I knew the doctor was at fault, at times I couldn't help doubting my own feelings. But now I had the satisfaction of knowing I wasn't crazy and that in some small way he was being punished for what he did.

The majority of malpractice cases are settled out of court, but of those that do go to trial, most are won by the doctor. That can be a discouraging and costly ending to a lengthy, tedious, and emotion-filled process. Parents must decide if money and vindication can ever make up for the pain of losing a child or alleviate their anger. They must consider whether they can endure the rigors and expense of a trial. But if they undertake a suit, knowing all that is involved, they should be encouraged for pursuing what they believe to be their right.

Parents who wish to sue after a miscarriage, ectopic pregnancy, stillbirth, or early infant death have in some ways been at a particular disadvantage in our legal system. Fortunately, this situation is slowly changing. The courts in some states are beginning to recognize the right of parents to sue for the wrongful death of their expected baby.

Nevertheless, as long as many of the laws and practices involved in medical malpractice suits continue to discourage people from suing, those who believe they have been wronged should have the possibility of recourse to a different procedure, one that has been designed for cases with small financial awards. In these cases, some approach such as binding arbitration might work best. At present, arbitration is not often used in malpractice cases.

Parents who feel they want to sue should consult a lawyer and explore all their options, given their particular situation and the state in which they live. If a legal solution is not possible simply because the laws of their state do not allow for a suit or because there may not be sufficient awards to justify the cost, there are other possible courses of action open. They could file complaints with state and county medical societies, ethics panels where they exist, or with the hospital administration. They might obtain some satisfaction with the help of local health and consumer groups. Otherwise, until the circumstances involving medical malpractice cases are changed, many families with legitimate grievances are likely to be deprived of justice through the courts.

15

Possible Causes

Is Progress Killing Our Babies?

New Delhi (AP) A state health minister said today that 36 pregnant women spontaneously aborted and that six gave birth to deformed babies after the toxic gas leak at the Union Carbide plant in Bhopal here in December.... Autopsies conducted on 27 other stillborn babies indicated the possibility that their deaths had been caused by methyl isocyanate gas that leaked from the pesticide plant.

The New York Times,
July 16, 1985

Hidden in the back pages of the newspaper, news items such as this report the increasing evidence of an explosive drama. Sometimes in the least likely places, unexpectedly high rates of birth tragedies are becoming apparent.

Pregnant women are the modern version of the canaries which were sent into coal mines to test the safety of the air. If a canary died, the miners knew the mine was unsafe. Similarly, if an unusually high number of miscarriages or birth defects appear in one location or workplace, this is a clue that the environment is toxic.

Hundreds of such clusters of birth tragedies have been reported, but in most instances the causes are still unknown. Will these cases be thoroughly studied by researchers who are supported by government grants to uncover the source of this tragic picture? More likely, they will just be added to the list of statistical anomalies, never understood, and soon forgotten. Unless attitudes change, pregnant women and their babies will continue to be like the canaries, but their warnings are given in vain.

The death or deformity of an infant is in every case a profoundly personal tragedy. But it is also much more. Increasingly, it is becoming clear that there are patterns to many of the tragedies, that they are far from random occurrences. The effects on pregnancy of medication, diet, alcohol and tobacco consumption, and exposure to hazards in the environment and in the workplace are beginning to be understood, and, as a result, the occurrence of the failure of pregnancy is increasingly having political, economic, and legal repercussions.

We take pride in the major advances in both medical technology and in the standard of living that have resulted in dramatically lowered rates of infant loss during this century. The statistics used are almost always those of infant mortality—the proportion of babies born alive who die in the first year of life. Those who do not survive until birth are not so accurately counted. What the statistics conceal, as well, is the possibility that fetal and infant deaths caused by the environment—by pollution, radiation, and chemicals—are actually increasing.

Because the reasons for these events are as yet so poorly understood, miscarriage, ectopic pregnancy, stillbirth, fetal deformities, and infant death are still often treated as mysteries, as flukes of nature. There is not yet enough research being done to try to uncover their causes, and the results of existing research are not often translated into effective preventive measures.

Where there has been research, it has focused mostly on the behavior and psychological makeup of the individual mother. This type of research is easier to do. It is also easier to blame the mother than to uncover the external causes of her suffering. Bereaved parents feel guilty enough about the loss of their child; and since they have few answers, when the answers that do exist seem to point to their own actions, they blame themselves even more:

> Over and over I wondered what could have caused our baby's deformities. The doctor said the malformations were not caused by our genes, but were "freak accidents of nature," that some-

thing had gone wrong during my first month of pregnancy. I keep
looking for reasons. Did I drink too much diet soda? Did I have a
cold and take aspirin? Did they spray our fruit trees that spring?
Was I particularly nervous about the new job I started? What did
I do? It had to be something!

Most of us are no longer willing to accept "nature" or "God"
as the causes of events when we know that there are often
specific reasons that can be identified. It is essential to discover
the real sources of loss during pregnancy in order to help these
parents and to prevent so many tragedies from occurring in the
future.

When causes linked to an individual's behavior are known,
preventive action must be taken. Recent evidence emphasizes the
harmful effects on a fetus of smoking, excessive drinking, and
poor nutrition. Yet young people continue to be bombarded by
advertising for products that are dangerous. The tobacco industry says to women: "You've come a long way, baby," associating
smoking with progress and freedom. The American government
continues to subsidize the tobacco industry. And many doctors
fail to advise pregnant patients about the importance to the
baby's health of what they consume.

The focus on the mother's psychological problems appears
particularly in studies of repeated miscarriage. The women who
experience this terrible situation are described as rejecting their
femininity, being hostile toward their mothers, or unconsciously
wishing not to have children. These explanations are particularly cruel in light of the growing evidence of environmental and
medical reasons for miscarriage. They also sometimes ignore the
fact that the miscarriages themselves may have psychological
effects on the women and those effects might be wrongly inter-
preted as causes.

Some of the most dramatic evidence of environmental causes
of birth tragedies comes not from scientists but from the victimized
families themselves. Women who have experienced these events
have begun to compare their experiences with one another and
to uncover some startling connections.

Perhaps the first well-publicized example was that of Love

Canal in Niagara Falls, New York. Neighbors in the area surrounding Love Canal became aware that their children were
becoming seriously ill and soon realized that many women were
experiencing what seemed to be unusually high rates of miscarriage, stillbirth, and birth defects. They discovered that the public elementary school was built on top of a chemical graveyard
and that those chemicals had been seeping up through the ground
and into their water supply for years. The families immediately
surrounding the dump site were finally evacuated, and the school
was closed. The women of Love Canal succeeded not only in
explaining their own tragedies; they focused national attention
on the fact that toxic wastes have been and continue to be
disposed of throughout the country in ways which threaten the
health and happiness of countless families.

Another example of families finding a common cause for their
grief took place in Oregon in the late 1970s. Several women
discovered that they and their neighbors were experiencing an
unusually high number of miscarriages, especially in the spring.
They found that it was no coincidence. The excessive rates of
miscarriage appeared in areas which, each spring, were sprayed
with a herbicide called 2,4,5–T containing the chemical dioxin.
The toxic effects of this chemical had already been suspected for
several years. As an ingredient of Agent Orange, best known for
its use to defoliate the Vietnamese countryside during the Vietnam war, it has been linked to excessive rates of miscarriage,
stillbirth, birth defects, and cancer among the Vietnamese and in
the families of American soldiers. In 1970, the United States
stopped spraying Vietnam with Agent Orange because of the
publicity on its unexpected effects. Yet the same ingredients
continued to be used to clear land in other parts of the world,
including Oregon. Some families had moved there in search of a
clean and simple environment; instead they found disease and
heartache.

The women of Oregon organized; they had to fight the timber
industry, Dow Chemical—the manufacturer of 2,4,5–T—and the
government. One difficult task was convincing government regulators that the observations of nonprofessionals who had experienced tragedy could have any scientific validity. Bonnie Hill, an

Oregon schoolteacher and mother who had a miscarriage in 1975, testified in Congress about the struggle she waged:

> It was ironic to me that while scientists have not been willing to study humans who have been exposed to various chemicals, many of them will not lend credence to what people have to say about how they have been affected because their evidence is "anecdotal" or "circumstantial." What else is there left, besides people who are able to observe things that are happening around them, and who are able to reason that certain relationships are most certainly possible. . . . Somehow, we ordinary folk are left to "prove" that we have been adversely affected by a foreign element in our environment to which we are exposed without our consent.

Bonnie Hill and women like her were successful in presenting their case and stopping the use of 2,4,5–T in Oregon. But other dangerous chemicals continued to be used. When community representatives met with officials of one company involved in the spraying of 1981, they were told that "babies are replace-able" and that they should plan their pregnancies to avoid conceiving during the spraying season.

How many other pregnancy-related tragedies are caused by unknown exposure to chemicals whose effects are not yet obvious enough to provide research, protest, and regulation? Environmentalists are finding new sources of chemical pollution all the time—in our air, in our water supply, and underground.

In the spring of 1979, the accident at the Three Mile Island nuclear power plant in Pennsylvania drew the nation's attention to another important source of fetal damage: radiation. Debate continues around the health effects of the accident, with a number of scientists pointing to evidence of increased infant mortality rates in the area around the plant and in the state of Pennsylvania as a whole.

The disastrous 1986 explosion at the Chernobyl nuclear plant in the Soviet Union once again brought public attention to the potential dangers of radiation for human health. Recent revelations have raised concern about the possible ill effects of radon in homes. There is also a growing awareness of the difficult problem of radioactive wastes generated from other sources, such as hospitals and processing plants. These wastes cannot as yet be safely disposed of, and they may increase the risks to pregnant women and their developing infants.

The fear of damage to a fetus is extremely stressful for expectant parents living in areas thought to be hazardous. Pregnant women were evacuated from the Three Mile Island region after the accident, and many left a year later when radioactive gas was vented into the atmosphere. One reporter who covered the Three Mile Island story decided afterward to have an abortion rather than take the risk of bearing an unhealthy child. Some women in Seveso, Italy, a town that was covered by the accidental release of dioxin gas, also sought abortions afterward; they were terrified by the thought of what the exposure to dioxin would do.

One location where the exposure of pregnant women to dangerous substances has produced considerable controversy is the workplace. For example, a study of one computer factory reported in 1987 by the University of Massachusetts School of Public Health found the miscarriage rate among women who etch computer chips with acids and gases to be thirty-nine percent, or at least twice the national average for miscarriages.

With an increasing number of women working and our growing awareness of occupational hazards, employers have sought to reduce their liability for dead and deformed infants by excluding women of childbearing age from certain kinds of jobs. Some women have responded by undergoing sterilization to keep their jobs or by suing to protect their rights to equal employment and to a safe workplace.

What employers have failed to respond to is the growing evidence that fetal death and deformity can also be caused by exposure of the fathers to dangerous work environments. This is possible because some substances (referred to as mutagens) damage not only the ovum but also the sperm before conception even occurs; men are therefore very susceptible to hazards that can damage their future children.

One study carried out early in this century is especially dramatic in demonstrating this common effect: of thirty-two pregnancies begun by the wives of a group of male lead workers, eleven ended in miscarriage, one in stillbirth, and thirteen in infant death. Only two children survived to adulthood.

More recent studies indicate that male workers exposed to a variety of solvents and other chemicals have sharply reduced sperm counts and are at higher risk of infertility and of fathering children with birth defects. The workplace must be made safe for everyone, not just for fertile women.

Often an embryo is normal at conception but then is damaged by exposure of the mother to harmful substances (teratogens). One workplace known to be hazardous to a fetus but from which, not surprisingly, women workers have not been excluded, is the hospital. Ironically and tragically, medical care and medications have become recognized as important sources of birth tragedies. Exposure to radiation and anesthesia can create risks for men and women working in hospitals, as well as being unexpectedly damaging to the patients they are intended to help.

Doctors have begun to warn that any woman of childbearing age admitted to a hospital for diagnosis or treatment be tested first for pregnancy. They have discovered that many newly pregnant women—not knowing that they have conceived and unaware of the risks—are being subjected to hazardous X rays, anesthesia, and medication.

The effects of all kinds of medications, even aspirin, are becoming increasingly evident. Everything ingested by the mother can affect a fetus in some way, and, in the case of some medications, the effect can be permanent deformity or death.

One terrible example of the effects of medication is seen in the use of the hormone DES (diethylstilbestrol). In the 1940s and 1950s it was given to many pregnant women whose doctors believed they might miscarry. Not only did it have no impact on the likelihood of miscarriage, but many of the children born from those pregnancies are suffering the effects as adults. Daughters of women given DES have higher rates of cervical abnormalities and are thought to have an increased risk of developing vaginal cancer. Research also indicates that the same daughters have a greater likelihood than other women of experiencing miscarriage, stillbirth, and premature—and therefore risky—delivery.

*   *   *

The most surprising source of tragic birth outcomes is the mis-use of new obstetrical techniques that, paradoxically, were de-veloped to increase the safety of childbirth. Ultrasound, for example, which is increasingly used routinely during pregnancy, is still not proven completely safe. A panel of experts convened by the National Institutes of Health in 1984 recommended cau-tion in using ultrasound, citing some animal studies which showed that it might produce birth defects or slow fetal growth.

Some techniques, which were intended for use in high-risk births, are too often used automatically in all deliveries and have been attacked as causing unnecessary damage to infants. Rou-tine induction of labor, excessive Caesarean surgery, unneces-sary use of medication and anesthesia, and the placement of the delivering mother in a position which reduces the oxygen supply to the infant—these are the major examples of practices that sometimes backfire, harming the child they are intended to help. The women's health movement—which includes obstetricians, childbirth educators, nurses, and concerned parents—has at-tempted to spare the mother whose pregnancy and labor pro-ceed normally from the dangers of unnecessary technology. They point to the striking experience of European countries, where there are more at-home or midwife-assisted births and also lower infant death rates than in the United States.

In attempting to explain the higher infant mortality rates in the United States, Americans sometimes claim the difference is due to the more "homogeneous" composition of European popu-lations. What they actually mean is that there are more poor and minority people in the United States and that these groups are responsible for the higher rates of infant death. In this country, black women are twice as likely as white women to experience the death of an infant. Infant mortality has actually increased in the 1980s in areas of the United States with high levels of unemployment and poverty. Income, education, occupation, and race do correlate strongly with pregnancy outcomes, but that is hardly an acceptable excuse.

Poor people in this country are much more susceptible to many kinds of diseases than are middle- and upper-income people, and disease during pregnancy does increase the risk to the baby. High blood pressure and malnutrition—serious problems for a pregnant woman and her baby—are much more common among the poor. Poor women are less likely to receive proper prenatal care and skilled delivery services. They have even less control than other women over the kind of care they receive. And the poorer classes are much more likely to be exposed to hazards at work.

To attribute the high rates of fetal and neonatal death in the United States to the large percentage of poor women is to ignore the true causes and to pretend that nothing can be done to alleviate the conditions that contribute to their suffering.

Tobacco, pollution, chemicals, radiation, medication, poverty. These are some of the factors that illustrate our growing awareness that fetal and infant death are not simply medical problems. The source of so much anguish is all too often found in our class system, in the workplace, the hospital, and in the air we breathe.

Yet the research, the technology, and the money are focused on saving a baby who is already in distress when born. The years preceding that baby's conception—and even the first crucial months just after conception—are all but ignored. Many doctors tell pregnant women that they need no medical attention until the third month, and even then the doctors often give little advice about proper diet and potential hazards to the baby. And federal and state regulators are often unwilling to challenge the economic power of industrial polluters and the owners of dangerous factories.

Parents' fears during pregnancy are magnified by the knowledge that they can never eliminate every potential danger to their baby:

> I know that the next time I will be extremely careful about everything I do and about what I eat, even more cautious than I was the last time. But how can I really protect that baby? I don't know what's in the water supply or in the air around me. How can I be sure there isn't another Love Canal just waiting to be discovered in my own neighborhood?

With the help of enlightened physicians and the support of growing scientific evidence, organized consumer groups and women's health advocates are beginning to bring these issues to light. Fighting the causes of unnecessary tragedies can unite groups of women with very different political views to bring pressure on the political, economic, and medical powers-that-be. Until then, growing numbers of individual families will still face tragedies and wonder if they are to blame.

Margie Gaffron, a woman living in Pennsylvania at the time of the Three Mile Island nuclear power plant accident, put her fears into powerful words of poetry:

I am a woman who carries a child,
A child of three inches who this day
Grows liver, kidney, heart, finger, face, bone,
This day when rain falls and wind blows
From the south, from Harrisburg.

I am a woman who can build a good fire,
Mend tears of cloth or skin,
Who in a summer's growing fills
A winter's worth of jars, baskets, cans, crates, stomachs.

I am a woman who sings with children,
Who with care attends each small growth and budding,
Who daily weaves each luminous strand
Into the delicate cloth of family and home.

I am a woman who watches the rain
This day fall upon the soil my fingers cherish,
Sink into the soil that is our life,
Innocent rain, carrying what small death.

I am a woman who chooses not to flee,
Whose fear grows heavy in this rain,
Who envelops yet does not protect the tiny embryo
Growing toe, thumb, or small fingernail.

I am a woman who labors in this understanding
So difficult to grasp in its entirety,
We have left no place in this earth
Safe for the growing of seed or child.

I am a woman who carries a child,
Who can never again embrace the rain as it falls in total friendship,
Who must learn to distrust the soil and its offerings,
Who must teach children to both love and comprehend,
To stand in their humanity with strength and dignity,
To fashion from their fear
Tools for creation.

I am a woman who carries a child.

V
WHAT NEXT?

16

Recovering
Changes, Activities, and Support Groups

"I am a different person from the young woman I was just before my child died. I don't feel changed in a radical sense, but I am changed. It's sometimes difficult to relate to that person: to the youth, invincibility, and near simplicity. Sometimes I have difficulty remembering that young woman who was the mother of two children. . . . It was a good time, laced with all the happiness and minor dissensions that are part of living.

"And in one hellish moment, all of that changed. Changed as swiftly as if a bomb had been dropped into the core of our lives. Changed on a bright, sunny summer morning when I picked up the rigid, lifeless, distorted body of our young son."

Carolyn Szybist wrote these thoughts after her three-month-old son died of Sudden Infant Death Syndrome. Life changes for most couples after the baby they wished for dies, whether before or soon after birth. Tragedies jolt people into taking a deeper look at their lives, their beliefs, their feelings. For many parents there is a new appreciation of life and of the family they have. They say:

My values changed. I have a different feeling about what is important. I don't care as much about material things.

I'm less selfish now, more aware of other people's suffering.

For the first time I understand the feelings of people who can't have children.

Although they may welcome these new insights, they wonder if a tragedy is the only way to gain different perspectives.

Some people become embittered and toughened by the experience. They no longer believe in a just God, or they are angry at the whole world. They feel unfairly marked for suffering.

For almost all parents there are heightened fears that something else might happen, that they are jinxed now. An example is the comment made by the mother of a stillborn daughter:

> I kept having this premonition that my husband would die suddenly just as the baby had. Every time he was a minute late coming home from work, I would go crazy. I was sure that he had had a car accident or a heart attack.

Usually these fears subside over time. Yet the confidence, even innocence, of earlier days can never be entirely recaptured.

Emotional changes are only a part of what happens to families after the loss of their baby. In many cases there are changes in life-style as well. For the mother especially, the failure of pregnancy may dramatically alter the life she had expected. The woman who has given up her career or other involvements, in anticipation of becoming a mother for the first time, must make the biggest readjustment. Without either her career or baby she is faced with important decisions at a time of great distress. She is likely to be unsure about what to do next. Should she return to her former job or try something entirely different? Should she get pregnant again? Her ideas may change completely from one day to the next. One woman described her confusion after her stillbirth:

> I couldn't bear facing new people, asking for a job, going to all those interviews, and then being turned down. I just didn't have the strength or the confidence. And the work seemed so meaningless to me. I wanted to get pregnant soon, so I also did not want to start something new, only to quit again. Since I couldn't decide, I didn't do anything. All I remember about that time is watching a lot of television. It was pretty depressing.

In coping with this emptiness, some women find that it helps to pamper themselves. They buy new clothes, redecorate the house, join a pool or health club, buy the pet they always wanted, go on vacation. All of these are attempts to restore some sense of well-being, to erase the feelings of shabbiness and failure.

Almost any activity that contributes to greater self-confidence, no matter how trivial it may seem, can help the parents in recovering from the terrible blow that they have been dealt. In time, as they gradually feel ready to become involved in new activities, they may look for more substantial changes. This presents an unexpected opportunity for some parents to rethink their goals, to reorganize their priorities, and to move in new directions. It takes time and patience; the healing process is slow.

Sometimes the tragic experience itself becomes the source of a variety of creative outlets. Some individuals organize support groups or seek training in counseling in order to help others. Some become involved in environmental and political activism related to the causes of their loss. Others write stories and poems; a number of outstanding women authors such as Mary Shelley, Anaïs Nin, and Harriet Beecher Stowe all created great literature out of their experiences with infant loss.

In the past decade, a wide variety of books, seminars, and counseling services has become available to women seeking career changes or reentry into the labor force. Adult education courses have also expanded to offer them greater opportunities to obtain or complete a degree. And a multitude of organizations, consumer groups, political coalitions, and charitable or religious institutions eagerly seek committed volunteers.

A woman who took a maternity leave from her job or who is still working, or who already has other children at home to take care of, has the option of continuing what she was doing before her pregnancy. Women in this situation feel fortunate that they have something to keep them busy, just as do most men who continue with their work.

Nevertheless, it is difficult at first for both men and women to concentrate on their work or their other children at a time when they are still grieving for the baby they lost. Friends or relatives may try to distract them, but sometimes they wish they could withdraw and be alone to cry or to think. Parents who are busy with work, child care, or housekeeping responsibilities do not always have the opportunity they need for grieving. One man whose son died two days after birth commented:

> I work in a large room surrounded by people. Everyone knew the baby died, and I felt really awkward since I knew they were watching me to see if I was all right. I just wanted a chance to be left alone to deal with my own feelings.

How do people gather up the pieces and go on? How do they get over the nagging memories and begin to concentrate on other activities? Sometimes supportive friends and family or personal strength just aren't enough. For some, a social worker or psychologist is needed to help them to put their lives back together.

Even when professional counseling is not necessary, discussions with others who have also experienced the loss of an infant can help tremendously in the recovery. Organized support groups can put such parents in touch with each other.

The number of support groups—or self-help groups—has grown rapidly throughout the United States in the last decade. Professionals such as physicians, social workers, and clergy have been instrumental in organizing these groups, where individuals meet with others who understand their troubles from personal experience. Often it is only by sharing their emotions with those in the same situation that they can believe their own reactions are normal, that they are not going crazy.

Only in the last few years have families who have undergone a tragic pregnancy had an opportunity to meet and share their feelings. Some groups now in existence were organized by maternity nurses, social workers, and clergy. They often have the most immediate contact with bereaved parents in the hospital, so they can encourage them to meet with others soon after the infant's death in order to help them through the early stages of grieving.

In contrast, groups have been organized and run by parents outside of the hospital setting. Compassionate Friends is one such group for families who have lost a child at any age. There are local chapters in many parts of the United States. Although most of the parents grieve for a son or daughter whose death came at a later age, the parents of infants are also welcome.

AMEND (Aiding a Mother Experiencing Neonatal Death) was one of the first organizations that responded to the specific needs of families after infant death. In addition to group meetings, parents who have lost their infants in the past are trained to speak with and counsel the newly bereaved. These counselors meet regularly for lectures and discussions. Groups are being organized throughout the country, and their numbers are growing steadily. (See Appendix A for names and addresses.)

Probably the most active organization nationally for helping parents with all types of pregnancy loss is SHARE, based at St. Elizabeth's Hospital in Belleville, Illinois. Started by a remarkable woman, Sister Jane Marie Lamb, as a local support group, SHARE has grown to be the center of a network of hundreds of groups in the United States. It is an excellent source of information about available resources and of assistance in starting a new group.

These support groups are usually most helpful for parents going through the normal grief process. They do not offer intensive therapy but rather provide a setting where feelings can be expressed and will be understood. On occasion, they also present speakers who provide information on a variety of subjects that are important to the family. Some groups are more formal and organized than others. Some have a public meeting place, newsletter, and leaders who plan the meetings. In others, parents meet informally to discuss their feelings. In all groups, the atmosphere is one of acceptance, of allowing people to speak or simply to observe as they wish.

Many families find that they are not yet ready to become involved; they are reluctant to expose their open wounds so quickly to others. Fathers especially are less likely to participate in groups, perhaps because many of them prefer to keep their feelings to themselves.

For some parents, it may be frightening at first to attend a meeting. They do not know what to expect. One mother talked about this feeling:

> I had a name to call for Compassionate Friends, yet picking up the phone was very difficult. What would I say? Could I talk comfortably to someone I didn't even know? It took a few months of thinking about it and needing someone to talk to before I could bring myself to call her.

When parents do eventually decide to participate, it may be months after the event. Sometimes friends or relatives discourage involvement. Perhaps they are afraid that talking to others will revive the intense grief of the first days and weeks. But it is precisely at the time when others may be tired of listening and think that the mourning period should be over that the parents may need a sympathetic ear the most.

If there is no group available in the area, some individuals may wish to form their own. They should contact existing groups in other areas for suggestions on how to get started. Professionals in local hospitals may be able to provide contacts with other families and even meeting space and program ideas.

For Carolyn Szybist, whose son died of crib death, the support group she organized three years later was the key to her coming to terms with the tragedy. A magazine article about crib death led her to contact other people who had experiences similar to her own. She found that by talking to them—even though they were strangers—she could express her long-hidden feelings about the event:

> . . . the release inside of me of so many locked up feelings can only be described as nearly exhilarating. It was a strange blend of hearing other people say what I had been feeling, and feeling along with them what I was hearing them say. When we all finally met as a group, it can only be described as a warm reunion of very old friends.

This feeling, that only someone else who has been through a similar experience can truly understand, has made support groups an important part of the recovery process for many parents. It is one way in which they can begin to overcome the terrible isolation of their personal grief.

17

Another Baby?
Feelings and Options

Should we try again? How long should we wait? What if something goes wrong this time? These questions are the source of great anxiety for almost all families who have had a pregnancy that ended in tragedy.

Often there is an overwhelming desire to have another child quickly. Some parents feel the ache of empty arms, the sadness of an empty crib. They had been preparing for a child, making room for one in their lives. Only another baby could fill the enormous void.

As time goes by, the urgency of this feeling subsides. The couple begins to readjust to living without the expected child. The mother, especially, may become reluctant to conceive again quickly, even if she desperately wants a baby. She is still recovering physically from being pregnant; she realizes that she is the one who will have to endure, once again, the stresses of pregnancy, and her body will remind her daily of the last one that failed.

However, if the woman is over thirty, she may feel the pressure of time and worry that she will be too old to bear children if she waits much longer. There may be additional pressure from her husband, who urges her to become pregnant again soon. Friends and family may also encourage them to try again, hoping that a live baby will erase the pain.

If the cause of their tragic loss is not known, they can be

particularly anxious about conceiving again. Then it becomes essential to seek a full understanding of whatever might have contributed to the disastrous ending of the previous pregnancy and what the chances are of its happening a second time.

When a couple asks how long they should wait before getting pregnant, they are likely to receive a wide variety of views from friends and physicians. This confusion is seen in the comment of a mother who had a miscarriage in the fifth month:

> I wanted to get pregnant again as soon as I had my first period, but then one of my friends told me of someone who did just that and had a second miscarriage. I wondered if maybe it would have happened anyway. But how could I be sure? Another friend who became pregnant soon after her miscarriage had a healthy baby. Everyone's doctor had a different idea about this—it was very hard to know what to do.

The length of the previous pregnancy, the type of delivery, and the age and health of the mother are important factors in deciding how long to wait. Some obstetricians feel very strongly that two pregnancies spaced closely together might be detrimental to the second infant. They suggest a wait of three to six months after a miscarriage or abortion and six to twelve months after a stillbirth or infant death. Their recommendations are based on the belief that the mother's body is not yet physically ready to carry another fetus, and that both mother and father need a chance to mourn for the first baby before preparing themselves to accept a new one.

If the couple have not recovered from their grief, the next baby may not be loved for him- or herself and may be—even subconsciously—compared with the one who died. Some physicians warn parents against the possibility of this "replacement child syndrome." As one doctor said:

> I tell parents how important it is to give each child a separate identity. If the one who died was their second child, the next one should be thought of as the third, not the second again. And they should give the next baby a new name and make it as different as possible in their minds so there won't be any confusion.

When parents are aware of the problem of the replacement child and still feel physically and emotionally ready for another pregnancy, many physicians encourage them to conceive again without waiting a specific length of time. They believe that, under these circumstances, the next child will not suffer any ill effects.

No matter what they decide to do, parents are bound to worry. The next pregnancy, whether it occurs in a few months or a few years, is a time of great anxiety and fear. Will tragedy happen again?

They hold their breath as each important stage passes. If a miscarriage occurred at three months, then getting beyond that point is the first important goal. If the baby who died was premature, the weeks still left until the second due date are counted carefully and recounted until the time of danger has passed.

Every sign, every symptom becomes important. The doctor's face is scrutinized for any indication of trouble. If the baby who died was breech, the next one's position is carefully felt. One mother said after her miscarriage: "I was terrified all during my next pregnancy. Every time I went to the bathroom, I was sure I would see blood."

Many couples try to make the next pregnancy as different as possible from the one that ended tragically. They may give up certain activities they enjoyed during the first pregnancy. Some buy all new maternity clothes. Some refrain from planning or talking about the baby or even setting up the crib until a much later time than they had before. They may seek constant reassurance from each other and from the doctor that this time everything will be okay.

Sometimes they may have to face another tragedy, for once in a while lightning does strike twice. After a second tragedy, it is much harder to have hope, and the strain can be intense. They had told themselves that they could not possibly handle another loss, but somehow they do. They survive; they grieve again; and again they may try for the baby they want so much.

Friends may criticize them as foolish for trying again. A case

in point is the comment from a mother whose first pregnancy
ended in miscarriage:

> When I got pregnant again, everyone was excited and very en-
> couraging. But then I had amniocentesis and found out the baby
> would be seriously deformed, so we decided to have an abortion.
> It was horrible, but we were determined to try one last time. I
> was amazed that this time when I got pregnant, no one said a
> word of congratulations. One friend even told me I was crazy to
> try again.

What parents need at this time is understanding of the courage it
requires to take such an emotional risk.

For some parents, there is no next time. Some are unable to
conceive again. Some are too afraid of the risks of another
pregnancy. The mother may feel that she is too old or be
convinced that the same thing will happen again. Perhaps, angry
at her loss and determined never to be pregnant again, or simply
because she was unaware that her baby was critically ill, she
had her tubes tied at the time of birth. For some couples, divorce
intervenes or time simply passes without the decision to try
again ever being made.

Those families must go through the painful process of adjusting to a new and unexpected reality: a life without children or
with fewer children than they had hoped for. They, perhaps even
more than other families, will always wonder how different their
lives might have been. One father recalled:

> We already had two children, and soon after the third died my
> wife decided to have her tubes tied. She said she never wanted to
> be pregnant again and have to live through the horrors of that
> experience. We're happy with our two, but we often talk about
> what it would have been like to have another. Sometimes I
> wonder if we should have adopted a child.

For the parents who cannot or do not wish to conceive again,
adoption is a possibility. However, adopting a healthy baby has
become very difficult in the United States. Because of legalized
abortion, the increased availability of contraception, and the
greater social acceptance of single parents who choose to keep

their babies, fewer babies are available for adoption now than ever before. Some adoption agencies have such long waiting lists of prospective parents that they no longer accept applications.

There are, however, legal ways of adopting still available. Some agencies in the United States continue to arrange adoptions, while many parents have turned to other countries, mostly in Asia and Latin America, to find children. In some states it is permissible to adopt privately through a lawyer. For families considering adoption, there are now many informative resources available (see Appendix B and references for this chapter). Other families who have already adopted can offer essential information and support for beginning the process.

Whatever route is chosen, adoption involves complicated paperwork, a "home study" consisting of lengthy interviews with social workers, and sometimes a period of residence in another country. The waiting and uncertainty can be very frustrating; and once a specific child is selected, the concern about his or her well-being is similar to that of a couple expecting a natural child. As one mother explained:

> We had decided to adopt a baby after our daughter died from a terrible genetic disease. But we were very frightened. We learned from our first baby that there are no guarantees in life. I worried throughout the whole adoption process. One day I worried that the baby would never come, and the next day I would worry about the stories I had heard of adopted kids arriving seriously ill. Sometimes I wondered if getting pregnant again wouldn't have been easier after all—at least I would know how long it would last. It wasn't until he finally came that I could feel some sense of relief and begin to feel good about our decision. Then I knew it was worth all the worry—our new son is wonderful!

For couples who prefer not to adopt but are having difficulty conceiving again, there are fertility clinics where the causes of their problem can be investigated and where a variety of treatments can be explored. Ordinarily, these clinics can be contacted through an obstetrician or medical school. There is also a national organization—RESOLVE—which provides information and support for infertile couples.

Some couples hesitate to become pregnant again because they worry that the next child will have the same condition as the previous baby. Genetic counseling, discussed in chapter 4, offers the possibility of investigating the likelihood of future problems.

The arrival of a new, healthy baby ends the long waiting and worry over pregnancy or adoption. But certain fears linger. After their previous tragedy, parents may worry that they are overprotective or anxious about their new child, because the life of any child seems so terribly fragile to them. They may think that they have to be perfect parents, never feeling the normal ambivalence of new parents toward this new demanding person in their lives. And they find it difficult not to compare this child with the one who isn't there. Would he have been cuter? Would she have cried less?

Especially if the new baby has arrived soon after their tragedy, parents must face the fact that this new child might not be there had it not been for the untimely death of another. "We were extremely upset when Joan miscarried," one husband recalled. "But we know we would not have had Amy; and what would our lives be like without her?"

Having another child can never erase the memories or make up for the loss. And comparing one infant with another is almost inevitable. But the new child will grow and develop a unique identity of his or her own. Parents are aware of how precious this next child is, how much he or she was wanted, how miraculous it is that life can still be created and grow and thrive. Another child, a healthy baby, brings joy and celebration. There is enormous relief. As one woman who had miscarried described her response to her new baby: "I felt whole again."

VI
EPILOGUE

Epilogue

While we were writing this book we became mothers again. But this second time the outcome was completely different. Judy gave birth to Shira in June, and Susan's daughter, Laura, arrived from South Korea the following January at three months of age. The time of waiting for their arrival was difficult for each of us, as it is for any parent who has lost a baby. Once again our experiences differed, but once again we shared similar feelings, this time ones of relief and delight.

Judy:

During the first few weeks after our baby Elana died I was completely in a daze. I cried going to sleep, and each morning as I woke up the reality of what had happened struck me all over again. There were visitors, our families and friends, offering distraction and comfort. Their presence was much more important than their words. But no one could take away the hurt.

I returned to work gradually. I was doing my work as I had before, and I would guess most people thought that I was getting quickly back to normal. No one saw the tears that appeared when I was alone in the car, driving to and from work. And no one knew how often the thought passed fleetingly through my mind to drive off the side of the road. There were some very bad moments then. But Barry was wonderful at cheering me up. And the knowledge that our baby had been healthy until the birth sustained me for a while. Later it would make me angry, but now

I held onto it as the hope I needed that the next time we would be successful.

The idea of being pregnant for another nine months was frightening. Yet many people encouraged us to get pregnant again immediately, citing examples of others who had lost babies and now were happy because they had another child. Sometimes it seemed like I was being told that it was like falling off a bike—if only I got right back on and started riding again, I would forget how badly my knees were scraped. I listened eagerly for the stories but didn't really believe them. I also felt pressed for time; at my age I didn't have the luxury to wait very long to have more children.

Three months after the baby's death I was pregnant again. I felt elated, and momentarily lifted out of the terrible depression which had been weighing me down. But I also began nine months of worry and anxiety. First I worried that it was too soon. Would the baby be okay? If something went wrong again, could I stand the guilt I would surely feel for having conceived so quickly? Sometimes my husband and I felt that the anxiety was too much to bear, that we would never survive those nine months. Yet we knew more certainly than ever that we wanted a child.

Inevitably we compared this pregnancy to the last one. We were much more cautious in every way, conservative in activities and reluctant to expect too much. We made no preparations for a baby's room and barely practiced the Lamaze techniques which we had studied so carefully a year before. When the day came on which I had decided I should feel kicking, and it went by without any movement appearing, I began to panic. I was sure something was wrong. But when the baby began to move, and the kicking was more vigorous and frequent than the first baby's, I was greatly relieved.

Of course I still worried that something would go wrong. And I was beginning to feel as though I had been pregnant forever, that I would always be huge and awkward and going to the doctor.

Right on schedule, Shira was born, and it was the beautiful, exciting, labor-room birth I had hoped for. But, more important, this time a baby was born who was alive and healthy. I had been sure that I would cry, but I didn't. I just kept saying, "I can't believe it" over and over again. I didn't even bother to look or ask if it was a boy or a girl. All I wanted was to hear a cry, to see the baby breathe. She cried and she breathed and she was healthy. It felt like a miracle had happened.

Later I did cry for Elana, for I knew what in my worst pain I had not fully understood a year earlier—how wonderful it is to hold a living baby, to nurse her and rock her and love her. So I mourned once again for the baby who wasn't there and delighted at the same time in the one who was. It was a confusing time, tied up with all the normally intense emotions after birth. But it was mostly a time for great joy and celebration.

People who see me doting over Shira and being entranced by my wonderful baby probably tell others now what they told me then—she was unhappy but then she had another baby and forgot all about it. I still grieve for Elana, and I am still angry about her needless death. But I also cannot imagine not having Shira. I hope she will not be hurt by my hurt. But surely our lives will always be different because of it.

Susan:

I had gone through seven and a half months of a very difficult pregnancy. I had given up my job when my back pains became unbearable. Then I watched my first-born baby die. And now what was left? For two months I was confined to the house from complications after my Caesarean. I felt that I had failed at everything I had tried so hard to accomplish—a career and motherhood. Those days were empty and lonely for me as I watched my husband leave for work each morning. Life seemed to continue for everyone but me.

As time passed I felt I would have to start all over. Yet I didn't have the energy for the awesome task of looking for a new job, and I was unsure that a second pregnancy would end any differently. Somehow, after what seemed like forever, I was beginning to recover from the physical effects of the birth. As I started to go out of the house and see people, I would tell them what had happened, even if they didn't ask or even if I hardly knew them. I realized that I must have seemed crazy, but it was a way for me to work out my feelings.

I also talked to Judy often. We would talk constantly about our feelings—unlike others, we were never bored by hearing the minute details of each other's experience over and over again. More than that, we could understand each other's feelings and even laughed together at the inappropriate remarks some people had made to us. Soon after, we started writing this book and continued our talks even more frequently.

Judy was pregnant at the time. For the first three months after Shira was born, she brought her along while we worked. As I listened to her talk about her new daughter and saw her cuddle and kiss her, I believed that I would never be so lucky as to have an infant.

Even so, I certainly was going to try to have another baby. Certain that we wanted a healthy baby as quickly as possible, and unwilling to go through a second pregnancy so soon again, my husband and I decided we would adopt our next child. Since our only niece was adopted from South America and we love her very much, adoption seemed like a very natural step. We began by contacting adoption agencies around the country. Our initial attempts were met with frustrations. We found out that many agencies were closed or lists were full. It took persistence until we found an agency that had children available and would accept us.

The adoption procedure seemed endless. We were interviewed at length about our lives, our relationship, and our families, our feelings about having a child from another country, and our son Daniel's death. We completed applications and financial statements. We obtained marriage and birth certificates, photographs and letters of recommendation. We went to the police station to be fingerprinted and to the Immigration and Naturalization Service for a visa. All of these were part of the long process.

It seemed unreal to think that all of these bureaucratic activities would produce a child for us. But her picture finally arrived. Laura was one month old, looking healthy and content. We knew at first sight that we wanted her. We signed more documents and were told that she would be coming by the end of the year.

Now we were frantically beginning to get ready for her. We painted the room, set up the crib, bought some clothes, and found a pediatrician. Last-minute changes in the paperwork, the assassination of the South Korean president—all caused panic. Would she ever be here?

Christmas came and went, then New Year's and still no word about Laura's arrival. Then, finally, in mid-January the phone call came. Laura would be in New York in two days.

A year after our son Daniel's death, Laura arrived at Kennedy Airport from Seoul, South Korea. There wasn't a cloud in the sky that day. My stomach was jumping as we went to the airport. She arrived at 11:30 at night and smiled as she was given to me. She seemed so healthy—sturdy, happy, and beautiful.

She still smiled as we changed her and fed her. All of a sudden we were parents. We left the airport with her, expecting somehow to be stopped and asked whose baby we had taken. But to everyone else, we were just another family on our way home.

In the spring of 1979 we wrote the accounts of our experiences that appear in the prologue. It was spring again a year later as we wrote this epilogue. A much happier spring. Our work was interrupted by anecdotes of our daughters' growth and accomplishments and much less often by the memories of our first babies' deaths. We exchanged toys, clothes, and helpful advice rather than remembering the moments of sorrow and anger. We struggled harder to recapture the feelings of those first days and months of terrible pain. The memories were still there, but we had new memories too, the joyful thoughts of Shira's and Laura's arrivals, the incredible experience of watching them grow.

It is spring once again, eight years later, as we meet to revise this book. During that time, we have each given birth again. Susan's daughter Margo, born prematurely after a difficult pregnancy, is now a thriving five-year-old, and Judy's daughter Ariella is a terrific three-year-old. Both pregnancies were filled with anxiety; we knew too much about all that could go wrong. As we watch our four girls play together now, we are very aware of how precious they are. Yet we still often wonder what our lives would be like if Daniel and Elana were here too.

We have spent these years talking with families and professionals about loss and writing a book on infertility. We know that our own reactions—how we felt then and how we feel now—are shared, with variations, of course, by countless other families.

Our "unblessed events" are just two among the millions that occur each year throughout the world. Insignificant in the scale of history, two statistics for the government's records. But for us they will always be important. And those little babies will always be part of us.

VII
REPORT OF
NEW RESEARCH

Report of New Research on Pregnancy Loss

by Judith Lasker, Susan Borg,
and Lori Toedter

When Judy moved to Lehigh University in the fall of 1981, not long after the book was first published, she was fortunate to meet Lori Toedter, a clinical psychologist with extensive survey research experience, who had also recently experienced a miscarriage. It seemed like an ideal team to try to carry out a more systematic investigation into pregnancy loss. The research and experience we wrote about in the first edition of *When Pregnancy Fails* formed the basis for this project. They gave us many valuable insights, but there were many questions for which we wanted more precise answers. Who seems to cope best with loss and why? Which people have the most difficulty, and what can be done to help them? How different is the emotional impact of a miscarriage from that of a stillbirth? Do bereaved parents appreciate the interventions that are being recommended for medical staff to implement? How many people's lives and relationships are significantly changed by the loss?

THE STUDY

A proposal to investigate these questions was submitted to the National Institute of Child Health and Human Development, one of the National Institutes of Health. We were funded for three years and then received additional funding for two more years in order to complete the study.

Many of the physicians and hospital clinic staffs in the area where we live—the Lehigh Valley, which includes Allentown, Bethlehem, and Easton, Pennsylvania, and the surrounding rural areas—cooperated in the study by referring people to be interviewed. We wanted to be sure that the sample represented all social classes in the region, and therefore we included four hospital obstetrical clinics and a city health bureau as well as eighteen private OB/GYN practices.

At each referral source, one or two people, usually nurses, asked every woman who came in for her checkup in the four to six weeks after a loss if she would be willing to participate in the study. All together, 74.6% of those who were asked were actually interviewed. We compared the social characteristics of people who agreed to those who refused. There were no significant differences between the two, suggesting that the people we interviewed are very much like other women in this region who have suffered losses.

We interviewed a total of 138 women who had experienced losses. This number includes 63 women who had miscarriages, 18 who had ectopic pregnancies, 39 who had stillbirths, and 18 who had losses of newborns. Our study includes approximately 31% of all people who had stillbirths or newborn deaths in the two counties we included during the two years we were collecting referrals.

The women in the study ranged in age from 15 to 42, the average being 28.5 years. The great majority (82.6%) were married. They came from a wide range of social classes and occupations, including students, professionals, housewives, single mothers on welfare, secretaries, and factory workers. Two-thirds came from Western European ethnic origins, and less than six percent were Black or Hispanic, reflecting the makeup of the region. Almost all of those interviewed, in filling out a rating form after the interview, indicated that the experience had been a positive one for them.

The interviewers asked each woman if her partner would be willing to participate in the study. Fifty-six men participated in the interview, or 40.6% of the partners of all women who had a steady partner.

The interview was long, lasting at least three hours and in

some cases much longer. We asked for a description of the circumstances surrounding the loss and the responses of friends, family, and professionals following the loss. We gave people forms to complete which assessed the quality of their relationships with their partners and their social support from others. They also rated their religious involvement, their mental health in general, and their children's responses to the loss. A grief scale reflected emotions specific to the loss. People were also asked about other stresses in their lives, about previous losses, and about their hopes and expectations for the future.

A comparison group of pregnant women and their partners was selected from the same clinics and practices. Two hundred fifteen women and 102 men participated in this part of the study. They were asked all of the same questions except those pertaining to pregnancy loss. The pregnant women were very similar in age, race, marital status, social class, and length of pregnancy to the women who had losses. We did these interviews in order to give us a picture of what people would have been like before the loss, to see how the tragedy changed them. The comparison group also served as a check of the loss group's remembrance of how they felt and how much support they received during the pregnancy. Since the answers of both groups were similar, we have confidence in the validity of the loss group's recall, so that changes due to their loss can be accurately assessed.

The purpose of the study was to follow people over time, to measure both short-term and long-term effects of the loss. Therefore, everyone who participated in the first loss interview was contacted approximately one year later and asked if they would be willing to be interviewed again. This interview was somewhat shorter because it did not include the detailed description of the loss again. One hundred eleven women (80.4%) and thirty-seven men (60.3%) agreed to be interviewed a second time. Some of the original group had moved away or could not be reached; others did not have the time or were not willing to discuss the loss again.

A third wave of interviews is now complete, with people being contacted approximately one year after the second interview, or between twenty-six and thirty months after the loss. In addition, the men and women in the comparison group are being contacted for a second interview, which is timed to fall twenty-six to thirty months following their due date.

In this report, we will summarize what we have found so far from the first round, and highlight a few findings available from the second round.

RESULTS

Grief

Social scientists are still a long way from agreeing on the best way to measure grief; there is some question about whether it can be measured at all. Most people who try to assess levels of grief use indicators of depression or mental and physical symptom checklists. Others use a psychiatric interview and rely on their clinical judgment to decide who is having the most difficulty in coping with bereavement. Based on our review of the literature and our own understanding of grief after pregnancy loss, we constructed a scale of 104 items. This was based on some questions used by other researchers and on twenty-one aspects of grief which we felt to be most important, e.g., shock, sadness, anger, guilt, jealousy. Participants were asked to rate each item on a five-point scale ranging from strongly agree to strongly disagree. After analyzing the results of this scale, we narrowed it down to thirty-three questions that, based on the way people answered them, fell into three distinct categories. We call these *active grief, difficulty coping,* and *despair.*

Active grief includes sadness, crying, and missing the baby. This is what some people might call "normal" grief. *Difficulty coping* describes the situation of people who perceive themselves as being more withdrawn from others and as having difficulty functioning in their daily lives. *Despair* is how we describe the feelings of those people who identified most with such statements as "The best part of me died with the baby" and "I feel worthless since he/she died." The people who rated themselves high in *difficulty coping* and *despair* seemed to be the ones having the hardest time and needing the most attention. There were other people who were very sad about their loss and ranked high on *active grief,* but they indicated from their responses that they were able to function and were not filled with a sense of hopelessness. We expect to find in the second round that these people have coped well with their losses.

It is perhaps not surprising that women had higher average scores than the men. This was particularly striking for "active grief." Yet there was no difference between them on "despair," and there were some men whose scores on "despair" were significantly higher than their wives' scores. It may be that women and men have different styles of responding to loss.

Why did some people report much more intense grief than others? For the grief scale as a whole, women who suffered losses later in pregnancy tended to report more intense responses. Also, the more troubled their relationship was with their partner, the more grief they experienced. The women who described their overall physical health and their emotional state as poor or who felt unsupported by their friends also had the highest levels of grief.

There is a striking difference in the pattern of results for those who had miscarriages and ectopic pregnancies compared to those who suffered stillbirths or infant losses. For the first group, perception of support from friends was the most important determinant of the intensity of grief. Concerns about fertility and about the likelihood of a successful future pregnancy also played a role in the grief of women who had early losses. In addition, the quality of the partner relationship was important. In contrast, the grief of women who had losses in the latter part of the pregnancy was based largely on their assessment of their overall state of physical health, as well as on relationship quality, mental health, and the length of the pregnancy.

Older women and those of higher social class generally had lower grief scores. It may be that they had more resources for coping with their situation. Also, the older women were more likely to already have children, and this seems to have helped some of them cope with the loss.

We were surprised that a history of previous loss was not associated with grief, and for those with stillbirths and newborn deaths, concerns about fertility or future pregnancies were also not related to grief. This may be because at six or eight weeks after a loss, the event by itself is more important than its possible meaning for the future or in relationship to the past.

In addition to the grief scale, we asked people how often they were overwhelmed by grief. They could check "never," "rarely," "sometimes," or "frequently." Their answers for the first two rounds are given in Table One:

TABLE ONE
"SOMETIMES" OR "FREQUENTLY" OVERWHELMED BY GRIEF

	MISCARRIAGE AND ECTOPIC PREGNANCY		STILLBIRTH AND EARLY INFANT DEATH	
	Women	*Men*	*Women*	*Men*
6–8 weeks after loss	61.7%	33.3%	82.5%	57.7%
14–18 months after loss	34.7	5.6	61.5	29.4

It is striking that in every category, scores are higher for women than for men. On average, men and women with later losses rate their emotions as more intense than do those with early losses. Every group experienced a decline in score between the first interview and the second, but a large number of people were still very much affected by the feelings of bereavement up to a year and a half after the loss. It should be noted that since not everyone who was interviewed in the first round also participated in the second round, comparisons between the two are based on slightly different groups of people.

Help

We asked people what helped them cope with their feelings of grief. Table Two presents the most common responses.

Some interesting contrasts appear in this table. The presence of other children is more consoling to women who have early losses than it is to their partners, while the opposite is true for later losses—the men are more likely to mention their children

TABLE TWO
WHAT HAS HELPED YOU COPE WITH THE LOSS?

	MISCARRIAGE AND ECTOPIC PREGNANCY		STILLBIRTH AND EARLY INFANT DEATH	
	Women	*Men*	*Women*	*Men*
Support of spouse	23.5%	16.6%	26.4%	11.5%
Thinking a pregnancy is still possible	13.5	20.0	3.6	3.8
Presence of other children	16.0	6.6	10.6	15.5
Contact by others who have had a loss	9.8	16.6	15.8	7.7
Supportive friends	9.8	3.3	21.1	7.6
Supportive family	4.9	13.4	21.1	11.4
Keeping busy	7.4	0.0	1.8	15.3
Spiritual beliefs	8.6	6.6	12.4	7.7

than other sources of help. Thinking that another pregnancy is possible helps both men and women with early losses more than it helps men and women who had stillbirths and newborn deaths. And while women in both groups cite the support of their spouses as most important, the men more often list other responses. Apparently women look more to their spouse and friends to help them cope with the loss. Men look to other children (those already living or those who may be born in the future) and to activities to distract them.

Friends, relatives, and professionals all play an important part in helping bereaved parents to recover. We asked people about the kinds of help they received from others following the loss. When we asked who was most helpful to them, the majority said it was their spouse or partner. Table Three shows the results.

It is obvious that the spouse (or partner) is a crucial person in the time following a loss. This is particularly true for the women, as indicated earlier. Family members (parents, in-laws, and sisters in particular) are next in importance. Interestingly, family members also rated high in some people's responses to the question of who was least helpful.

In addition to asking the open-ended questions about who

TABLE THREE

WHO HAS BEEN MOST HELPFUL TO YOU IN DEALING WITH THE LOSS?

	MISCARRIAGE AND ECTOPIC PREGNANCY		STILLBIRTH AND EARLY INFANT DEATH	
	Women	*Men*	*Women*	*Men*
Spouse	62.8%	55.2%	64.7%	46.2%
Family members	18.0	17.2	23.6	30.8
Friends	15.4	6.9	11.8	15.4
Doctor	1.3	10.3	0.0	0.0
No one	2.6	10.3	0.0	7.7

was most and least helpful, we also listed a number of categories of people and asked how helpful each of them was in dealing with the loss. Spouse (or partner) received the highest rating, with relatives, funeral directors, and friends and co-workers next in order. Then came physicians, other bereaved parents, nurses, neighbors, clergy, and last in order, church members.

Professionals play a very important role in the experience of loss. Fortunately, most parents were very satisfied (63.9%) or satisfied (25.3%) with the care they received. When asked if there was anything they wished had been done differently for them, the comments revolved mostly around the desire for more rapid and attentive care, more sensitivity, and a preference not to be in the labor and delivery or maternity area following the loss. Comments such as these were made by just over half the people.

We also gave each person a list of what we called "hospital and ritual experiences" which they might have experienced, a list which was somewhat different for each type of loss. These experiences are generally the ones which have been recommended in this book and incorporated into hospital programs for helping people at the time of the loss. We wanted to know whether people had had these experiences and whether they considered them to be essential for people suffering losses such as theirs. Tables Four and Five show what percentage of each group checked that the experience was essential.

TABLE FOUR

HOSPITAL AND RITUAL EXPERIENCES CONSIDERED ESSENTIAL
(Miscarriage and Ectopic Pregnancy)

	MISCARRIAGE		ECTOPIC PREGNANCY	
	Women (63)	Men (23)	Women (18)	Men (7)
Cause of loss explained	85.7%	91.3%	100.0%	85.7%
Grief process explained	82.5	54.5	94.4	28.6
Have lab tests done	63.5	71.4	64.7	60.0
Option of hospital floor	41.7	52.4	64.7	85.7
Contact by chaplain	23.8	28.6	55.6	28.6
Contact by support group	37.1	45.0	55.6	14.3
Contact by social worker	17.7	30.0	33.3	14.3
Know what happened to remains	38.7	18.2	50.0	14.3
See remains of pregnancy	27.4	22.7	16.7	14.3
Baptism	16.7	10.0	6.3	28.6
Other ritual	10.0	10.0	6.7	14.3
Placed on maternity floor	16.4	5.0	11.1	14.3

There were a number of items on the list which were rated as essential by many people who had not actually experienced them. For women who had had stillbirths and newborn deaths, the experiences they would have wanted were: the option of which hospital floor to be placed on; having the grief process explained; contact by chaplain, social worker, or support group; touching and/or holding the baby after death; touching and/or holding the baby while still alive; being alone with the baby after death; being alone with the baby while still alive; and having written materials on loss provided. Large gaps between what had happened and what was desired were also reported by women with early losses on such experiences as having the option of which hospital floor to be placed on, knowing what happened to the remains, explanation of the grief process and the cause of the loss, and contact by a support group. The major areas then in which many bereaved parents do not get what they want are: the opportunity to be with and hold the baby, information about grief and the loss, and contact by supportive

TABLE FIVE

HOSPITAL AND RITUAL EXPERIENCES CONSIDERED ESSENTIAL
(Stillbirth and Newborn Death)

	STILLBIRTH		NEWBORN DEATH	
	Women (39)	Men (17)	Women (18)	Men (9)
Cause of death explained	79.5%	64.7%	88.9%	100.0%
Grief process explained	84.6	56.3	83.3	55.6
See baby while still alive	——	——	94.4	100.0
Touch and/or hold baby while still alive	——	——	94.4	88.9
See baby after death	74.4	64.7	83.3	77.8
Touch and/or hold baby after death	73.5	76.9	83.3	66.7
Provided written materials on loss	76.5	50.0	88.9	66.7
Be alone with baby while still alive	——	——	83.3	66.7
Be alone with baby after death	58.8	76.9	77.8	66.7
Have picture taken	60.6	46.2	83.3	77.8
Picture given to parents	56.3	58.3	83.3	66.7
Baby named by parents	58.8	76.9	83.3	88.9
Baby's name on death certificate	50.0	40.0	81.3	62.5
Keepsakes given to parents	42.4	50.0	83.3	55.6
Funeral service held	55.9	53.8	66.7	55.6
Mother attended funeral	62.5	77.8	81.3	55.6
Burial arranged by parents	56.7	53.8	76.5	55.6
Baptism	54.1	37.5	66.7	66.7
Have autopsy performed	56.8	56.3	43.8	44.4
Memorial service	42.4	53.8	47.1	22.2
Have option of hospital floor	47.4	41.2	66.7	44.4
Contact by chaplain	45.9	33.3	61.1	66.7
Contact by support group	48.6	33.3	61.1	55.6
Contact by social worker	27.8	26.7	61.1	55.6
Placed on maternity floor	21.1	43.8	35.3	55.6

personnel. The one item experienced that was thought undesirable but which often occurred was placement on the maternity floor.

Many parents received counseling from their physicians, nurses, and other hospital personnel following the loss. When asked what they found most helpful about the counseling, they focused on the sympathetic responses, reassurance about future pregnancies, being told that the parent was not responsible for the loss, assurance that grieving is normal, and the provision of concrete information about the cause of the loss. Insensitivity and lack of information were the most frequent complaints about the responses of professionals.

Changes

We also asked people about the ways in which the loss had changed them and their relationships with others. Table Six gives the answers regarding change in relationship to one's spouse or partner.

What is most notable about this table is that there is little change over time, with similar percentages in each category at both the first and the second interview. The only exception is women who had stillbirths and newborn deaths, some of whom apparently experienced a deterioration in their relationships during the time between the two interviews. For the most part, however, people said the experience had brought them closer

TABLE SIX

HOW HAS THE LOSS AFFECTED YOUR RELATIONSHIP WITH YOUR SPOUSE OR PARTNER?

	MISCARRIAGE AND ECTOPIC PREGNANCY		STILLBIRTH AND EARLY INFANT DEATH	
	Women	*Men*	*Women*	*Men*
Positive Change				
6–8 weeks after loss	56.6%	49.8%	80.8%	66.8%
14–18 months after loss	58.3	47.3	61.5	69.2
Negative Change				
6–8 weeks after loss	15.1	13.6	8.5	19.2
14–18 months after loss	13.9	10.5	28.2	7.7
No Change				
6–8 weeks after loss	28.3	36.4	10.6	14.3
14–18 months after loss	27.8	42.2	10.3	23.1

together and made them more appreciative of each other. Those who referred to negative changes mentioned that they were having more arguments and more difficulty talking to each other. Four of the women (3.6%) had separated from their partners.

Relationships with other people were not affected as much as was the relationship to spouse or partner. Most people said that their other relationships had not changed, and this was even more true for the second interview than for the first. Although some people did indicate a deterioration of their relationships with others, more of those who thought there had been a change said they felt closer to friends and relatives and more appreciative of them because of the loss. Twenty-six percent of the women who experienced stillbirths and newborn deaths reported this positive change at the time of both interviews.

We also asked people how the loss changed their attitude to religion. Again, the majority responded that there was no change. People who experienced losses later in pregnancy reported more change, both positive and negative, in their attitude toward religion than did those who had early losses. In both groups, early and late, the men spoke of more positive changes at the time of the first interview (e.g., beliefs strengthened, closer to the church) than did the women, who were more likely to say that they had lost faith and were angry with God. By the second interview, the opposite pattern appeared, with the men's accounts of greater faith dropping, and the women's increasing. Some people mentioned that they were initially angry with God but that this did not last, and it may be that some of the women in particular turned back to faith and to their church over time.

We also asked people how they felt the loss had changed them, and as Table Seven shows, most of the responses suggested a positive change. Although the bereaved parents were distressed by their experiences, most of them looked at what they had gained from the tragedy.

TABLE SEVEN

CHANGES IN ONESELF AS A RESULT OF THE LOSS*

	MISCARRIAGE AND ECTOPIC PREGNANCY		STILLBIRTH AND EARLY INFANT DEATH	
	Women	*Men*	*Women*	*Men*
More appreciative of life, of family, of spouse	39.3%	43.3%	49.2%	61.3%
More understanding of losses and sympathetic to others	17.2	13.2	30.1	23.0
More aware of fragility and insecurity of life	14.9	13.2	17.8	15.4
Stronger, experienced personal growth	17.2	3.3	7.2	11.5
More in touch with feelings	8.6	6.6	3.6	3.8
More depressed, irritable	15.9	0.0	14.2	18.6
More cautious about pregnancy	8.6	6.6	7.1	3.8

*Since the question was open-ended and it was possible to give more than one answer, the percentages may add up to more than 100%.

The last question we asked in the interview was what advice the parents would give to others experiencing similar losses. The advice took on a very positive tone, one of sympathy, encouragement, and understanding.

The bereaved people we interviewed clearly recognized the value of seeking support from others. Talking with friends about feelings can help parents enormously in coping with their grief. This coincides with our finding that women who were highest on the dimensions of despair and difficulty coping were those who felt least supported by friends.

A striking result in this study is that although many people felt that contact by a chaplain would be helpful, very few said that their religious faith was important in dealing with grief. Being more religious did not make grief any less intense; clergy and church members were not considered very helpful; and spiritual beliefs were rarely mentioned as important tools for coping.

TABLE EIGHT

WHAT WOULD BE YOUR ADVICE TO SOMEONE EXPERIENCING A LOSS SUCH AS YOURS?*

	MISCARRIAGE AND ECTOPIC PREGNANCY		STILLBIRTH AND EARLY INFANT DEATH	
	Women	*Men*	*Women*	*Men*
Rely on and talk to others	59.1%	46.6%	79.1%	72.8%
Be positive, put it in perspective, go on with your life, hang in there, you'll survive	32.0	56.5	32.0	53.5
Accept grieving, know your needs, it will get better, everyone grieves in own way, you're not alone	19.8	23.3	24.8	19.1
Don't blame yourself	23.5	20.1	10.7	7.6
Try again	23.4	10.0	5.4	11.5
Rely on faith	9.8	6.6	8.9	7.6
Get good medical care, understanding doctor	4.8	0.0	5.3	0.0

*Since the question was open-ended and it was possible to give more than one answer, the percentages may add up to more than 100%.

When we returned for the second interview, fourteen to eighteen months after the loss, just over half the women were pregnant or had already given birth. Another ten percent had had a subsequent loss, one woman had adopted a child, and most of the others were planning to or trying to become pregnant. By the third interview (twenty-six to thirty months after the loss) many more women had given birth successfully, some more than once.

Friends and relatives do help, and so does time. We have seen by the second interview, and even more so by the third, that people were much less likely to feel overwhelmed by their loss. The memories are there, but the intensity and frequency of feelings have diminished. Some are finding it difficult to go on, but most people are looking ahead to new babies, career changes, and continuing the ongoing pattern of their lives.

APPENDIX A

Support Groups for Families After Miscarriage, Ectopic Pregnancy, Stillbirth, and Infant Death

NATIONAL SUPPORT ORGANIZATIONS

SHARE
c/o Sister Jane Marie Lamb
St. Elizabeth's Hospital
211 S. 3rd St.
Belleville, IL 62222
(618) 234-2120

The most complete source of information on local support groups and resources of all kinds

The Compassionate Friends, Inc.
National Headquarters
P. O. Box 3696
Oak Brook, IL 60522
(312) 990-0010

A self-help organization of bereaved parents helping each other; local chapters exist throughout the world

National Sudden Infant Death
  Syndrome Foundation
8200 Professional Place, Suite 104
Landover, MD 20785
(301) 459-3388

Information and referral for parents regarding crib death

LOCAL SUPPORT GROUPS

Alabama

SHARE
Family Resource Center
2914 Linden Avenue
Birmingham, AL 35209
(205) 879-1717
Marty Eason
(205) 967-3706

AMI Brookwood Hospital
c/o Elaine Hickman, Chaplain
2010 Brookwood Medical Center
  Drive
Birmingham, AL 35209

Alaska

SHARE
Michelle & Rus Cunningham
SRA Box 6754-8
Palmer, AK 99645
(907) 745-8476

SHARE
Elizabeth McWilliams
P. O. Box 14-2874
Anchorage, AK 99514
(907) 562-3494

Arizona

COMPASSIONATE FRIENDS—
INFANT GROUP
Cindy Chambers
3221 E. Campobello Drive
Phoenix, AZ 85032
(602) 971-6018

SHARE
Elizabeth Winkler
4466 E. Sylvane
Tucson, AZ 85711
(602) 790-5954
(602) 887-6491

Arkansas

SHARE
Cindy Westcott
University—Arkansas Med. Science
4301 W. Markham Slot #518
Little Rock, AR 72205-7199
(501) 661-5000

AMMEND
c/o The Parent Center
7107 12th Street
West Park Bldg. 1, Suite 103
Little Rock, AR 72207
(501) 666-6833
Contact: Sarah Faitak
(501) 225-2930

AMEND OF NORTHWEST
ARKANSAS
c/o Sandra Hopkins
1680 E. Shadowridge Drive
Fayetteville, AR 72701
(501) 521-1860

AMEND
Box 7062
Jonesboro, AR 72403

RESOLVE THROUGH SHARING
Quachita Memorial Hospital
Olive at Broadway St.—Box 1137
Hot Springs, AR 71901
Sylvia Tharp-contact person
(501) 624-5702 (hospital)
(501) 321-1000 (Sylvia's work)

California

SHARE
Julie Lehman
St. Agnes Medical Center
1303 East Herndon Avenue
Fresno, CA 93710
(209) 449-3591

SHARING PARENTS OF KERN
COUNTY
Mary Bezdek
7417 Eliso Court
Bakersfield, CA 99309
(805) 397-0874

SHARING PARENTS
Attn: Leslie Massey, RN
Marshall Hospital
Marshall Way
Placerville, CA 95667
(916) 626-2679

SHARE
Ginger Scherck
3064 Lejeune Circle
29 Palms, CA 92278-1151
(619) 368-9511
or
Dr. Dianne Gerard
(619) 368-6344

SHARING PARENTS OF SAN
JOAQUIN COUNTY
Anita Freyman-Danielsen
1683 Kingwood Avenue
Manteca, CA 95336
(209) 239-1071

HOPING & SHARING OF LONG
  BEACH (A SHARE GROUP)
Marie Teague
5335 Carita Street
Long Beach, CA 90808
(213) 425-4889

SHARE
Emily Rivera
Keweah Delta Hospital
400 West Mineral King
Visalia, CA 93291
(209) 625-2211

HAND OF SANTA CLARA
  COUNTY
P. O. Box 341
Los Gatos, CA 95031
Pam Puetsch
(408) 732-3228

SHARE OF SONOMA COUNTY
Joyce Giles, Coordinator
Home Hospice of Sonoma County
1811 Fourth Street
Santa Rosa, CA 95404
(707) 542-5045

HAND OF MONTEREY COUNTY
c/o Children's Services Center
484 Lighthouse Avenue
Monterey, CA 93940

SHARING PARENTS
P. O. Box 838
Carmichael, CA 95609-0838
(916) 381-0745
(916) 424-5150

RESPOND/CHICO
Kathy Sorrels
10 Forest Creek Avenue
Chico, CA 95926

HOPE-EUREKA
Debra Jones
911 Third Street
Eureka, CA 95501

HAND OF THE PENINSULA
Emily Corpos, Coordinator
257 Fir Street
San Carlos, CA 94070
(415) 591-0283
Daly City to San Mateo
  (415) 877-8585
Belmont to Menlo Park
  (415) 363-2111
On the Coast (415) 726-2111

AMEND
Aida Feria
P. O. Box 30
Harbor City, CA 90710
(818) 877-7999

HAND OF SANTA CRUZ
Lisa Jones
4382 Ranchero Drive
Soquel, CA 95073
(408) 475-4188

STILLBIRTH/MISCARRIAGE
  SUPPORT GROUP
Alice Yamada
559 Marsh Street
San Luis Obispo, CA 93401
(805) 544-2266

PACS—PARENTS ADJUSTING
  THROUGH CARING
Dianne Van Loon
YWCA—8172 Magnolia
Riverside, CA 92504
(714) 688-5531

HOPING OF COLTON/SAN
  BERNARDINO
Marilyn Noordhof
752 Plumwood Street
Colton, CA 92324
(714) 825-2469

HOPING OF ORANGE COUNTY
Cherie Beckmeyer
11022 Flynn
Garden Grove, CA 92640
(714) 635-4486

PARENTAL LOSS GROUP
Janice and David Phillips
222 S. Russ Street
King City, CA 93930
(408) 385-4457

HOPING OF SAN GABRIEL
    VALLEY
Debbie McMahon
2225 Junipero Serra Drive
San Gabriel, CA 91776
(213) 943-7971

EMPTY CRADLE—SUPPORT
    GROUP
Ann Nickel
6497 Decanture Street
San Diego, CA 92120
(619) 692-2144

HOPING OF SOUTH BAY/SANTA
    MONICA
11620 Freenan Avenue, No. B
Hawthorne, CA 90250

MOMENT BY MOMENT
Patsy Jones, RN
c/o Cedars–Sinai Medical Center
8700 Beverly Blvd.
Room 3506
Los Angeles, CA 90048
(213) 855-5357

BEREAVED PARENTS OF
    INFANTS
Susan Newton
3508 Dale Road, Suite D
Modesto, CA 95356
(209) 578-4863

SAIL (SUPPORT AFTER INFANT
    & PREGNANCY LOSS)
Eden Hospital
20103 Lake Chabot Road
Castro Valley, CA 94546
(415) 537-1234, Ext. 5043
Debra Linder
(415) 838-8431

BEREAVED PARENTS SUPPORT
    GROUP
Sabra S. Hudson
P. O. Box 223139
Carmel, CA 93923
(408) 625-0666

COPING
Yvonne Fundingsland
561 Northview Road
Santa Barbara, CA 93105
(805) 682-8020, 682-7529

PARENTS BEREAVEMENT
    OUTREACH (any age child)
Lee Schmidt, RN
535 16th Street
Santa Monica, CA 90402
(213) 825-2450

EMPTY ARMS
Lori Lingenfelter
8773 Comet Street
Cucumonga, CA 91730
(714) 982-6074

BEREAVEMENT PARENTS &
    MOURNING AFTER
Santa Rosa Memorial Hospital
1165 Montgomery Drive
Santa Rosa, CA 95402
(707) 546-3210

HAND (Helping After Neonatal
    Death)
c/o Apple Growing Family Center
80 Skyview Terrace
San Rafael, CA 94903
Gretchen Kucserka
(415) 453-0115

SAND (Support After Neonatal
    Death)
Janet Kirksey, RN
Alta Bates Hospital
3001 Colby Street at Ashby
Berkeley, CA 94705
(415) 540-1571

SAND
Children's Hospital
3700 California
San Francisco, CA 94118
(415) 387-8700
Niva Jones
Department of Social Services

GRIEF COUNSELING
Susan Breed
P. O. Box 4852
Walnut Creek, CA 94596
(415) 944-0645

HOPING
8200 Owensmouth Avenue #14
Canoga Park, CA 91304

HAND—San Francisco
P. O. Box 3805
San Francisco, CA 94119

SHARE
Sofia Close
3347 Courtland Avenue
Oakland, CA 94619

Colorado

SHARE
Frank and Linda Pavlak
11470 W. Powers Avenue
Littleton, CO 80127
(303) 978-9517

SHARE
Rhonda Welch
3512 Lilac Lane
Evans, CO 80620
(303) 330-1629

HUMANA—SHARE
Kathy McGraw, Director, Social Ser.
1501 S. Potomac Street
Aurora, CO 80012
(303) 695-2600

FETAL & NEWBORN LOSS
   SUPPORT GROUP
Dorothea Graham Cicchinelli,
   BASW
Rose Medical Center
4567 E. Ninth Avenue
Denver, CO 80220
(303) 320-2713

STILLBORN/NEWBORN LOSS
   SUPPORT GROUP
Boulder County Hospice
Marcia Lattanzi
2825 Marine Street
Boulder, CO 80303
(303) 449-7740

HOPING OF LARIMER COUNTY
402 Stover
Fort Collins, CO 80524
(303) 484-4318

COMPASSIONATE FRIENDS
   INFANT LOSS SUPPORT
   GROUP
Marcia Richardson
16 E. Platte Avenue
Colorado Springs, CO 80903
(303) 576-2395

HOPING
Joyce Boyles
11070 Hardy Road
Colorado Springs, CO 80908

HOPING
Kathy Morrissey
2445 Courtney Drive
Loveland, CO 80537

SHARE
Rita Beam, RN, ACCE
The Women's Center
Humana Hospital
9191 Grant Street
Thornton, CO 80229
(303) 450-4520

Connecticut

SHARE
Robin Wheeler, RN
227 Stadley Rough Road
Danbury, CT 06811
(203) 744-4658

SHARE
Mary Hanka
48 Chestnut Street
Willimantic, CT 06226
(203) 456-8101

AID
c/o Nancy Baranowski
21 Canterbury Lane
Monroe, CT 06468
(203) 452-0709

NEWBORN DEATH SUPPORT
  GROUP
Donna Goldman
Women's Center of Southeastern Ct.
120 Broad Street
New London, CT 06320
(203) 447-0366

UPHOLD
Mary Lou Greer
100 Teeter Road
Trumbull, CT 06611

AID IN INFANT DEATH
Susan Braren
27 Anderson Road
Tolland, CT 06084
(203) 872-0326

SHARE
Ilga Baker
P. O. Box 806
Salisbury, CT 06068
(203) 364-5544

AID
c/o St. Francis Hospital & Med.
  Ctr.
114 Woodland Street
Hartford, CT 06105
(203) 548-4000

SHARE
OBS Unit, Sharon Hospital
Sharon, CT 06069
Judy Dietz
(203) 364-5511, Ext. 2240

HOPE
89 Maple View
Woodbridge, CT 06525
Nancy Walker
(203) 397-5200

SHARE
c/o Mary Beth Pratt
1960 Bucks Hill Road
Southbury, CT 06488
(203) 264-7644

SURVIVING YOUR BABY'S
  DEATH
Char Stabinsky
152 E. Avenue
Norwalk, CT 06851

Delaware

PARENTS' SUPPORT GROUPS
Pat Ohrams
Delaware Medical Center
1902 Gheen Road
Wilmington, DE 19808
(302) 994-9287

LOVING ARMS
  PARENTS' SUPPORT GROUP
Marie E. Hughes
The Medical Center of Delaware
P. O. Box 6001
Newark, DE 19718
(302) 733-2375

UNITE, INC.
April Palekar, RN
Beebe Hospital
Lewes, DE 19958

SHARE
Lydia Garnick
Rt. 1, Box 213C
Marydel, DE 19964

HOPING
Rev. Walters
Grace United Methodist Church
Wilmington, DE 19801

Florida

SHARE
Chris Pfeffer
Baptist Hospital, Patient Ed. Dept.
8900 N. Kendall Drive
North Miami, FL 33176
(305) 596-1960, Ext. 6658

NEONATAL AND EARLY
  INFANT DEATH SUPPORT
  GROUP
Shelly Wortman, MS
Center for Counseling Services
140 South University Drive
Plantation, FL 33324
(305) 475-1371

SHARE
Judy Fisher
7465 Overton Drive
Leesburg, FL 32788
(904) 728-2227

SHARE
Ann Torrance Backmann
c/o Neonatal Stepdown
Orlando Regional Medical Center
1414 South Kuhl Avenue
Orlando, FL 32806-2093
(305) 841-5111

SHARE
Maureen Shea
Jackson Memorial Hospital
Social Work Department
1611 North West Twelfth Avenue
Miami, FL 33136
(305) 325-7429

SHARE
Pat Stauber
North Shore Medical Center
1100 N.W. 95th Street
Miami, FL 33150
(305) 835-6162

SHARE
Ms. Terry S. Johnson, RN
All Children's Hospital
801 Sixth Street South, Box 600
St. Petersburg, FL 33701
(813) 898-7451

HOPING
Evelyn Beno
941 Adelphia Court
Fort Myers, FL 33907
(813) 481-8173

CARING FRIENDS
Jennifer Kunz
4809 Figwood Lane
Orlando, FL 32808
(305) 293-1766

COPES (CARING FOR OTHER
  PARENTS EXPERIENCING
  SORROW)
Pat Burt, CPNP
232 Riverbeach Drive
Ormond Beach, FL 32074
(904) 677-4453

EMPTY ARMS
Nancy Brubaker
3505 65th Street West
Bradenton, FL 33529
(813) 792-3729

AMEND
Karen Frazier
5104 127th Avenue
Tampa, FL 33617
(813) 959-0323 or 977-2090

HOPES
c/o Sandi Poston
P. O. Box 1143
Lutz, FL 33617

CARING FRIENDS
Margie White
Seminole County
104 Moss Road
Winter Springs, FL 32708
(305) 327-0347

CARING FRIENDS
Dolores McCrory
Lake County
Star Route 3, Box 844
Eustis, FL 32726
(904) 357-9876

AMEND
Kim Petrie, Director
5241 Rowe Trail
Pace, FL 32571
(904) 994-4368

RESOLVE THROUGH SHARING
Memorial Medical Center
3625 University Blvd. S.
P. O. Box 16325
Jacksonville, FL 32216
Sandra Mays
(904) 399-6111

RESOLVE THROUGH SHARING
St. Vincent Medical Center
1800 Barrs Street, Box 2982
Jacksonville, FL 32203
Jamie Zachary
(904) 387-7300

HOPING
Evelyn Hetanek
469 Ena Road 708
Fort Myers, FL 33907

Georgia

SHARE
Larry M. Connolly, Chaplain
Piedmont Hospital
1968 Peachtree Road, NW
Atlanta, GA 30309
(404) 350-2222

SHARE
Marcia McGinnis
c/o The Link Counseling Center
218 Hilderbrand Avenue
Sandy Springs, GA 30328
(404) 256-9797

PREMIE PARENTS' SUPPORT
  GROUP
Lisa Cohen
Northside Hospital
1000 Johnson Ferry Road, NE
Atlanta, GA 30042
(404) 851-8000, beeper 238

Hawaii

HOPING
c/o Judy Boomer, RN
46–398 Holopu Place
Kaneohe, HI 96744
(808) 834-5333, Ext. 9902 or 9903

Idaho

SHARE OF IDAHO
Nanci Hyneman
P. O. Box 1225
Boise, ID 83701
(208) 342-7226

Illinois

SHARE OF RUSHVILLE
Melissa Mathis
114 North Jackson Street
Browning, IL 62624
(217) 322-4321

SHARE
Sandra Fisk
Galesburg Cottage Hospital
695 N. Kellogg Street
Galesburg, IL 61401
(309) 343-8131, Ext. 210

SHARE
Kathy Shank
Passavant Hospital
1600 W. Walnut Street
Jacksonville, IL 62650
(217) 245-9541, Ext. 184

SHARE
Laura Blickensderfer, RN
St. Mary's Hospital
1800 E. Lake Shore Drive
Decatur, IL 62526
(217) 429-2966, Ext. 2206

SHARE
Linda Whited, RN
718 Ashton Lane South
Champaign, IL 61820
(217) 359-5480
or
Champaign, Illinois Group
Mercy Hospital
Urbana, IL
(217) 337-2226

SHARING PARENTS
Janet Pugh—OB Department
Oliver Anderson Hospital
Highway 162
Maryville, IL 62062
(618) 288-5711, Ext. 466
(618) 656-5598 (Home)

SHARING OF OLNEY, ILLINOIS
Richland Memorial Hospital—OB
  Dept.
800 East Locust
Olney, IL 62450
(618) 395-2131
or
Chris Carter
Rt. 1, Box 44-A
Louisville, IL 62858
(619) 665-4029

EMPTY ARMS (A SHARE
  GROUP)
Nancy Pormenter
Illinois Valley Community Hospital
925 West Street
Peru, IL 61354
(815) 223-3300, Ext. 443

ILAC (I LOST A CHILD)
Jane Rose, RN
Memorial Hospital
404 West Main Street
Carbondale, IL 62920
(618) 549-0721, Ext. 5202

HELP FOR PARENTS LIVING
  WITH LOSS
St. Joseph's Medical Center
Jan Reeder, MSW
2200 East Washington
Bloomington, IL 61701
(309) 662-3311
Jim Turner, Pastoral Care

GRIEVING PARENTS' SUPPORT
  NETWORK
Cindy Scroggins
1419 Chadwick Drive
Normal, IL 61761
(309) 454-7000

MIS (MISCARRIAGE, INFANT
  DEATH & STILLBIRTH)
Lois Wahrenburg
2402 Lohman Road
Peoria, IL 61604
(309) 674-0213
(309) 685-5010

SHARE
Debbie Vrtis
1709 Pleasant Avenue
McHenry, IL 60050
(815) 344-0756

AMEND
Jane Borman
Madison County Amend
2209 Gillis
Alton, IL 62002
(618) 466-7129

EMPTY ARMS (A SHARE
  GROUP)
Charlene K. Basham, CTRS
Director of Ed/Activity Therapy
Community Hospital of Ottawa
1100 E. Norris Drive
Ottawa, IL 61350
(815) 433-3100 (day) or
(815) 434-2152 (eve.)

SHARE
Sister Jane Marie Lamb
St. Elizabeth's Hospital
211 S. Third St.
Belleville, IL 62222
(618) 234-2120

SHARE
Doris Thouvenin, RN, Nursing Serv.
St. Elizabeth's Hospital
211 S. Third Street
Belleville, IL 62222
(618) 234-2120, Ext. 1293

SHARE
Social Service Department
Sarah Bush Lincoln Health Center
P. O. Box 372
Mattoon, IL 61938
(217) 258-2392

SHARE
Jean Strausbaugh
Social Worker
St. Francis Hospital
1215 E. Union Avenue
Litchfield, IL 62056
(217) 324-2191

SHARE—BLESSING HOSPITAL
Ingrid Prunkl, RN
Broadway at Eleventh Street
Quincy, IL 62301
(217) 223-5811

SHARE
Debbie Rubach
St. Anthony's Memorial Hospital
503 N. Maple Street
Effingham, IL 62401
(217) 342-6690 (home)

SHARE
Diane Nelson, Dept. of Neonatology
Rockford Memorial Hospital
2400 N. Rockton Avenue
Rockford, IL 61103
(815) 968-6861, Ext. 5060

SHARE
Elizabeth Johnson
409 W. Eighth
Belvidere, IL
(815) 544-4704
        or
Debbie Dreckney
437 Garden Drive
Belvidere, IL 61008

SHARE
Cindy Waters
McDonough District Hospital
525 E. Grant Street
Macomb, IL 61455
(309) 833-4101

SHARE (Moline, Illinois)
Quad Cities Group
Tricia Horst
618 33rd Avenue
E. Moline, IL 61244
(309) 755-1945

SHARE
Heart of Illinois
St. Francis Medical Center
Billie Rocke
530 N. E. Glen Oak
Peoria, IL 61637
(309) 655-2090

ILLINOIS SHARE
Clairann Nicklin
Methodist Medical Center
211 N. E. Glen Oak
Peoria, IL 61636
(309) 672-4850
(309) 686-5806

SHARE
Linda Bronersky, Social Worker
Loyola University Medical Center
2160 S. First Avenue
Maywood, IL 60153
(312) 531-4044
(312) 531-3056 (Rev. Peg Shultz)

COMPASSIONATE FRIENDS
   INFANT GROUP
Joanne Matzke
5N625 Santa Fe Trail
Bartlett, IL 60103

THE COMPASSIONATE FRIENDS
Parents of Infants
P. O. Box 3696
Oak Brook, IL 60522
(312) 990-0010

GRIEF & GROWTH GROUP
Chaplain Tim Arnold
Lutheran General Hospital
1775 Dempster Street
Park Ridge, IL 60068
(312) 696-6395

CARETAKERS (any age or type loss)
Robert Hanson
Rev. Michael McMillen, Pastoral Care
West Suburban Hospital
Erie at Austin Blvd.
Oak Park, IL 60302
(312) 383-6200, Ext. 6401

PARENTS WHO HAVE LOST A CHILD
Rabbi Robert J. Marx
540 Frontage Road, #301
Northfield, IL 60093
(312) 835-5605

CARING/UNDERSTANDING TEAM
Chaplain Margaret Heinz, O. P.
Ravenswood Hospital Medical Center
4500 N. Winchester at Wilson
Chicago, IL 60640
(312) 878-4300, Ext. 4400

COPING AID
Judy Friedrichs, Coordinator
7 Jones Special Care Nursery
Rush-Presbyterian St. Luke's Medical Center
1753 Congress Parkway
Chicago, IL 60612
(312) 942-5068

THE CARING CONNECTION
Sherry Miller
Christ Hospital
4440 West 95th Street
Oak Lawn, IL 60453
(312) 857-5175

TOGETHER IN THE LOSS OF A CHILD (TLC)
Linda Given
333 East Superior
Chicago, IL 60611
(312) 908-7600 or 908-7225

HOUDAL KROVITT PERINATAL LOSS SUPPORT GROUP
Ray Silverstein, Pediatrics
Evanston Hospital
2650 Ridge Avenue
Evanston, IL 60201
(312) 492-4570 (days)
(312) 835-1346 (nights/weekends)

TOUCH
Barbara Julion, RN
Bethany Hospital L & D
3435 W. Van Buren
Chicago, IL 60624
(312) 854-3401

For Hispanic Parents:
Eva Hernandez
Erie Family Health Center
1347 West Erie
Chicago, IL 60622

COFFEE AND COMFORT
Orland Park Christian Church
7500 W. Sycamore Drive
Orland Park, IL 60462
(312) 460-1392

MT. VERNON SHARE
Carol Hughey
Good Samaritan Hospital
605 N. Twelfth
Mt. Vernon, IL 62864
(618) 242-4600, Ext. 5540

SHARE
St. Joseph's Hospital
OB Department
Jamestown Road
Breese, IL 62230-0099
Helen Essenpreis, RN, BSN
(618) 526-4511, Ext. 423

RESOLVE THRU SHARING
Maralee Kaufman
Freeport Mem. Hospital OB/GYN
1045 W. Stephenson Drive
Freeport, IL 61032

SHARE
Mary Kay Frey
Katherine Shaw Bethea Hospital
403 E. First Street
Dixon, IL 61021

COMPASSIONATE FRIENDS
N.W. Suburban Chapter
800 W. Central Road
Arlington Heights, IL 60005
(312) 259-1000

TCF (The Compassionate Friends)
Carl & Shirley Melin
Mercy Center
West Highland Street
Aurora, IL 60506
(312) 557-2930

Indiana

SHARE
Beth Kindler
323 Hamilton Street
West Lafayette, IN 47906
(317) 463-6605

SHARE
Joan Callahan, Chaplain
Community Hospital
1500 North Ritter Avenue,
    Dept. 670
Indianapolis, IN 46219
(317) 353-5505

HOPE
Elkhart General Hospital
600 East Blvd.
Elkhart, IN 46515
Attn: Rita Walker, RN
Head Nurse, OB
(219) 294-2621, Ext. 3273

PROJECT COMFORT
Parkview Hospital
2200 Randalia Drive
Fort Wayne, IN 46805
(219) 484-6636

COMPASSIONATE FRIENDS
Nancy Prange
2606 Pleasant Street
South Bend, IN 46615
(219) 233-5915

SHARE OF MUNCIE INDIANA
    INC.
Susan Yingling
Ball Memorial Hospital
2401 W. University Avenue
Muncie, IN 47303
(317) 747-3111
(317) 724-7655

SHARE
Margaret Risley
Bartholomew County Hospital
2400 East Seventeenth Street
Columbus, IN 47201
(812) 379-4441

SHARE
Mary Beth Lodato
St. Mary's Medical Center
3700 Washington Avenue
Evansville, IN 47750
(812) 479-4624

SHARE OUTREACH
Sherry Hutchins
103 West Diamond Street
Kendallville, IN 46755
(219) 347-3209 or (219) 347-3826

RESOLVE THROUGH SHARING
St. Francis Hospital
1600 Albany Street
Beech Grove, IN 46107
Michele Kuntz Wood
(317) 787-3311

RESOLVE THROUGH SHARING
St. Vincent Hospital & Health Care
    Center
2001 W. 86th Street
Indianapolis, IN 46260
Judy Marich
(317) 871-2345

SHARE
Pat Parr
305 N. Detroit Street
LaGrange, IN 46761
(219) 463-7266

PROJECT COMFORT
Marcia & Greg Schroder
310 E. 2nd Street
Bloomington, IN 47401

Iowa

SHARE
Glenda Ferguson, RN
Fort Madison Community Hospital
2210 Avenue H
Fort Madison, IA 52627
(319) 372-6530

SHARE
Pat Williams
Mercy Hospital
500 Market Street
Iowa City, IA 52240
(319) 337-0658

SHARE
Quad Cities Group
Anita Purcell
2128 Madison
Davenport, IA 52804
(319) 322-2651 or (309) 755-1945

SHARE
Jack and Cindy Myers
1120 Tenth Street
Sheldon, IA 51201
(712) 324-4720

SHARE
Vicki & Steve Rall
807 W. Mills
Creston, IA 50801
(515) 782-7752

SHARE
Hospice of Pella
Shirley Borgman
404 Jefferson
Pella, IA 50219
(515) 628-3456

EMPTY ARMS SUPPORT GROUP
Covenant Medical Center
Sister Lou Marie Fideler, Chaplain
3421 W. Ninth
Waterloo, IA 50702
(319) 236-4111

PARENTS SUPPORT GROUP
Russell C. Striffler, Chaplain
St. Luke's Methodist Hospital
1026 A Avenue N. E.
Cedar Rapids, IA 52402
(319) 369-7347

PARENT SHARE AND SUPPORT,
  INC.
Mary Olson, RN
Palmer Memorial Hospital
112 Jefferson Street
West Union, IA 52175
(319) 422-3775

BEREAVEMENT SUPPORT
  GROUP
Burlington Medical Center
618 N. Fourth Street, Room 1
Burlington, IA 52601
Rev. Richard Gilbert, BMC Chaplain
(319) 753-3011

SHARE
Evan & Ann Terhorst
RR 2, Box 72
Ireton, IA 51027
(712) 722-2079

PARENT SHARE
Marjorie Evans
1001 E. Pennsylvania Avenue
Ottumwa, IA 52501

Kansas

SHARE
Rev. Harry Tyson
Asbury Hospital
400 South Santa Fe
Salina, KS 67401
(913) 827-4411, Ext. 362

SHARE
Infant Loss Support Services of
  Greater Kansas City
P. O. Box 9516
Shawnee Mission, KS 66201
Daren Archer, RN
  or
Largo Callenbach
(816) 331-6222
(816) 322-2944

Kentucky

SHARE
Sarah Moore, RN
The Medical Center
P. O. Box 56
Bowling Green, KY 42101
(502) 781-2150

SHARE
Phyllis Tuttle, RN
P. O. Box 2799
Owensboro Daviess Co. Hospital
Owensboro, KY 42302
(502) 926-3030, Ext. 117

CONSOLING PARENTS
Humana Hospital University
530 S. Jackson Street
Louisville, KY 40202
(502) 589-4313

NORTON CHILDREN'S
   HOSPITAL
c/o Chaplain Wayne Willis
P. O. Box 35070
Louisville, KY 40232

SHARING SESSIONS
Judy Dickey
110 Southridge Drive
Somerset, KY 42501
(606) 679-4297

COMPASSIONATE PARENTS
Alice Higgins, Dir. of Patient
   Services
206 W. South Street
Mayfield, KY 42066
(502) 247-5211

CARING FRIENDS: A SUPPORT
   GROUP FOR GRIEVING
   PARENTS
Judy Neal, Social Services
Madisonville Regional Medical
   Center
Hospital Drive
Madisonville, KY 42431
(502) 825-5100

CONSOLING PARENTS
c/o Francis E. Englander
1114 Hilliard Avenue
Louisville, KY 40204
(502) 452-9138

BEREAVED PARENTS SUPPORT
   GROUP
Western Baptist Hospital
Kentucky Avenue
Paducah, KY 42001
(502) 575-2100
Anne Freeland & Marsha Puckett
(502) 898-8059

Louisiana

SHREVEPORT—BOSSIER
   CHAPTER OF SHARE
Patricia Thompson
Northwestern State University
College of Nursing Prof.
1800 Line Avenue
Shreveport, LA 71101
(318) 677-3030
(318) 929-2892

SHARE
Humana Hospital
4200 Nelson Road
Lake Charles, LA 70605
(318) 474-6370
Joann Owen, RN

RESOLVE THROUGH SHARING
Pendleton Memorial Methodist
   Hospital
5620 Read Blvd.
New Orleans, LA 70127
Wendy Guichard
(504) 244-5100

RESOLVE THROUGH SHARING
Ochsner Foundation Hospital
1516 Jefferson Highway
New Orleans, LA 70121
Ann Richardson
(504) 838-3000

INFANT–LOSS SUPPORT GROUP
Woman's Hospital
Susan Eaton, MSW
Beth Manning
P. O. Box 95009
Baton Rouge, LA 70895-9009
(504) 927-1300

Maine

EMPTY ARMS (A SHARE
   GROUP)
Kathy Hobson
P. O. Box 104
Alna, ME 04535
(207) 443-4082
Robyn Corsman
(207) 443-9425

Maryland

LABOR OF LOVE
Wendy Hite
Rt. 1, Box 139
Fairplay, MD 21733
(301) 582-3697

HOWARD COUNTY SHARE
Kathleen Liparine, RN
Childbirth Ed. Assn. of Greater
   Washington, Inc.
10436 Schoolmaster Place
Columbia, MD 21044
(301) 997-2670
Ellen Byrd, (301) 797-1705

THE COMPASSIONATE
   FRIENDS SUPPORT GROUP
   FOR PREGNANCY LOSS
Susan G. Phillips
Star Route 1, Box 246
Prince Frederick, MD 20678
(301) 535-4341

THE COMPASSIONATE
   FRIENDS INFANT GROUP
Harford County Group
Debbie O'Connell
1315 Mayflower Drive
Bel Air, MD 21014
(301) 836-2252
or Pat Parfrey, (301) 838-7417

MIS (Miscarriage, Infant death,
   Stillbirth)
Sharon Covington
Shady Grove Adventist Hospital
9715 Medical Center Drive #5013
Rockville, MD 20850
(301) 460-6222, (301) 279-9030
or SUBSEQUENT PREGNANCY
   GROUP
Sue Abrams
(301) 294-0146

COMPASSIONATE FRIENDS
Anna Ruhrbaugh
44 River Drive
Annapolis, MD 21403

Massachusetts

SHARE
Jeanie Sullivan
87 Keddy Blvd.
Chicopee, MA 02010
(413) 534-1526
(Group meets in Springfield, MA)

FAMILY SUPPORT CENTER
295 Longwood Avenue
Boston, MA 02115
(617) 232-8390

NICU BEREAVEMENT GROUP
Bernadette Reilly-Smorawski, RN
Anne Armstrong, RN, BSN
Massachusetts General Hospital
Burnham 6—NICU
Fruit Street
Boston, MA 02114
(617) 726-3315

PARENTS GROUP
Tamar May, MSW, MCSW
Bringham & Women's Hospital
75 Francis Street
Boston, MA 02115
(617) 732-6462

REACH
Diane Naventi
P. O. Box 280
Pittsfield, MA 01202
(413) 243-3116

NEONATAL DEATH SUPPORT
  GROUP
Sally Fields
Ornac Street
Concord, MA 01742
(617) 369-1400, Ext. 434

LOSS (LIFTING OTHERS SOR-
  ROWFUL SPIRITS)
Louise Hunt, MSW
c/o Social Service Dept.
Beverly Hospital
Heather and Herrick Streets
Beverly, MA 01915
(617) 922-3000, Ext. 2710

THE BEREAVED PARENT
  SUPPORT GROUP
Cindy Gallup
c/o Anna Jaques Hospital
25 Highland Avenue
Newburyport, MA 01950
(617) 462-6601, Ext. 394

HOPE
Michelle Austin
23 Wampum Road
E. Falmouth, MA 02536
(617) 337-7011, Ext. 332

HOPE
Winchester Hospital
Barbara Bryant, LICSW
Social Service Department
41 Highland Avenue
Winchester, MA 01890
(617) 729-9000, Ext. 3103, 3104

HOPE (HELP OTHER PARENTS
  ENDURE)
c/o S. Harrington, RN
South Shore Hospital
South Weymouth, MA 02190
(617) 659-7131

HOPE
Kathy Kineen, Social Service
Lawrence General Hospital
1 General Street
Lawrence, MA 01842
(617) 683-4000, Ext. 2550
        or
Pam Bureau, 35 Blossom Road
Windham, New Hampshire 03087
(603) 432-0069

SHARE
c/o Dashevsky
41 Churchill Street
Springfield, MA 01108
(413) 736-3546

SHARE
Wanda Roberge
340 Dickinson Street
Springfield, MA 01108

COMMUNITY BIRTH LOSS SUP-
  PORT GROUP
P. O. Box 582
Shrewsbury, MA 01545
Carol Geary

LOSS
Waltham Western Medical Center
Hope Avenue
Waltham, MA 01108
Paulette Melarson, RMC
(617) 647-6311

SHARE
Cynthia W. Kusisto
Franklin Medical Center
164 High Street
Greenfield, MA 01301
(413) 772-0211, Ext. 2303

Michigan

HOPING
Carolyn Wicklam
E. W. Sparrow Hospital
1215 E. Michigan, P. O. Box 30480
Lansing, MI 48909-9986
(517) 483-3873 or (517) 483-2344

HOPING
Linda Thomas
661 Michigan
Marysville, MI 48040
(313) 364-5532

HOPING
Mary Reed
1009 Robert Avenue
Mt. Pleasant, MI 48858
(517) 773-6219

HOPE
Judy O'Toole
Saginaw General Hospital
1447 N. Harrison
Saginaw, MI 48602
(517) 771-4153 or 771-4496

CARE
George & Kay Brown
304 S. Lane Street
Blissfield, MI 49228
(517) 486-4102

NEW BEGINNINGS
Tom Zerbel
321 S. 15th Street
Escanaba, MI 49829
(906) 786-2609

HEART
Gwen & David Stellmach
12883 Wormer
Redford, MI 48239
(313) 532-0712

SOUL (SURVIVING OUR LOSS)
Rev. Lucille Kness
Hutzel Hospital
4707 St. Antoine Blvd.
Detroit, MI 48201
(313) 745-7279

BEREAVED PARENTS GROUP
Maria Boehm
Providence Hospital
16001 W. 9 Mile Road
Box 2043
Southfield, MI 48037
(313) 424-3113

PEND (PARENTS EXPERIENC-
ING NEONATAL DEATH)
c/o Kim Meyers
Butterworth Hospital
100 Michigan Street
Grand Rapids, MI 49501
(616) 774-1523

BEREAVED PARENTS SUPPORT
GROUP
Lori Glick, MSW
William Beaumont Hospital
3601 W. 13 Mile Road
Royal Oaks, MI 48072
(313) 288-7288

GREATER HOLLAND PARENT
GRIEF SUPPORT GROUP
Karen Ann North
Holland Community Hospital
602 Michigan Avenue
Holland, MI 49423
(616) 392-5141

SHARE
Mary E. Bates
223 Schuring Road
Portage, MI 49002
(616) 327-7844
or
Ruth Kavalherna, Neonatal Dept.
Bronson Hospital
Kalamazoo, MI 49000
(616) 327-7844

THE COMPASSIONATE FRIENDS
Cindy Royer
900 River Street
Alpena, MI 49707
(517) 356-3636

PREGNANCY & NEWBORN
LOSS SUPPORT GROUP
Rev. Richard Feigenbaum, OSFS
Oakwood Pastoral Office
18101 Oakwood Blvd.
Dearborn, MI 48123-2500
(313) 593-7200
Sr. Ann Foley
Oakwood Hospital
18101 Oakwood Blvd.
Dearborn, MI 48123-2500
(313) 593-7200

FRIENDS SUPPORTING
PARENTS
Cindy Melitz, Chairperson
1289 Mulberry
Mt. Clemens, MI 48043
(313) 468-5199

MISCARRIAGE, NEWBORN &
  LOSS SUPPORT GROUP
611 Church Street, Suite 307
Ann Arbor, MI 48105
(313) 761-4402
Mary G. Schuman, ACSW

BEREAVED PARENTS SUPPORT
  GROUP
Jeff & Sharon Wickey
63322 N. M.—66
Sturgis, MI 49091

FRIENDS SUPPORTING FRIENDS
P. O. Box 206
Roseville, MI 48066-0206

Minnesota

SHARE—ST. JOSEPH'S
  HOSPITAL
Ann L. Ropp, RN
St. Joseph's Hospital
69 West Exchange Street
St. Paul, MN 55102
(612) 291-3000

SHARE
Amy Evavold
801 S. Sheridan
Fergus Falls, MN 56537
(218) 739-2162

CHILDRENS HOSPITAL
Social Work Department
Jean London/Sue Lamoureux
345 North Smith Avenue
St. Paul, MN 55102
(612) 452-4110
Michelle Leoxley
(612) 298-8720

PERINATAL BEREAVEMENT
  SUPPORT GROUP
Abbott/Northwestern Hospital
800 E. 28th Street
Minneapolis, MN 55407
(612) 874-4428 (work)

EMPTY ARMS INFANT
  SUPPORT GROUP
Alice Rademacher/Penny Rae
349 38th Avenue North
St. Cloud, MN 56301
(612) 253-1143 or (612) 253-0669

PREGNANCY AFTER A LOSS/
  MISCARRIAGE AND SUPPORT
  GROUP
Shari Perlman, MSW
4300 Manor Court Road
Minnetonka, MN 55345
(218) 933-0713

AIID (AID IN INFANT DEATH)
Barbara and Ron Madole
Box 1043
Moorhead, MN 56560
(406) 248-2056
(Meet in Fargo, ND)

PREGNANCY & INFANT LOSS
  CENTER OF MN
Sherokee Ilse, Director
1415 W. Wayzata Blvd. #22
Wayzata, MN 55391
(612) 473-9372
24-hour helpline: (612) 292-1184

PARENTS GRIEF SUPPORT
  GROUP
Ben Wolfe, Director
St. Mary's Hospital
407 E. Third Street
Duluth, MN 55805
(218) 726-4402

GRIEF SUPPORT GROUP (any
  type loss, any age)
Gail Noller or Chaplain B. Pederson
4050 Coon Rapids Blvd.
Mercy Medical Center
Coon Rapids, MN 55433-2586
(612) 427-2200

TLC SUPPORT GROUP
Marilyn Weedman
7088 5th Avenue E.
Alexandria, MN 56308
(612) 762-1489

Meeting Place:
Douglas County Hospital
c/o Education Department
Alexandria, MN 56308
(612) 762-1511, Ext. 294

FRIENDS WHO CARE
Jean Ruff
1011 Third Avenue NE
Grand Rapids, MN 55744
(218) 326-8876

PERINATAL DEATH GROUP
Diane Black
Rochester Methodist Hospital
201 West Center Street
Rochester, MN 55902
(507) 286-7890

RESOLVE THROUGH SHARING
Community Memorial Hospital
855 Mankato Avenue
Winona, MN 55987
(507) 457-4345 or (507) 452-9511

EMPTY ARMS
Ann and Dennis McCoy
772 Humphrey
Box 116
Lake Crystal, MN 56055
(507) 726-6072
Camille Koonce
126 W. 8th
Mankato, MN 56001
(507) 387-5108

EMPTY ARMS
P. O. Box 764
Thief River Falls, MN 56701
Myrna Lane, (218) 681-3263
Judy Melby, (218) 681-7194
Laurie Crist, (701) 469-2105

GRIEF SUPPORT GROUP
St. Mary's Hospital Hospice
2414 S. 7th Street
Minneapolis, MN 55454
Chuck Ceronsky
(612) 337-4000

Mississippi

TCF (The Compassionate Friends)
P. O. Box 20018
Jackson, MS 39209
(601) 982-3363

SOCIAL SERVICES
   DEPARTMENT
Boliver County Hospital
Highway 8E
Cleveland, MS 38732

Missouri

SHARE INFANT LOSS SUPPORT
   SERVICES (Kansas City Group)
c/o Daren Archer, RN
7402 E. 132nd Terrace
Grandview, MO 64030
(816) 761-8890 (home)
(816) 761-2333 (work)

SHARE
Karen Sutton, RN/Laura Hely
St. Mary's Health Center OB/GYN
6420 Clayton Road
St. Louis, MO 63117
(314) 768-8000, -8780, -8349

(SHARE) PREGNANCY LOSS &
   STILLBIRTH
(Ft. Leonardwood, MO group)
Mrs. Jennifer Stever
Rt. 1, Box 105
Waynesville, MO 65583
(314) 774-5668

SHARE
Linda Logan
Southeast Missouri Hospital
1701 Lacey Street
Cape Girardeau, MO 63701
(314) 651-5560

SHARE
c/o Linda Jones, Dir. Social Service
Golden Valley Memorial Hospital
Jct. Hwy. 7 and 13 North
Clinton, MO 64735
(816) 885-5511, Ext. 187
or (816) 696-2591

SHARE
Nancy Trombley
Box 222
Trenton, MO 64683
(816) 359-3656

EPS
Nancy Watrous
2410 N. Garth Avenue
Columbia, MO 65201

MOTHERS IN CRISIS
Cheryl Rabe, MA
Freeman Hospital
1102 W. 3rd Street
Joplin, MO 64801
(417) 623-2801 or (417) 782-1412

AMEND
Maureen Connelly
4324 Berrywick Terrace
St. Louis, MO 63128
(314) 487-7582

AMEND
Dianne Donahue
16043 Clarkson Woods Drive
Chesterfield, MO 63017
(314) 532-3888
        or
Linda McGrath
2164 Golden Rain Drive
Chesterfield, MO 63017
        or
Mrs. Peggy Springer
P. O. Box 174
Columbia, MO 65201

COMPASSIONATE FRIENDS
    GREATER OZARK CHAPTER
Pat Haas
4308 East Catalpa
Springfield, MO 65804
(417) 882-6313

COMPASSIONATE FRIENDS
    INFANT GROUP
Judy Hanley
3065 Harness
Florissant, MO 63033
(314) 837-4610

AMEND
Neida Gill
Manchester, MO 63011

Montana

SHARE
Peggy Hanson
c/o Janette Corp.
Northern Montana Hospital
Havre, MT 59501
(406) 265-5200

SHARE
Lois Lamber
2324 Spruce
Billings, MT 59101

Nebraska

SHARE
Jane Parks
Rt. #2, Box 225
Hastings, NE 68901
(402) 462-8683

HOPE (A SHARE GROUP)
Marv and Joy Johnson
4902 Happy Hollow Blvd.
Omaha, NE 68104
(402) 553-1200
        or
HOPE (A SHARE GROUP)
Dave Weeks
First Christian Church
63rd Dodge Street
Omaha, NE 68114
(402) 558-1939

TCF (The Compassionate Friends)
Theresa Wielgus, MSW
Columbus Community Hospital,
    Inc.
3111 19th Street
Columbus, NE 68601
(402) 563-9632

PREGNANCY & INFANT LOSS
    SUPPORT GROUP
Dee Dee Przymus
223 S. Potash
Alliance, NE 69301
(308) 762-7419

BRIDGES (Bereavement-Resources-
Infant Loss-Death-Grief-
Encouragement-Support)
St. Elizabeth Community Health
Center
Joanne Bronson
2845 Manse Avenue
Lincoln, NE 68502

PREGNANCY & INFANT LOSS
SUPPORT GROUP
Barb Hill
HC 65, Box 25
Wauneta, NE 69045
(308) 882-4002

PROMISE
Greg & Shirley Clayton
3534 Laura Avenue
Lincoln, NE 68510
(402) 477-5853

New Hampshire

HOPE
Pam Burzay
35 Blossom Road
Windham, NH 03087
(603) 432-0069

New Jersey

SHARE
Mary McTigue, RN
Elizabeth General Med. Center
925 E. Jersey Street
Elizabeth, NJ 07201
(201) 289-8600, Ext. 8485

SHARE
Kay Peterson-Guadagno
Monmouth Medical Center
300 Second Avenue
Long Branch, NJ 07740
(201) 222-5200, Ext. 3399

FRIENDS OF PARENTS
Salem/Cumberland County
Salem County Memorial Hospital
Salem, NJ 08079
(609) 935-4357

BEREAVEMENT GROUP
Lori Postal, RN
Pascack Valley Hospital
Old Hook Road
Westwood, NJ 07675-3181
(201) 690-0441

HOPE (HELPING OTHER
PARENTS ENDURE)
Marsha & Ed Roger
314 Salem Court
Somerville, NJ 08876
(201) 722-7726

HOPE
Ellen & Andy Forte
Our Lady of Fatima Church
499 New Market Road
Piscataway, NJ 08854
(201) 968-5555

ST. BARNABAS PERINATAL
BEREAVEMENT
Margaret Miele, ACSW
St. Barnabas Medical Center
Old Short Hills Road
Livingston, NJ 07039
(201) 533-5745

HOPING OF SOUTH JERSEY
Susan Skelly, RN
Zurbrugg Memorial Hospital
Rancocas Valley Division
Willingboro, NJ 08046

HOPING (HELPING OTHER
PARENTS IN NORMAL
GRIEVING)
Willingboro/Mt. Holly/Burlington
(609) 811-4700
(609) 267-8500
(609) 234-8888

HOPING OF GREATER
CAMDEN AREA
(609) 667-3000
(609) 757-3506

HOPING OF EASTERN CAMDEN
CITY
(609) 667-3000
(609) 861-6200

HOPING OF SOUTHERN
    CAMDEN CITY
(609) 435-2416

HOPING OF SALEM COUNTY
(609) 935-4357

EMPTY ARMS
Washington Division
J. F. Kennedy Memorial Hospital
Hurffville-Cross Keys Road
Turnersville, NJ 08012
(609) 589-3300

HELPING HANDS
Judith Schmeek, RN
Newcomb Medical Center
65 S. State Street
Vineland, NJ 08360
(609) 691-9000 Ext. 6179

SHARE
Marge Dempsey
43 E. Shore Trail
Stockholm, NJ 07460
(201) 697-2178

HOPING
Janet Millspaugh, RN
W. Jersey Hospital (Eastern Div.)
Evesham Road
Voorhees, NJ 08043
(609) 772-5150

MIDS (Miscarriage, Infant Death,
    Stillbirth)
Essex County
Lisa Calabria
15 Clover Street
Nutley, NJ 07110
(201) 235-1364

MIDS
Morris County
Janet Tischler
16 Crescent Drive
Parsippany, NJ 07054
(201) 236-6730

MIDS
Passaic County
Cindy De Rosa
151 Vreeland Road
W. Milford, NJ 07480
(201) 728-2998

MIDS
Union County Chapter
Debbie Donner
315 High Street
Cranford, NJ 07016
(201) 276-5397 or (201) 464-4310

MIDS
Bergen County Chapter
Pam Tyler
Holy Name Hospital School of
    Nursing
Teaneck, NJ 07666
(201) 864-3867

MISCARRIAGE SUPPORT
    GROUP
Bonnie Phillips
United Methodist Church
Bethel Road
Somers Point, NJ 08244
(609) 927-9294

MIDS
Sue Maher-Dziemian (Nursery)
Englewood Hospital
Englewood, NJ 07631
(201) 894-3152
(201) 384-8258 (evenings)
    or
Karen Frank
(201) 894-3142

HOPING
Hackettstown Community Hospital
Willow Grove Street
Hackettstown, NJ 07840
Beth Van Meter
(201) 852-5100

PRIDE (PARENTS RESOLVING
    INFANT DEATH EXPERIENCE)
Jersey Shore Medical Center
1945 Corlies Avenue
Neptune, NJ 07753
Kate Luscombe, RNC
(201) 775-5500, Ext. 5616

UNITE, INC.
Medical Center
Princeton, NJ 08540
Eileen Stewart, RN
(609) 896-2941
Mary Wallace
(201) 359-7812

New Mexico

SHARE
Ida Turner, Secretary
Trinity Lutheran Church
Box 1113
Hobbs, NM 88240
(505) 392-5407

HOPING
Karen Phillips
Route 3, Box 739
Los Lunas, NM 87031
(505) 869-2261

New York

SHARE
Lois Sugarman
6726 Gleason Place
Fayetteville, NY 13066
(315) 446-1262

SHARE OF GENESSEE COUNTY
Irene Burns
127 North Street
Batavia, NY 14020
(716) 344-1288

SHARE
Sheila Vester, RN
Mercy Hospital
565 Abbott Road
Buffalo, NY 14220
(716) 826-7000, Ext. 416 or 417

SHARE
Sr. June Szumowski
St. Peter's Hospital
315 S. Manning Blvd.
Albany, NY 12208
(518) 454-1602

SHARE
Rosemary Hoffman, RN or
Theresa Locilent, RN
Queen's Hospital Center
82-68 164 Street
Jamaica, NY 11432
(718) 990-2551 or (718) 990-2838

BUFFALO AREA SHARE
Patricia A. Gugliuzza
University Christian Church
66 Englewood Avenue
Buffalo, NY 14214
(716) 881-5182 or (716) 878-7673

SHARE
Sandra Dolan, RN, Newborn
   Nursery
Staten Island Hospital
475 Seaview Avenue
Staten Island, NY 10305
(718) 390-9797

BEREAVEMENT CLINICS
Nancy O'Donahue
Kings County Hospital
451 Clarkson Avenue
Brooklyn, NY 11203
(201) 857-2464

BRONX BEREAVED PARENTS
(Not limited to newborn)
Judy Losecco
2417 Mickle Avenue
Bronx, NY 10469
(212) 881-3852

NEONATAL BEREAVEMENT
   GROUP
Sharon S. Pantel, CSW
Downstate Medical Center
450 Clarkson Avenue
Brooklyn, NY 11203-2908
(718) 270-2006 or (718) 270-1189

MISCARRIAGE/STILLBIRTH SUP-
   PORT GROUP
c/o Dorothy Hai
209 York Street
Olean, New York 14760
(716) 375-2111

EASE
(Empty Arms Support Effort)
Albany Medical Center
Rm. E-501, New Scotland Avenue
Albany, NY 12208
Ginnie LaJuene, (518) 864-5093
Linda Raydo, (518) 664-2729
Cindy Russell, (518) 377-9618
Sharon Therrien, (518) 372-8031

PARALLEL INC.
Karen Betteridge
P. O. Box 41045
Rochester, NY 14604
(716) 442-6121

SHARE
P. O. Box 5148
Utica, NY 13505
Toni Britten
(315) 736-6406

CRISIS SUPPORT GROUP
Lorraine Lee, RN
UHS Wilson Hospital
3357 Harris Street
Johnson City, NY 13790
(607) 770-6101

GRIEF GROUPS
Dr. Roberta Temes
262 Coleridge Street
Brooklyn, NY 11235
(212) 646-5537

PERINATAL BEREAVEMENT
  GROUP
Mercy Hospital, Pastoral Care Dept.
1000 N. Village Avenue
Brooklyn, NY 11571
(718) 255-2241

INFANT BEREAVEMENT
  GROUP
Mary Wasacz
172 Madison Road
Scarsdale, NY 10583

PREGNANCY LOSS
Ingrid Kohn, Peer Counseling Group
Jewish Women's Resources Center
9 East 69th Street
New York, NY 10021
(212) 535-5900

LOST MIRACLES
Arlene Campisi or Georgette
  Debiase
St. Adalbert Parish
52-20 84th Street
Elmhurst, NY 11373
(212) 639-0212

TOGETHER LOSS OF A CHILD
Laurie Britt
29 S. White Street
Poughkeepsie, NY 12601
(914) 473-7795

HELP
Nancy Bruck
4944 Cedarvale Road
Syracuse, NY 13215

SHARING PARENTS
St. Mary's Hospital
427 Guy Park Avenue
Amsterdam, NY 12010
(518) 842-5841

BEREAVEMENT SUPPORT
  GROUP
Ann Kutudis-Kenien
Lourdes Hospital, Hospice Unit
169 Riverside Drive
Binghamton, NY 13905
(607) 798-5708

HELP WITH EMOTIONS AFTER
  LOSS OF PREGNANCY
Kathy Meritheu
113 N. Woodland Drive
Liverpool, NY 13088
(315) 457-9623

HAVEN OF SCHENECTADY
  (INFANT DEATH SUPPORT
  GROUP)
Dana Tessitore
1101 Parkwood Blvd.
Schenectady, NY 12308
(518) 370-1666

EASE
Kris Clements
P. O. Box 2223
Glen Falls, NY 12801
(518) 587-7904

North Carolina

SHARE
Stanley Memorial Hospital
OB Department
Albermarle, NC 28001
(704) 463-7894

SHARE OF WAYNE COUNTY
Lu Saulmon
P. O. Box 10303
Goldsboro, NC 27530
(919) 735-7043

SHARE OF HAYWOOD COUNTY
Julie Anduze
Rt. 1, Box 523
Canton, NC 28716
(704) 648-4966

SHARE
Pitt County Memorial Hospital
P. O. Box 6028
Greenville, NC 27834
(919) 551-4470
Donna Weeks or Linda Roy

PROP (PARENTS REACHING
    OUT TO OTHER PARENTS)
Senior Chaplain
Naval Hospital
Jacksonville, NC 28542
(919) 451-4070

COMFORT
Terri Burleson
Moses H. Cone Memorial Hospital
Room 6057
1200 N. Elm Street
Greensboro, NC 27401-1020
(919) 379-4374

TLC (TENDER LOVING CARE)
Jeri Conner
Rt. 4, Box 161-A
Rutherdforton, NC 28139
(704) 248-2261

AMEND
1711 Independence Road
Greensboro, NC 24708
Susan Ridenour

BEREAVED PARENT SUPPORT
    GROUP
Margaret S. Miles, RN, Ph.D.,
    FAAN
c/o Triangle Hospice
3605 Shannon Road
Durham, NC 27707
(919) 942-8597

SHARE OF AVERY COUNTY
P. O. Box 636
Newland, NC 28657
Janet Johnson
(704) 733-2061 or (704) 733-4202

FAMILIES WITH HEALING
    HEARTS
Robin L. Kivett
4042 Pleasant View Drive
Fayetteville, NC 28301
(919) 483-6964 or
(919) 323-4155

North Dakota

SHARE
c/o Joey Melling, M.S., R.D.
Community Memorial Hospital
Route 2, Box 124
Hettinger, ND 58639
(701) 567-4561

SHARE
Melodie Zach, Share Meeting Coord.
1127 Hoover Street
Dickinson, ND 58601
(701) 264-7111

SHARE
Karen Bendell, RN
3rd Street, SE & Burdick Express
Minot, ND 58701
(701) 857-2000

AIDE IN INFANT DEATH
Mary Jo Horsager
Lutheran Social Services
1325 11th Street, South
Fargo, ND 58102
(701) 235-7341

COMPASSIONATE FRIENDS OF
THE FM AREA
Box 389
Fargo, ND 58107
(701) 235-7341
Syl & Marge Loegering
(701) 282-8714

SHARE
Darlene Frey
Diane Heupel
R.R. 1, Box 79
Mott, ND 58646
(701) 584-2661

Ohio

FRIENDS SUPPORTING
PARENTS
Chrislyn Shelhart, RN
Kathy Brzuchalski, RN
Riverside Hospital
1600 North Superior Street
Toledo, OH 43604
(419) 729-6000, Ext. 6416

SURVIVORS NEWBORN &
CHILD DEATH
Lucy Savory
2325 Shetland Road
Toledo, OH 43617
(419) 841-5406

REMEMBER ME
James and Janet Osborne
c/o St. Charles Hospital
2600 Navarre Avenue
Oregon, OH 43616
(419) 698-7460
(419) 385-6524

PRECIOUS PARENTS
P. O. Box 0655
Cuyahoga Falls, OH 44222
or
Sheryl Sheatzley
(216) 923-7216

PATIENT AND FAMILY
COUNSELING
S. Joan Carole Schaffner, ACSW
Good Samaritan Hospital
3217 Clifton Avenue
Cincinnati, OH 45220-2489
(513) 872-1400

PARENTS' SUPPORT GROUPS
Father Ken Czillinger
Immaculate Heart of Mary Church
7820 Beechmont Avenue
Cincinnati, OH 45230
(513) 474-5570

PARENTS REACHING OUT
Betty Teall, RN
St. Vincent's Medical Center
2213 Cherry Street
Toledo, OH 43608
(419) 321-2856

PEND
Ann Crute
Rainbow Babies & Children's
Hospital
2101 Adelbert Road
Cleveland, OH 44106
(216) 844-3754

TIFFIN SUPPORT GROUP
Tim and Jane Distel
33 Clinton Avenue
Tiffin, OH 44883
(419) 448-0093

CARE
June Henderson
4300 Leffler Drive
Lima, OH 45806
(419) 999-3415

CARE (CARING & RESTORING
EACH OTHER)
Dr. Irwin Weinfeld, MD
Center for Women and Children
2142 North Cove Blvd.
Toledo, OH 43606
(419) 473-4218 (Hospital Operator)

HOPE
Connie Kloppenhofer, RN
Fulton County Hospital Center
725 South Shoop Avenue
Wauseon, OH 43567
(419) 335-2015, Ext. 357

SOLACE
St. Paul's Catholic Church
433 Mission Drive
Akron, OH 44301

FEELINGS AFTER
Donna Naso, RN
Health Education Center
7300 State Road
Parma, OH 44134
(216) 886-0330

HOPE
400 Vine Street
Archbold, OH 73502
Georgia Kohart
(419) 445-1602

SHARE
Marilyn Miller Graef
1272 Indian Hill Drive
Bolivar, OH 44612
(216) 874-3100

SHARE OF NEWARD OHIO
Cheryl Holton
8132 Weaver Road, N.E.
St. Louisville, OH 43071

SHARE
Susan P. Sulzer, RN
St. John West Shore Hospital
29000 Center Ridge Road
West Lake, OH 44145
(216) 835-6094

SHARE
Ruth Detchon
Route 1
Amsterdam, OH 43903
(614) 543-3264

SHARE—TRUMBULL CHAPTER
Cindy Kares
Work: Trumbull Memorial Hospital
   1350 E. Market
   Warren, OH 44484
   (216) 841-9321
Home: 1007 Woodglen
   Newton Falls, OH 44444
   (216) 872-5985

SHARE OF LAKE COUNTY
Elsie Slaw, RN
Lake County Memorial Hospitals
Washington at Liberty Street
Painesville, OH 44077
(216) 354-2400

SHARE
Kirsten Hagesfeld, ASCW
Lake County Mental Health Center
8445 Munson Drive
Painesville, OH 44077
(216) 255-6701

SHARE
Childbirth Education Coordinator
Bethesda Hospital
2951 Maple Avenue
P. O. Box 1575
Zanesville, OH 43701-0551
(614) 454-4628

SHARE
Victoria Metz
Trumbull Memorial Hospital
1350 E. Market
Warren, OH 44482
(216) 898-2172 (Home) or
(216) 841-9880 (Work)

PARENTS HELPING PARENTS
Connie Harmon
33803 Electric E2
Avon Lake, OH 44012
(216) 933-7150

SHARE THE LOSS
Marilyn M. Melison, RNC
Euclid General Hospital
101 East 185th Street
Euclid, OH 44119
(216) 531-9000, Ext. 227

FEEL (FAMILIES EXPERIENCING
   EARLY LOSS)
Kathy Daum-Woods, RN
   (Facilitator)
c/o Fairview General Hospital
18101 Lorain Road
Cleveland, OH 44111-5856
(216) 476-7278

HEAL
Louise Aurilio, RNC
St. Elizabeth Hospital Medical
   Center
1044 Belmont Avenue
Youngstown, OH 44503

PARENTS GROUP FOR COPING
    WITH PERINATAL LOSS
Nancy Thomas, RN
The Children's Medical Center
1 Children's Plaza
Dayton, OH 45404-1815
(513) 226-8300

BEREAVED PARENTS SUPPORT
    GROUP
Agnes Barnes
145 Cornell Drive
Toledo, OH 43614
(419) 385-5063

BEREAVED PARENTS SUPPORT
    GROUP
3136 Ellet Avenue
Akron, OH 44312

CINCINNATI HOPING
Karen Young
1007 Windzag
Cincinnati, OH 45242

SHARE
Brenda S. Nickells, RNC, BSN
Intensive Care Nursery
Miami Valley Hospital
1 Wyoming Street
Dayton, OH 45409
(513) 223-6192, Ext. 3641

PARENTS WHO SHARE
Jim & Jane Linbon
1573 Westgate Drive
Defiance, OH 43512

SHARE
Linda Stratton
3550 SR 47 West
Bellefontaine, OH 43311

SHARE
Nancy Miller
462 Vancouver
Cincinnati, OH 45224

SHARE
Mary Mason
34490 Ridge Road, Box 124
Willoughby, OH 44094

HOPING
Linda Ward
Ohio State University
Columbus, OH 43210

Oklahoma

PRIDE (Parents Responding to In-
    fant Death Experience)
Ann Cooper, RNC
Connie Furrh, RN
Deaconess Hospital
5501 N. Portland
Oklahoma City, OK 73112
(405) 949-6122

PRIDE
Cheryl Boatright
Lisa Wulz, RN
Mercy Hospital
4300 West Memorial Road
Oklahoma City, OK 73120
(405) 752-3763 or
(405) 752-3784

PRIDE
Joan E. Morehead, LPN
Norman Regional Hospital
901 N. Porter, Box 1308
Norman, OK 73070
(405) 321-1700, Ext. 3500 or 1015

COMPASSIONATE FRIENDS
Norman Oklahoma Chapter
Betty Smith
4400 West Main, Box 120
Norman, OK 73072
(405) 329-4280 (home) or
(405) 360-4287

COMPASSIONATE FRIENDS
Cheryl Hille
7205 Crown Point Road
Oklahoma City, OK 73132
(405) 670-1159

AMEND
Cindy Wilcox
1344 E. 26th Place
Tulsa, OK 74100

Oregon

EMPTY ARMS
Sharon Ferren
441 Tenth Avenue
Coos Bay, OR 97420
(503) 267-6593 or
(503) 756-4502
Helpline 24 hrs/day: (503) 269-5910

PARENTS SUPPORTING
  PARENTS
Judy Klier
17345 SW Thistlebrook
Tigard, OR 97224
(503) 620-0936

Pennsylvania

SHARE
Thelma Garrett, MSW, Social
  Service
Abington Memorial Hospital
1200 Old York Road
Abington, PA 19001
(215) 576-2570

CAPITAL AREA SHARE
Suzanne Woods
P. O. Box 2521
Harrisburg, PA 17105
(717) 236-5999

SHARE
Nancy Sauder
P. O. Box 961
Lancaster, PA 17603
(717) 396-9613

SHARE
Jane Callan
Altoona Hospital
Howard Ave. & Seventh Street
Altoona, PA 16603
(814) 949-3146

SHARE
Rose Marie Stein
1305 Fairlane Drive
York, PA 17404
(717) 848-8175

SHARE
Judith W. Nowak, RN
Marilyn Gross
Mercy Hospital
360 Canal Street
Wilkes-Barre, PA 18634
(717) 826-3100
(717) 826-3682

SHARE
Carmen Anderson
5081 Rosecrest Drive
Pittsburgh, PA 15201
(412) 362-8670

SHARE
Barbara Antinora, Florence Shearer
Lee Hospital
320 Main Street
Johnstown, PA 15901
(815) 255-3605

SHARE
Beverly Clark, RN
Lebanon Valley General Hospital
4th & Willow Streets
Lebanon, PA 17042
(717) 273-8521

SHARE
(Washington, PA Group)
Patti Mounts
Rt. 1, Box 260
Clayville, PA 15232
(412) 948-3842

SHARE
Attn: Andrea F. Joubert
Allegheny General Hospital
320 E. North Avenue
Pittsburgh, PA 15212
(412) 359-4292

SHARE
Faye Dorney-Magitz
221 Willow Street
Macungie, PA 18062
(215) 966-3891
              or
Kathy Kuhn
RR 1
New Tripoli, PA 18066
(215) 285-6144

HOPE (HELPING OTHER
  PARENTS ENDURE)
Oskana Leader, RN
Box 934
Chambersburg, PA 17201-0934
(717) 264-5171
(717) 264-1025

EMPTY ARMS
Judy Howell
Geisinger Medical Center
Danville, PA 17822
(717) 271-6567
(717) 437-3720

EMPTY ARMS
Patty McGuinness
6416 Wyndham Court
Erie, PA 16505
(814) 838-6346

EMPTY ARMS
Andrea Martz
P. O. Box 212
Oneida, PA 18242
(717) 384-3790

UNITE
Janis Heil
7600 Central Avenue
Philadelphia, PA 19111
(215) 728-3777
(215) 728-3082

UNITE, CHESTER COUNTY
Beverly Kipp
9 Green Hill Way
Chester County Hospital
Thorndale, PA 19372
    or
Andrea Evan
(215) 869-8961

UNITE, LOWER BUCKS COUNTY
Katie Popp, RN
St. Mary's Hospital—Langhorne
Langhorne-Newton Road
Langhorne, PA 19047
(215) 750-2118

UNITE OF DELAWARE COUNTY
Krista Russel
Social Services
Fitzgerald Mercy Hospital
Lansdowne Avenue & Baily Road
Darby, PA 19023
(215) 237-4750

UNITE OF PHOENIXVILLE, PA.
Ruth Bell
Work: (215) 645-4927
Home: (215) 265-6818

ASPO LAMAZE PERINATAL
  LOSS SUPPORT LINE
c/o Sally Herr
117 Collins Drive
Pittsburgh, PA 15235
(412) 793-7545

GRIEVING PROCESS GROUP
Pat Christensen
Franklin Maternity Hospital
Philadelphia, PA 19131
(215) 878-7800, Ext. 655

TIOGA COUNTY BEREAVED
  PARENTS SUPPORT GROUP
Kaye Galloway
31 Meade Street
Wellsboro, PA 16901
(717) 724-5329

SHARE OF THE LEHIGH VALLEY
Allentown, PA 18102
Kathy Kuhn
(215) 285-6144
Faye Dorney—Magitz
(215) 966-3891
Diane Brown
(215) 820-3866

PA SIDS CENTER
M. D'Antonio, Ph.D.
Children's Hospital of Philadelphia
34th & Civic Center Blvd.
Philadelphia, PA 19104
(215) 386-0264

PA SIDS CENTER
Roseann English, RN, Exec. Dir.
P. O. Box 42280
Philadelphia, PA 19101
(215) 722-SIDS
(215) 222-1400

COMPASSIONATE FRIENDS
Mary Kay Steele
Parents of Infants
R.D. #1
Falls Creek, PA 15840
(814) 375-1045

PREGNANCY & INFANT LOSS
  SUPPORT GROUP
Nancy Yost, RN, BSN
Staff Education Dept.
Sewickley Valley Hospital
Blackburn Road
Sewickley, PA 15143-1498
(412) 749-7356

RESOLVE THROUGH SHARING
Diane Carp
Grandview Hospital
700 Lawn Avenue
Sellersville, PA 18960
(215) 256-6415

PARENTS SUPPORT GROUP
c/o Social Science
Deborah Lewis Melone
Bryn Mawr Hospital
Bryn Mawr, PA 19010
(215) 896-3214

South Carolina

CARING
Joyce Green
Dept. of Obstetrics & Gynecology
Acc. II, Section 4
Richland Memorial Hospital
3301 Harden Street
Columbia, SC 29203
(803) 765-6029

SHARE
Sharon Young, RN
Trident Regional Medical Center
9330 Medical Plaza Drive
Charleston, SC 29418
(803) 797-7000

SHARE OF NEWBERRY
Biff Riebe
66 Nance Street
Newberry, SC 29108
(803) 276-3672

South Dakota

SHARE
Mary R. Johnson, Social Worker
Sacred Heart Hospital
501 Summit
Yankton, SD 57078
(605) 665-9371, Ext. 176

FAMILIES OF STILLBORN
  CHILDREN
Doug Soule & Mary Weigelt
School of Medicine
University of South Dakota
800 East 21st Street
Sioux Falls, SD 57101
(605) 339-6785

BEREAVED PARENTS GROUP
Mary Beshara
324 St. Anne Street
Rapid City, SD 57701

Tennessee

SHARE
Don Ferguson
Ft. Saunders Medical Reg. Center
1901 Clinch Avenue S.W.
Knoxville, TN 37916
(615) 546-2811

HOPING
Diane Hawkins, RN
Holston Valley Hospital
Kingsport, TN 37662

SHARING
Derenda Hodge, RN, CNS
Vanderbilt University Hospital
  4C-NI
Nashville, TN 37232
(615) 322-5000
Emergency: (615) 322-0953

GRIEF SUPPORT TEAM
Cynthia Spears, RN
c/o OB Education
Erlanger Medical Center
975 East Third Street
Chattanooga, TN 37403
(615) 778-6103

COMPASSIONATE FRIENDS
  INFANT GROUP
c/o Barbara Heflin
Social Work Services
Memorial Hospital
Clarksville, TN 37043-3160
(615) 552-6622

PEPD (PARENTS EXPERIENCING
  PERINATAL DEATH)
Barbara Turner
P. O. Box 38445
Germantown, TN 38138
(901) 372-5102

Texas

SHARE
Constance Clear
3534 Avenue B
San Antonio, TX 78209
(512) 822-4135

SHARE—PARENTS SUPPORT
  GROUP
Chaplain Raymond Wolfe
Methodist Hospital
P. O. Box 1201
3615 19th Street
Lubbock, TX 79408
(806) 793-7143

SHARE
c/o Harris Hospital H.E.B.
Lynne Moffatt, Chaplain
1600 Hospital Parkway
Bedford, TX 76022
(817) 283-1561 or (817) 571-3784
Kathy Hill
(817) 571-6523

SHARE
Kitty Trice
1409 Lazy Lane
Longview, TX 75604
(214) 297-0005
        or
Sharon Cook, ACSW
1114 Wind Song
Longview, TX 75604
(214) 297-0005

HAND
(HOUSTON'S AID IN
  NEONATAL DEATH)
Mrs. Karen Riley
3115 Stephens Creek Lane
Sugarland, TX 77478
(713) 980-7496

COPE'S ANGELS (CORPUS
  CHRISTI ORGANIZATION
  FOR PARENT EDUCATION)
1913 Thames
Corpus Christi, TX 78413
(512) 992-2661, Ext. 512
Hotline: Tina Kurtz (512) 992-3954
Mary Jane Hamilton (512) 993-0469
Cathy Pederson (512) 854-4931

PARENT TO PARENT
Fort Worth Children's Hospital
c/o Sharon Whitney, ACSW
1400 Cooper
Fort Worth, TX 76104
(817) 336-9861

Marie Okerson
12622 Pine Bough
Cypress, TX 77429
(713) 373-0105

EMPTY CRADLE
P. O. Box 171492
Arlington, TX 76003
L. Lambreth (817) 478-5812
Linda Watson (817) 572-0875

Utah

SHARE PARENTS OF UTAH
Christine Balderas
3118 S. 2850 E.
Salt Lake City, UT 84109
(801) 486-9804
(801) 942-3199

UTAH VALLEY REGIONAL
  HOSPITAL-SHARE
c/o Cynthia Gaufin
786 E. Redford Drive
Provo, UT 84604
(801) 225-8001

SHARE
Mckay Dee Hospital
St. Benedict's Hospital
c/o Margaret Wardle
610 W. Elberta
Ogden, UT 84404
(801) 782-5599

SHARE
Logan Regional Hospital
Susan Ericksen
1400 N. 500 East
Logan, UT 84321
(801) 753-4377

SHARE
Dixie Medical Center
c/o Heidi Stevens
1419 W. 490 N.
St. George, UT 84770

Vermont

"REACH OUT"
Susan Alward
North Country Hospital
Prouty Drive RFD #2
Newport, VT 05855
(802) 334-7331, Ext. 269

SHARE
Dotty McCarthy
52 Herrick Hill
Milton, VT 05468
(802) 893-1870

Virginia

SHARE
Jeanie Flinn, Social Worker
John Randolph Hospital
700 N. Fourth
P. O. Box 971
Hopewell, VA 23860
(804) 541-7494

SHARE
Susan Vierra, RN
DePaul Hospital
150 Kingsley Lane
Norfolk, VA 23505
(804) 489-5000

SHARE
Susan Finelli
Labor & Delivery
Mary Immaculate Hospital
800 Denbigh Blvd.
Newport News, VA 23602
(804) 599-5453

SHARE
Carol Mason
Mary Washington Hospital
14 Ridgemore Circle
Fredericksburg, VA 22405
(703) 371-3158

SHARE
Karen Phillips, RN
Maternal/Child Community
    Instructor
Virginia Beach General Hospital
1060 First Colonial Road
Virginia Beach, VA 23454
(804) 481-8141

PERINATAL LOSS SUPPORT
    GROUP
Gayle Hinton
P. O. Box 1284
Manassas, VA 22110
(703) 369-2071

PREGNANCY LOSS INFANT
    DEATH RESOURCE GROUP
Linda White
Rt. 4, Box A1, Hillman Highway
Abingdon, VA 24210
(703) 628-7721 or 2533

MIS (Miscarriage, Infant Death,
    Stillbirth)
Anne Smith
10143 Yorktown Drive
Great Falls, VA 22066
(703) 450-5227

MIS
Linda Huret
6486 Crayford Street
Burke, VA 22015
(703) 455-2877

COMPASSIONATE FRIENDS,
    CENTRAL VA.
121 Sailview Drive
Forest, VA 24551
Barbara Dimmick
(804) 525-6473

Washington

P.S. MY BABY DIED
Bill & Doreen Dolleman
P. O. Box 20552
Seattle, WA 98102
(206) 772-5338

PARENTS OF PREMATURES
c/o Lauri Lowen, President
13613 N.E. 26th Place
Bellevue, WA 98005
(206) 883-6040

P.S. MY BABY DIED
Carla D. Curtis, Secretary
3509 N.E. 33rd Street
Tacoma, WA 98422
(206) 838-9833

TACOMA PARENTS OF
    STILLBORNS
Tacoma General Hospital
315 S. K Street
Tacoma, WA 98422
(206) 659-9615

PARENTS OF STILLBORNS
Everett General Hospital
1321 Colby Street
Everett, WA 98201
Contact: Cynthia (206) 259-3384
Mary (206) 347-3437
Nancy (206) 659-9615

PARENTS OF STILLBORNS
Yakima Valley Hospital
2811 Tieton Drive
Yakima, WA 98902
Kay Long, Soc. Serv.
(509) 575-8046
Lynda (206) 877-6424

HOPING OF OLYMPIA
    (up to adult child)
Susan and Don St. George
413 N. Lilly Road
Olympia, WA 98506
(206) 459-4412

PREGNANCY LOSS SUPPORT
    GROUP
Rt. 2, Box 2242
Wapato, WA 98951
Linda Stepniewski
(509) 877-6424

SHARE
Laura Boysen
1006 Elm Street
Centralia, WA 98531
(206) 736-8747

West Virginia

SHARE
Donna McCartney
Rt. 12, Box 298
Morgantown, WV 26505
(304) 296-5667

SHARE OF MARIETTA-
    PARKERSBURG
c/o Susan Hickman
116 Maple Street
Williamstown, WV 26187
(304) 464-5549

SHARE
c/o Susan Spagnuolo
242 Gordon
Bridgeport, WV 26330
(304) 842-6802

Wisconsin

RESOLVE THROUGH SHARING
Bonnie Gensch, RN, MS
Lutheran Hospital/6th Fl. Maternity
1910 South Avenue
Lacrosse, WI 54601
(608) 785-0530, Ext. 31796

RESOLVE THROUGH SHARING
Sandy Giacommona
Luther Hospital
1405 Babcock
Eau Claire, WI 54701
(715) 839-3169, Ext. 3169, or
(715) 835-2858

RESOLVE THROUGH SHARING
Cheryl Jaeger
St. Michael's Hospital
2400 W. Villard
Milwaukee, WI 53209-4999
(414) 527-8000, beeper 228

RESOLVE THROUGH SHARING
Theda Clark
Regional Medical Center
130 Second Street
Neenah, WI 54956
(414) 729-3100

RESOLVE THROUGH SHARING
Lois Seefeldt
St. Francis Hospital
3237 S. 16th Street
Milwaukee, WI 53215
(414) 647-5000

RESOLVE THROUGH SHARING
Lynn Carey, MSN, RN
Waukesha Memorial Hospital
725 American Avenue
Waukesha, WI 53186
(414) 544-2252

RAY OF HOPE
Valerie Babcock
Tri-County M.H. Center
RR 2, Highway IRR
Mauston, WI 53148
(608) 847-4991

RESOLVE THROUGH SHARING
Beloit Memorial Hospital
1969 W. Hart Road
Beloit, WI 53511
Ann Harvieux
(608) 364-5011

RESOLVE THROUGH SHARING
Mount Sinai Medical Center
950 N. 12th
Milwaukee, WI 53233
Chris Van Mullem
(414) 289-8200

RESOLVE THROUGH SHARING
St. Agnes Hospital
430 E. Division
Fond du Lac, WI 54935
Patricia Weidman
(414) 929-2300

CONSOLING FRIENDS
551 Silverbrook Drive
West Bend, WI 53095
Patti Luedtke, Med. Social Worker
(414) 334-5533

COMPASSIONATE FRIENDS
Chequamegon Bay
Maple Lane Road
Ashland, WI 54806
Pat Vernier (715) 582-3818
Gordon Hillsman (715) 682-4563

TCF (The Compassionate Friends)
Barbara Stellmacher
1081 Van Dyne Road
Fond du Lac, WI 54935
(414) 922-5467

PARENTS CARING/SHARING
Phyllis Rozinski
St. Catherine's Hospital
3556 7th Avenue
Kenosha, WI 53140-1490
(414) 656-3316

SHARE
Char Buelow
St. Vincent's Hospital
P. O. Box 13508
Green Bay, WI 54301-3508
(414) 433-8546

SHARE
c/o Patty Williams
Rt. #2, Hwy. 81, Box 124
Beloit, WI 53511
(608) 365-1392

SHARE
Claudia Kornacki
St. Nicholas Hospital
1601 N. Taylor Drive
Sheboygan, WI 53081
(414) 459-8300, Ext. 4622

SHARE
Karen Olson
St. Francis Medical Center
700 West Avenue South
Lacrosse, WI 54601
(608) 785-0940

BEREAVED PARENTS GROUP
Dara L. Harings
St. Joseph's Hospital
2661 County Trunk I
Chippewa Falls, WI 54729
(715) 723-1811

BEREAVEMENT PERSONS
  SUPPORT GROUP
Carol Garner or Laurie Brown
St. Mary's Hospital
707 South Mills Street
Barron, WI 54812
(715) 537-9056

BEREAVED PARENT SUPPORT
  GROUP
Pat Krantz
3276 Maple Grove Drive
Route 2
Madison, WI 53711
(608) 845-9156

PARENTS CARING/SHARING
LuAn Wells
St. Luke's Hospital
1320 Wisconsin Avenue
Racine, WI 53403
(414) 636-2790

HOPE (HELPING OTHER
  PARENTS ENDURE)
Our Savior's Lutheran Church
Vicki Johnson
749 Bluff Street
Beloit, WI 53511
(608) 362-2623
(608) 365-1392

PARENTS SUPPORT GROUP
Marsha Fritsche, RN
Prairie du Chien Memorial Hospital
705 East Taylor Street
Prairie du Chien, WI 53821
(608) 326-2431

SAID
Joel and Rae Ann Sigal
409 Lakeview Drive
Wausau, WI 54401
(715) 842-0237

BEREAVED PARENTS SUPPORT
  GROUP
Holly Nelles
Children's Service Soc.
480 E. Grand Avenue, Suite 3
Wisconsin Rapids, WI 54494
(715) 421-0480

SHARE
Sacred Heart Hospital
900 W. Clairemont Avenue
Eau Claire, WI 54701
(715) 839-4121

TOGETHER, LEARNING TO
  COPE (TLC)
St. Joseph's Hospital
611 St. Joseph's Avenue
Marshfield, WI 54449
(715) 387-7890
Pam Sobkowiak, Social Services or
Judy Johnson, Nursing Service

TCF (The Compassionate Friends)
114 Woodside Court
Neenah, WI 54956
Sherry Nutcher
(414) 729-6375

AIID (Aid in Infant Death)
Katie Walker
5636 Burleigh
Milwaukee, WI 53210

AIID
Box 20852
Milwaukee, WI 53220

TCF
Ann-Marie Luker
St. Peter's Church
345 High Avenue
Oshkosh, WI 54901

BEREAVED PARENTS SUPPORT
  GROUP
Dick and Donna Clesigen
St. Michael's Hospital
911 Illinois Avenue
Stevens Point, WI 54481

BEREAVEMENT
Sr. M. Mulcady
St. Mary's Hospital
707 South Mills Street
Madison, WI 53715

Foreign Countries

Australia

AMEND
Alice Coleman
11 Parkland Avenue
Wondonga
Victoria, Australia 3690

SANDS (STILLBIRTH & NEONA-
  TAL DEATH SUPPORT)
Helen Wollender
Room G9 Agnes Walsh House
Bagot Road
Subiaco, W. Australia 6025
382-2687-Office 6008,
453-2310-Home

SANDS (STILLBIRTH & NEONA-
  TAL DEATH SUPPORT)
Janet Rankin, RN
2 Lawrence Street
Toowoomba, Queensland 4350
Australia

Canada

BEREAVED PARENTS SUPPORT
  GROUP
Marie Gallant, MSW
The Izaak Walton Killam Hospital
  for Children
5850 University Avenue
Halifax, Nova Scotia, Canada
  B3J 3G9
(Close to Maine)

COMPASSIONATE FRIENDS
  INFANT GROUP
Bernie and Diane Stadynk
44 Delaere Drive
Yorkton, Saskatchewan
Canada S3N 3H3
(306) 783-3179

CANADIAN MENTAL
  HEALTH—BEREAVEMENT
1226 Ouelette Avenue
Windsor, Ontario
Canada N8X 1J5

LOSING A BABY (Perinatal
  Bereavement Support Group)
Mrs. Marilyn Flook
2589 Cavendish Drive
Burlington, Ontario
Canada L79 4A9

PREGNANCY AFTER
  BEREAVEMENT
Mrs. Sandra Stubbs
311 Limerick Street
Oshawa, Ontario
Canada L1J 6K8
(416) 725-7030

THE COMPASSIONATE
  FRIENDS
Adaline Leir
Trevor and Audrey Roadhouse
101 Cameron Crescent
Regina, Saskatchewan
Canada S4S 2X3
(306) 586-0900 or
(306) 693-7645

COMPASSIONATE FRIENDS
   INFANT GROUP
Norm and Sheila Williams
1637 Grieg Avenue
Saskatoon, Saskatchewan
Canada S7N 2R1
(306) 373-7149

PERINATAL LOSS SUPPORT
   GROUP
Luba Serge
4060 Coloniale
Montreal, Quebec
Canada H2W 2C1
(514) 849-1060

England

SAND
Barnsley Branch
169 Clifton Crescent
Athersley North
Barnsley S71 3NL England
Ann Walker
Ian Senior
Phone: Barnsley (0226) 207498

Israel

YAD ELISHA
   (means in Memory Of)
c/o Allon
Rehov Hanania F
93106 Jerusalem
Israel
Phone: 02 632213

South Africa

SHARE
STILLBORN AND MISCARRIAGE
   ASSOC. (SAMA)
Miss Marlene Adams
167 Lawson Road
Belthorne Estate
Crawford, 7764
Cape Town, R.S. Africa

SHARE of S.A.
Anne Friedlander
28 Chateau Circle
Cape Town, South Africa

West Germany

SHARE
Linda Hebbees, RN
97th General Hospital
Social Worker Service
APO, New York 09757
(Frankfurt, West Germany)

MIS/SHARE
HHB 31 Div. Arty
APO NY 09036-1814
Shelley Lingemfelter
Phone: 09721-801044
(Schweinfurt, West Germany—
Help areas of Würzburg, Nürnberg,
   and Hamburg)

SHARE
c/o PSC Box 5376
APO NY 09109
Amanda J. Hoback
Phone: 06545-1407
Hahn Air Force Base

Organizations and Resources

RESOURCES FOR PREGNANCY LOSS

Pregnancy and Infant Loss Center
1415 E. Wayzata Blvd.
Wayzata, MN 55391
(612) 473-9372

Sympathy and loss announcement cards, information packets for Pregnancy and Infant Loss Awareness Month

Perinatal Bereavement Alliance
318 Groveland Avenue
Minneapolis, MN 55403
(612) 870-1242

Coalition of professionals working to promote better understanding and care of bereaved families

Association for Recognition of Life
  of Stillbirths
11470 W. Powers Avenue
Littleton, CO 80127
(303) 978-9517

Provides "certificate of life" with baby's name and date of delivery

Perinatal Loss Project
c/o Sandra Taylor
2443 NE 20th Avenue
Portland, OR 97212-2621
(503) 284-7426

Announcement cards, certificates of life, booklets in English and Spanish

Centering Corporation
Box 3367
Omaha, NE 68103-0367
(402) 553-1200

Books and pamphlets on grief

ADOPTION RESOURCES

AASK (Aid to the Adoption of
  Special Kids)
3530 Grand Avenue
Oakland, CA 94611
(415) 451-1748

Assists families in adoption of older and handicapped children

ARENA (Adoption Resource
  Exchange of North America)
67 Irving Place
New York, NY 10003
(212) 254-7410

National Committee for Adoption (NCFA)
2025 M Street, Suite 512
Washington, DC 20036
(202) 463-7559

A resource and lobbying organization that provides information about adoption agencies, adoption practices, and the impact of current adoption methods

North American Council on Adoptable Children (NACAC)
P. O. Box 14808
Minneapolis, MN 55414
(612) 333-7692

An organization that publishes Adoptalk and provides information about adoption and local parent groups in the United States and Canada

OURS (Organization for United Response)
3307 Highway 100 North
Suite 203
Minneapolis, MN 55422
(612) 535-4829

Organization of adoptive parents, providing information especially on international adoptions

Parents for Private Adoption
P. O. Box 7
Pawlet, VT 05761
(802) 645-0337

RESOURCES FOR CHILDBIRTH

American Foundation for Maternal and Child Health, Inc.
439 E. 51st Street
New York, NY 10022
(212) 759-5510

American College of Obstetricians and Gynecologists (ACOG)
600 Maryland Avenue SW,
Suite 300
Washington, DC 20024
(202) 638-5577

ASPO (American Society for Psychoprophylaxis in Obstetrics)
1840 Wilson Blvd., Suite 204
Arlington, VA 22201
(703) 524-7802

C/SEC, Inc.
22 Forest Road
Framingham, MA 01701
(617) 877-8266

Information and support concerning Caesarean birth

ICEA (International Childbirth Education Association)
P. O. Box 20048
Minneapolis, MN 55420
(612) 854-8660

Education and support for more satisfying birth experiences. Some of the 350 local groups sponsor services for parents after miscarriage, stillbirth, and infant death

La Leche League International
9616 Minneapolis Avenue
Franklin Park, IL 60131
(312) 455-7730

4400 local chapters throughout the world providing information and support for breastfeeding mothers

NAPSAC (National Association for Parents and Professionals for Safe Alternatives in Childbirth)
P. O. Box 429
Marble Hill, MO 63764
(314) 238-2010

National Perinatal Association
101½ S. Union Street
Alexandria, VA 22314
(703) 549-5523

Parent Care
50 N. Medical Drive, Room 2A210
Salt Lake City, UT 84132
(801) 581-5323

COUNSELING SERVICES

Family Service Association of
   America
1170 West Lake Park Drive
Milwaukee, WI 53224
(414) 359-2111

*Organization of 265 local family
counseling agencies throughout the
United States and Canada*

RESOURCES FOR ENVIRONMENTAL AND OCCUPATIONAL HEALTH

Citizens Clearinghouse for
   Hazardous Wastes
P. O. Box 926
Arlington, VA 22216
(703) 276-7070

Clearinghouse for Occupational
   Safety and Health Information
National Institute for Occupational
   Safety and Health
4676 Columbia Parkway
Cincinnati, OH 45226
(513) 533-8236

Coalition for a Non-Nuclear World
413 8th Street SE
Washington, DC 20003
(202) 488-7896

DES Action/National
Long Island Jewish Hospital
New Hyde Park, NY 10040
(516) 775-3450

*Fourteen local chapters throughout
the country to provide information
and assistance to individuals affected
by DES*

Environmental Action, Inc.
1525 New Hampshire Avenue, NW
Washington, DC 20036
(202) 745-4870

*Publishes monthly magazine on en-
vironmental issues*

National Women's Health Network
1325 G Street N.W.
Washington, DC 20005
(202) 543-9222

*Research, public education, and leg-
islative action on a wide variety of
women's health issues; coordination
of many related organizations*

Public Citizens Health Research
   Group
2000 P Street, NW, Suite 708
Washington, DC 20036
(202) 872-0320

*Ralph Nader–initiated research and
action group*

Toxic Substances Project
Environmental Action Foundation
1525 New Hampshire Avenue, NW
Washington, DC 20036
(202) 745-4870

Women's Environmental Network
and Directory
U.S. Environmental Protection
Agency
401 M Street, SW
Washington, DC 20460
(202) 829-3535

Women's Occupational Health
Resource Center
School of Public Health
Columbia University
60 Haven Avenue, B-1
New York, NY 10032
(212) 694-3464

*Extensive research library; public
education services*

WISH (Workers' Institute for Safety
and Health)
1126 16th Street, NW
Washington, DC 20036
(202) 463-6081
or
271 East State Street
Columbus, OH 43215
(614) 224-8271

RESOURCES FOR GENETICS AND ABORTION

National Abortion Federation
900 Pennsylvania Avenue SE 1011
Washington, DC 20003
(202) 546-9060
Consumer Information Hotline:
(800) 223-0618
New York State:
(800) 422-8178

*Provides information and referral
for first and second trimester abortion services*

National Abortion Rights Action
League
1101 14th Street, NW
Washington, DC 20005
(202) 371-0779

*Advocacy and political organizing
to promote the full range of fertility choices*

National Center for Education in
Maternal & Child Health
38th and R Streets, NW
Washington, DC 20057
(202) 625-8400

March of Dimes—Birth Defects
Foundation
1275 Mamaroneck Avenue
White Plains, NY 10605
(914) 428-7100

*Supports research into birth defects,
prenatal and genetic counseling services, improved neonatal care, and
public education*

National Genetics Foundation, Inc.
555 West 57th Street
New York, NY 10019
(212) 586-5800

*Referral service for individuals and
families concerned about genetic
problems*

RESOURCES FOR INFERTILITY

Resolve, Inc.
5 Water Street
Arlington, MA 02174
(617) 643-2424
Support and information concerning infertility

American Fertility Society
2131 Magnolia Avenue, Suite 201
Birmingham, AL 35256
(205) 251-9764

Dalkon Shield Information Network
c/o Karen Hicks
626 Center Street
Bethlehem, PA 18018
(215) 867-6577

Endometriosis Association
P. O. Box 92187
Milwaukee, WI 53202
(414) 962-8972

FILMS

"Alive Again" (¾" VHS and Beta, 30 minutes), St. Elizabeth's Hospital, 211 S. 3rd St., Belleville, IL 62222

"Children Only Die When We Forget Them" (16 mm, 12 minutes), Pat Schweibert, University of Oregon Health Sciences Center, Portland, Oregon.

"Death of a Newborn" (16 mm, 32 minutes), Polymorph Films, 118 South Street, Boston, MA 02111, (617) 542-2004.

"Death of a Wished-For Child" (16 mm, 28 minutes)
SIU Medical Library
801 N. Rutledge
Springfield, IL 62702
(217) 782-2658.
or
OGR Service Corporation
P. O. Box 3586
Springfield, IL 62708
(217) 544-7428.

"Empty Arms" (½" and ¾", 60 minutes), Centering Corporation, P.O. Box 3367, Omaha, NE. 68103-0367, (402) 553-1200.

"Memories" (¾" VHS and Beta, 28 minutes), St. John's Hospital, Care Video Productions, P. O. Box 45132, Cleveland, OH 44145, (216) 835-5872.

"Some Babies Die" (16 mm and Video), University of California Extension Media Center, 2176 Shattuck Avenue, Berkeley, CA 94704, (415) 642-0460.

"Still to be Born" (VHS), (about subsequent pregnancy), Pat Schweibert, University of Oregon Health Sciences Center, Portland, OR.

"To Touch Today" (¾" VHS and Beta, 28 minutes), Human Services Division, Creative Marketing, 2631 North Grand Avenue E, Springfield, IL 62702, (217) 528-1756; or, St. Elizabeth's Hospital, 211 S. 3rd St., Belleville, IL 62222.

General References

Berezin, Nancy. *After a Loss in Pregnancy*. New York: Simon & Schuster, 1982.

Berg, Barbara. *Nothing to Cry About*. New York: Seaview Books, 1981.

Boston Women's Health Book Collective. *The New Our Bodies, Ourselves*, rev. ed. New York: Simon & Schuster, 1985.

Burrow, Gerard, and Ferris, Thomas. *Medical Complications during Pregnancy*, 2nd ed. Philadelphia: W. B. Saunders, 1982.

DeFrain, John. *Coping with Sudden Infant Death*. Lexington, MA: Lexington Books, 1982.

Donnelly, Katherine Fair. *Recovering from the Loss of a Child*. New York: Macmillan Publishing Company, 1982.

Ewy, Donna and Roger. *Death of a Dream*. New York: E. P. Dutton, Inc., 1984.

Friedman, Rochelle, and Gradstein, Bonnie. *Surviving Pregnancy Loss*. Boston: Little, Brown, 1982.

Ilse, Sherokee. *Empty Arms: A Guide to Help Parents and Loved Ones Cope with Miscarriage, Stillbirth and Neonatal Death*. P. O. Box 165, Long Lake, MN 55356, 1982.

Jimenez, Sherry Lynn Mims. *The Other Side of Pregnancy: Coping with Miscarriage and Stillbirth*. Englewood Cliffs, NJ: Prentice-Hall, 1982.

Klaus, Marshall H., and Kennell, John H. *Parent-Infant Bonding*, 2nd ed. St. Louis: C. V. Mosby, 1981.

Peppers, Larry, and Knapp, Ronald. *How to Go on Living After the Death of a Baby*. Atlanta: Peachtree Publishers Limited, 1985.

Pritchard, Jack A. and MacDonald, Paul C. *Williams Obstetrics*, 17th ed. New York: Appleton-Century-Crofts, 1984.

Rando, Therese (Ed.). *Parental Loss of a Child*. Champaign, IL: Research Press, 1986.

Schwiebert, Pat. *When Hello Means Goodbye*. Portland: University of Oregon Health Sciences Center, 1981.

Wilson, Robert, and Carrington, Elsie Reed. *Obstetrics and Gynecology*, 7th ed. St. Louis: C. V. Mosby, 1983.

I. PROLOGUE

Bibring, Grete. "Some Considerations of the Psychological Processes in Pregnancy." *Psychoanalytic Study of the Child* 14 (1959): 113–121.

Dorfman, Sally Faith. "Epidemiology of Ectopic Pregnancy." *Clinical Obstetrics and Gynecology* 30 (1987): 173–180.

French, Fern E., and Bierman, Jessie M. "Probabilities of Fetal Mortality." *Public Health Reports* 77, no. 10 (October 1962): 835–847.

Klaus, Marshall H., and Kennell, John H. *Parent-Infant Bonding.* (See General References.)

Leridon, Henri. *Human Fertility: The Basic Components.* Translated by Judith F. Helzner. Chicago: University of Chicago Press, 1977.

Vital and Health Statistics. National Center for Health Statistics, U.S. Department of Health and Human Services, Hyattsville, Maryland. Monthly publications.

Wilkerson, Isabel. "Infant Mortality: Frightful Odds in Inner City." *New York Times,* June 26, 1987: Al, 20.

1. THE PARENTS' GRIEF

Benfield, Gary D., Leib, Susan A., and Vollman, John H. "Grief Response of Parents to Neonatal Death and Parent Participation in Deciding Care." *Pediatrics* 62, no. 2 (August 1978): 171–177.

Bugen, Larry A. "Human Grief: A Model for Prediction and Intervention." *American Journal of Orthopsychiatry* 47, no. 2 (April 1977): 196–206.

Cullberg, J. "Mental Reactions of Women to Perinatal Death." *Proceedings of the Third International Congress of Psychosomatic Medicine in Obstetrics and Gynecology.* Basel, Switzerland: Karger, 1972.

Dana, Jacqueline. *Et Nous Aurions Beaucoup d'Enfants.* Paris: Editions du Seuil, 1979.

Davidson, Glen W. *Understanding Death of the Wished-For Child.* Springfield, IL: OGR Corporation, 1979.

Deutsch, Helene. *The Psychology of Women. Vol. 2: Motherhood.* New York: Grune and Stratton, 1945.

Engel, George L. "Grief and Grieving." *American Journal of Nursing* 64, no. 9 (September 1964): 93–98.

Freud, Sigmund. "Mourning and Melancholia." *Collected Papers.* Vol. 4. London: Hogarth Press, 1934.

Kirkley-Best, Elizabeth. "Grief in Response to Prenatal Loss: An Argument for the Earliest Maternal Attachment." Doctoral Dissertation, University of Florida, 1981.

LaRoche, C., et al. "Grief Reactions to Perinatal Death: A Follow-Up Study." *Canadian Journal of Psychiatry* 29 (1984): 14–19.

Lewis, Emanuel. "Mourning by the Family after a Stillbirth or Neonatal Death." *Archives of Disease in Childhood* 54 (1979): 303–306.

Lewis, Thomas H. "A Culturally Patterned Depression in a Mother after Loss of a Child." *Psychiatry* 38 (February 1975): 92–95.

Lindemann, Erich. "Symptomatology and Management of Acute Grief." *American Journal of Psychiatry* 101 (1944): 141–148.

Lovell, Alice. "Some Questions of Identity: Late Miscarriage, Stillbirth and Perinatal Loss." *Social Science and Medicine* 17 (1983): 755–761.

M. A. "C'est Quoi, Une Maman Sans Bébé?" *F Magazine*, no. 26 (April 1980): 92.

Markusen, Eric; Owen, Greg; Fulton, Robert; and Bendiksen, Robert. "SIDS: The Survivor as Victim." *Omega* 8, no. 4 (1977–1978): 277–284.

Menning, Barbara Eck. *Infertility: A Guide for the Childless Couple.* Englewood Cliffs, NJ: Prentice-Hall, 1977.

O'Donohue, Nancy. "Facilitating the Grief Process." *Journal of Nurse-Midwifery* 24, no. 5 (September/October 1979): 16–19.

Osterweis, Marian; Solomon, Frederic; and Green, Morris (Eds.). *Bereavement Reactions, Consequences, and Care.* Committee for the Study of Health Consequences of the Stress of Bereavement, Institute of Medicine, National Academy Press, Washington, DC, 1984.

Parkes, C. M. "Bereavement and Mental Illness, Part 2. A Classification of Bereavement Reactions." *British Journal of Medical Psychology* 38 (1965): 13–26.

Parkes, Colin M. *Bereavement—Studies of Grief in Adult Life.* New York: International Universities Press, 1972.

Pollock, George. "Mourning and Adaptation." *International Journal of Psychoanalysis* 42, nos. 4–5 (1961): 341–361.

Pollock, George H. "Anniversary Reactions, Trauma, and Mourning." *The Psychoanalytic Quarterly* 39 (July 1970): 347–371.

Quirk, Tina R. "Crisis Theory, Grief Theory, and Related Psychosocial Factors: The Framework for Intervention." *Journal of Nurse-Midwifery* 24, no. 5 (September/October 1979).

Rich, Adrienne. *Of Woman Born: Motherhood as Experience and Institution.* New York: Norton, 1976.

Schiff, Harriet Sarnoff. *The Bereaved Parent.* New York: Crown, 1977.

Schoenberg, Bernard; Carr, Arthur C.; Kutscher, Austin H.; Peretz, David; and Goldberg, Ivan I. (Eds.). *Anticipatory Grief.* New York: Columbia University Press, 1974.

Solnit, Albert J., and Stark, Mary H. "Mourning and the Birth of a Defective Child." *Psychoanalytic Study of the Child* 16 (1961): 523–537.

Worden, J. W. *Grief Counseling and Grief Therapy: A Handbook for the Mental Health Practitioners.* New York: Springer, 1982.

Zahourek, Rothlyn. "Grieving and the Newborn." *American Journal of Nursing* 73 (May 1973): 836–839.

2. MISCARRIAGE

Berle, Beatrice, and Javert, Carl. "Stress and Habitual Abortion." *Obstetrics and Gynecology* 3 (1954): 298.

Billingsley, Janice. "The Child Who Never Arrived: A New Look at Miscarriage." *Ladies' Home Journal* 97, no. 11. (November 1980): 32–38.

Boston Women's Health Book Collective. *The New Our Bodies, Ourselves.* (See General References.)

Brody, Jane E. "Miscarriage: Myths Often Add to Grief." *The New York Times* (March 5, 1980): Cl.

Cain, Albert C.; Erickson, Mary; Fast, Irene; and Vaughan, R. A. "Children's Disturbed Reactions to Their Mother's Miscarriage." *Psychosomatic Medicine* 26 (January/ February 1964): 58–66.

Corney, Robert and Horton, Frederick. "Pathological Grief Following Spontaneous Abortion." *American Journal of Psychiatry* 131 (July 1974): 825–827.

Day, Randall, and Hooks, Daniel. "Miscarriage: A Special Type of Family Crisis." *Family Relations* 36 (1987): 305– 310.

Dickey, Richard. "Evaluation and Management of Threatened and Habitual First Trimester Abortion." *Advances in Clinical Obstetrics and Gynecology*, Vol. 2. Edited by Howard J. Osofsky. Baltimore: Williams & Wilkins, 1983.

Fallaci, Oriana. *Letter to a Child Never Born*. Translated by John Shepley. New York: Simon & Schuster, 1976.

Groll, Michael. "Endometriosis and Spontaneous Abortion." *Fertility and Sterility* 41 (1984): 933–935.

Guttmacher, Alan F. *Pregnancy, Birth and Family Planning*. Revised and updated by Irwin H. Kaiser. New York: E. P. Dutton, 1986.

Harger, James, et al. "Etiology of Recurrent Pregnancy Losses and Outcome of Subsequent Pregnancies." *Obstetrics and Gynecology* 62 (1983): 574–581.

Hart, Donn V.; Rajadhon, Phya Anuman; and Coughlin, Richard J. *Southeast Asian Birth Customs: Three Studies in Human Reproduction*. New Haven, CT: Human Relations Areas Files Press, 1965.

Ilse, Sherokee and Burns, Linda. *Miscarriage: A Shattered Dream*. Long Lake, MN: Wintergreen Press, 1985.

Moffitt, Perry-Lynn. "Miscarriage: The Baby Who Wasn't." *Parents Magazine* 62 (April 1987): 132–134, 214–217.

Malmguist, A., Kaij, L., and Nilsson, A. "Psychiatric Aspects of Spontaneous Abortion. I. A Matched Control Study of Women with Living Children. II. The Importance of Bereavement, Attachment and Neurosis in Early Life." *Journal of Psychosomatic Research* 13 (1969): 45–59.

Mann, Edward. "Spontaneous Abortions and Miscarriages." *Modern Perspectives in Psycho-obstetrics*. Edited by John G. Howell. New York: Brunner/Mazel, 1972.

Page, Tim. "Life Miscarried." *New York Times Sunday Magazine,* January 27, 1985.

Pizer, Hank and Palinski, Christine O'Brien. *Coping with a Miscarriage*. New York: Dial, 1980.

Potts, Malcolm; Diggory, Peter; and Peel, John. *Abortion*. Cambridge, England: Cambridge University Press, 1977.

Pritchard, Jack A., and MacDonald, Paul C. *Williams Obstetrics*. (See General References.)

Reinharz, Shulamit. "Controlling Women's Lives: A Cross-Cultural Interpretation of Miscarriage Accounts." *Research in the Sociology of Health Care*. Vol. 7. Edited by Dorothy Wertz. JAI Press, 1987.

Seibel, Machelle, and Graves, William L. "The Psychological Implications of Spontaneous Abortions." *The Journal of Reproductive Medicine* 25, no. 4 (October 1980): 161–165.

Shives, Vicki Ann. "Coping with a Miscarriage." *Parents* 55, no. 11 (November 1980): 56–66.

Stack, Jack. "The Psychodynamics of Spontaneous Abortion." *American Journal of Orthopsychiatry* 54 (1984): 162–167.

Stray-Pedersen, Babill, and Stray-Pedersen, Sverre. "Etiologic Factors and Subsequent Reproductive Performance in 195 Couples with a Prior History of Habitual Abortion." *American Journal of Obstetrics and Gynecology* 148 (January 15, 1984): 140–146.

Sullivan, Deborah H., and Hai, Dorothy. "The Silent Sympathy: A Study of Attitudes Towards Spontaneous Abortion." Presented at annual meetings of The American Public Health Association, New York, November, 1979.

Wal-Haas, Constance. "Women's Perceptions of First Trimester Spontaneous Abortion." *Journal of Obstetric Gynecologic and Neonatal Nursing* (1985): 50–53.

Welch, Mary S., and Herrmann, Dorothy. "Why Miscarriage Is so Misunderstood." *Ms.* (February 1980): 14–20.

3. ECTOPIC PREGNANCY

Brown, John. "Update on Ectopic Pregnancy." Letter to *Canadian Medical Association Journal* 130 (1984): 1262.

Centers for Disease Control. "Ectopic Pregnancy—United States, 1981–1983." *Journal of the American Medical Association* 255 (June 20, 1986): 3221–3222.

Corson, Stephen L., and Batzer, Frances R. "Ectopic Pregnancy: A Review of the Etiologic Factors." *Journal of Reproductive Medicine* 31 (February 1986): 78–85.

DeCherney, Alan H. (Guest Editor). "Ectopic Pregnancy." *Clinical Obstetrics and Gynecology* 30 (March 1987): 117–246.

DeCherney, Alan H., and Jones, Ervin E. "Ectopic Pregnancy." *Clinical Obstetrics and Gynecology* 28 (June 1985): 365–374.

Guttmacher, Alan. *Pregnancy, Birth and Family Planning*. Revised and updated by Irwin H. Kaiser. New York: E. P. Dutton, 1986.

Johns, Jeanine. "Ectopic Pregnancy." *Nurse Practitioner* (June 1984): 17–22.

Levin, Ann A., et al. "Ectopic Pregnancy and Prior Induced Abortion." *American Journal of Public Health* 72 (March 1982): 253–256.

Lindblom, B., et al. "Local Prostaglandin F22 Injection for Termination of Ectopic Pregnancy." *The Lancet* (April 4, 1987): 776–777.

Nagamani, Manubai, et al. "Factors Influencing Fertility After Ectopic Pregnancy." *American Journal of Obstetrics and Gynecology* 149 (1984): 533–535.

McKaughan, Molly. "The Ectopic Pregnancy." *Woman's Day* (April 3, 1984): 62–65.

Weinstein, Louis, et al. "Ectopic Pregnancy: A New Surgical Epidemic." *Obstetrics and Gynecology* 61 (June 1983): 698–701.

Wolfman, Wendy, and Holtz, Gary. "Update on Ectopic Pregnancy." *Canadian Medical Association Journal* 129 (December 15, 1983): 1265–1269.

4. PRENATAL DIAGNOSIS AND THE UNWANTED ABORTION

Bernard, Jessie. *The Future of Motherhood*. New York: Dial, 1974.

Daffos, F.; Capella-Pavlovsky, M.; and Forester, F. "A New Procedure for Fetal Blood Sampling in Utero: Preliminary Results of Fifty-Three Cases." *American Journal of Obstetrics and Gynecology* 146 (1983): 985–987.

Dembert, Mark, and Harisiades, James. "Prenatal Diagnosis of Neural Tube Defects." *American Family Physician* 27 (1983): 241–244.

Finegan, Jo-Anne K. "Infant Outcome Following Mid-Trimester Amniocentesis: Development and Physical Status at Age Six Months." *British Journal of Obstetrics and Gynaecology* 92 (1985): 1015–1023.

Harrison, Michael R.; Golbus, Mitchell S.; and Filly, Roy A. *The Unborn Patient: Prenatal Diagnosis and Treatment*. Orlando: Grune & Stratton, 1984.

Hogge, Joan S.; Hogge, W. Allen; and Golbus, Mitchell S. "Chorionic Villus Sampling." *Journal of Obstetric, Gynecologic, and Neonatal Nursing* (1986): 24–28.

Hubbard, Ruth. "Legal and Policy Implications of Recent Advances in Prenatal Diagnosis and Fetal Therapy." *Women's Rights Law Reporter* 7 (Spring 1982): 201–218.

Jones, O. W., et al. "Parental Response to Mid-Trimester Therapeutic Abortion Following Amniocentesis." *Prenatal Diagnosis* 4 (1984): 249–256.

Kolata, Gina. "Prenatal Diagnosis of Neural Tube Defects." *Science* 209, no. 4462 (September 12, 1980): 1216–1218.

Kolata, Gina. "First Trimester Prenatal Diagnosis." *Science* 221 (September 9, 1983): 1031–1032.

Lilford, Richard. "Chorion Villus Biopsy." *Clinical Obstetrics and Gynaecology* 13 (1986): 611–632.

Lorenz, Robert, et al. "Role of Prenatal Genetic Counseling Before Amniocentesis." *The Journal of Reproductive Medicine* 31 (1986): 1–3.

Mackenzie, W. E. and Rushton, D. I. "Spontaneous Abortion After Transcervical Chorionic Villus Sampling: A Case Report." *Prenatal Diagnosis* 6 (1986): 387–388.

Macri, James N. "Critical Issues in Prenatal Maternal Serum Alpha-Fetoprotein Screening for Genetic Abnormalities." *American Journal of Obstetrics and Gynecology* 155 (1986): 240–246.

Marwick, Charles. "Controversy Surrounds Use of Test for Open Spina Bifida." *Journal of the American Medical Association* 250 (1983): 575–577.

Maxwell, D., et al. "Transabdominal Chorionic Villus Sampling." *The Lancet* (January 18, 1986): 123–126.

McGovern, Margaret; Goldberg, James D.; and Desnick, Robert J. "Acceptability of Chorionic Villi Sampling for Prenatal Diagnosis." *American Journal of Obstetrics and Gynecology* 155 (1986): 25–29.

Michelacci, Laura, et al. "Psychological Distress and Amniocentesis." *Gynecologic and Obstetric Investigation* 18 (1984): 40–44.

Nielsen, Caroline. "An Encounter with Modern Medical Technology: Women's Experiences with Amniocentesis." *Women and Health* 6 (1981): 109–124.

Powledge, Tabitha M. and Fletcher, John. "Guidelines for the Ethical, Social and Legal Issues in Prenatal Diagnosis." *New England Journal of Medicine* 300 (January 25, 1979): 168–172.

Rapp, Rayna. "The Ethics of Choice: After My Amniocentesis, Mike and I Faced the Toughest Decision of Our Lives." *Ms.* (April 1984): 97–100.

Rothman, Barbara Katz. *The Tentative Pregnancy: Prenatal Diagnosis and the Future of Motherhood.* New York: Viking, 1986.

Stockton, William. *Altered Destinies: Lives Changed by Genetic Flaws.* Garden City, NY: Doubleday, 1979.

U.S. Department of Health, Education and Welfare, Public Health Service. *Antenatal Diagnosis.* Washington, DC: National Institutes of Health Publication (April 1979).

5. STILLBIRTH

Bourne, S. "Stillbirth, Grief, and Medical Education." *British Medical Journal* 1, no. 6069 (April 30, 1977): 1157.

Crout, Teresa Kochmar. "Caring for the Mother of a Stillborn Baby." *Nursing* 10, no. 4 (April 1980): 70–73.

Dudley, Denis K. L. and D'Alton, Mary E. "Single Fetal Death in Twin Gestation." *Seminars in Perinatology* 10 (1986): 65–72.

Godwin, Gail. "Dream Children." *Dream Children.* New York: Knopf, 1976, pp. 3–19.

Grubb, Carolyn. "Is the Baby Alive or Dead: Psychological Work of a Woman with an Intrauterine Fetal Death." *Maternal-Child Nursing Journal* 5, (Spring 1976): 25–37.

Hovatta, Outi, et al. "Causes of Stillbirth: A Clinicopathological Study of 243 Patients." *British Journal of Obstetrics and Gynaecology* 90 (1983): 691–696.

Kotzwinkle, William. *Swimmer in the Secret Sea.* New York: Avon, 1975.

Kowalski, K., and Bowes, W. "Parents' Response to a Stillborn Baby." *Contemporary OB/GYN* 8 (October 1976): 53–57.

Lewis, Emanuel. "The Management of Stillbirth: Coping with an Unreality." *The Lancet* 2 (September 18, 1976): 619–620.

Lewis, Emanuel, and Page, Anne. "Failure to Mourn a Stillbirth: An Overlooked Catastrophe." *British Journal of Medical Psychology* 51 (1978): 237–241.

Nin, Anaïs. *The Diary of Anaïs Nin, Vol. 1: 1931–1934.* New York: Swallow Press, 1966, pp. 338–349.

Saylor, D. "Nursing Response to Mothers of Stillborn Infants." *Journal of Obstetric, Gynecologic, and Neonatal Nursing* 6 (July/August 1977).

Seitz, Pauline, and Warrick, Louise H. "Perinatal Death." *American Journal of Nursing* 74 (November 1974): 2028–2033.

Swinton, Alan. "Grief and Stillbirth." *British Medical Journal* 1, no. 6066 (April 9, 1977): 971.

Whited, Linda. "Helping the Parents of a Stillborn." *Nursing* (May 1985): 63.

Wolff, John R.; Nielson, Paul E.; and Schiller, Patricia. "The Emotional Reaction to a Stillbirth." *American Journal of Obstetrics and Gynecology* 108 (1973): 73–77.

6. INFANT DEATH

Bocian, Maureen E., and Kaback, Michael M. "Crisis Counseling: the Newborn Infant with a Chromosomal Anomaly." *Pediatric Clinics of North America* 25 (August 1978): 643–650.

Brazelton, T. Berry. "When a Baby Is Born Too Early." *Redbook* 154, no. 1 (November 1979): 53, 119–121.

Brennan, Maeve. "The Eldest Child." *Women and Fiction: Short Stories by and about Women*. Edited by Susan Cahill. New York: New American Library, 1975, 173–179.

Burnell, George M. "Maternal Reaction to the Loss of Multiple Births." *When Children Die*. Edited by Loren Wilkenfeld. Dubuque, Iowa: Kendall/ Hunt Publishing Co., 1977.

Caplan, Gerald. "Patterns of Parental Response to the Crisis of Premature Birth: A Preliminary Approach to Modifying the Mental-Health Outcome." *Psychiatry* 23 (1960): 365–374.

Cohen, Marion. *"She Was Born, She Died." A Collection of Poems Following the Death of an Infant*. Omaha: Centering Corporation, 1983.

DeYoung, Pamela. "Born Too Soon." *Baby Talk* 45 (February 1980).

Donovan, Bonnie. *The Caesarean Birth Experience*. Rev. ed. Boston: Beacon Press, 1978.

Drotar, Dennis; Baskiewicz, Ann; Irvin, Nancy; Kennell, John; and Klaus, Marshall. "The Adaptation of Parents to the Birth of an Infant with a Congenital Malformation: A Hypothetical Model." *Pediatrics* 56 (1975): 710–717.

Duff, Raymond S. "A Physician's Role in the Decision-Making Process: A Physician's Experience." *Decision-Making and the Defective Newborn*. Edited by Chester A. Swinyard. Proceedings of a Conference on Spina Bifida and Ethics. Springfield, IL: Charles C. Thomas, 1978.

Duff, Raymond, and Campbell, A. G. M. "Moral and Ethical Dilemmas in the Special-Care Nursery." *New England Journal of Medicine* (October 25, 1973): 890–894.

Elliott, Barbara A. "Neonatal Death: Reflections for Parents." *Pediatrics* 62 (July 1978): 100–102.

Fletcher, John. "Ethics and Euthanasia." *American Journal of Nursing* 73 (1973): 50.

Friedman, Stanford; Chodoff, Paul; Mason, John W.; and Hamburg, David A. "Behavioral Observations on Parents Anticipating the Death of a Child." *Pediatrics* 32 (October 1963): 610–625.

Galinsky, H. *Beginnings*. Boston: Houghton Mifflin, 1976.

Giles, P. F. H. "Reactions of Women to Perinatal Death." *Australia and New Zealand Journal of Obstetrics and Gynaecology* 10 (1970): 207–210.

Gray, Pamela J. "Premature Babies, Premature Parents." *Johns Hopkins Magazine* (August 1979): 8–15.

Guillemin, Jeanne, and Holmstrom, Lynda L. *Mixed Blessings: Intensive Care for Newborns.* New York: Oxford University Press, 1986.

Hubbard, Ruth. "Caring for Baby Doe." *Ms.* 165 (May 1984): 84–85.

Jackson, Pat Ludder. "Chronic Grief." *American Journal of Nursing* 74 (July 1974): 1288–1291.

Kaplan, David, and Mason, Edward A. "Maternal Reactions to Premature Birth Viewed as an Acute Emotional Disorder." *American Journal of Orthopsychiatry* 30 (July 1960): 539–552.

Kennell, John H., and Rolnick, Alice R. "Discussing Problems in Newborn Babies with Their Parents." *Pediatrics* 26 (November 1960): 832–838.

Lyon, Jeff. *Playing God in the Nursery.* New York: Norton, 1985.

Massanari, Jared, and Massanari, Alice. *Our Life with Caleb.* Philadelphia: Fortress Press, 1976.

Meier, Paula. "Wee Babies: Nursing Care for Extremely Premature Infants." *Quarterly Review Bulletin* (September 1978): 22–27.

Moskop, John, and Rita Saldanha. "The Baby Doe Rule: Still a Threat." *Hastings Center Report.* 16 (April 1986): 8–14.

Patrick, Jane Gassner. "Little Murders: Who Has the Right to Commit Infanticide?" *New Times* 10, no. 7 (April 3, 1978): 32–37.

Rasminsky, Judy. "When a Baby Dies." *Reader's Digest* (April 1984), 25–32.

Rowe, Jane; Clyman, R.; Green, C.; et al. "Follow-up of Families Who Experience a Perinatal Death." *Pediatrics* 62 (August 1978): 166–169.

Sargeant, Kimbal J. P. "Withholding Treatment from Defective Newborns: Substituted Judgment, Informed Consent, and the *Quinlan* Decision." *Gonzaga Law Review* 13 (1978): 781–811.

Smith, David H. "On Letting Some Babies Die." *Death Inside Out.* Edited by Peter Steinfels and Robert Veatch. New York: Harper & Row, 1975, pp. 129–138.

Stinson, Robert, and Stinson, Peggy. *The Long Dying of Baby Andrew.* Boston: Little, Brown, 1983.

Zachary, R. B., and Leeds, M. B. "Ethical and Social Aspects of Treatment of Spina Bifida." *The Lancet* 2 (August 3, 1968): 274–276.

7. THE COUPLE

Archgill, Jim, and Archgill, Lucy. "A Marriage Encounter with Grief." Carmel, Ind.: Compassionate Friends, n.d.

Benfield, Gary D.; Leib, Susan A.; and Vollman, John H. "Grief Response of Parents to Neonatal Death and Parent Participation in Deciding Care." *Pediatrics* 62 (August 1978): 171–177.

"Bereavement and Marriage Stress." Commack, N.Y.: Compassionate Friends, 1978.

Helmrath, Thomas A., and Steinitz, Elaine M. "Death of an Infant: Parental Grieving and the Failure of Social Support." *The Journal of Family Practice* 6 (1978): 785–790.

Hendin, David, and Marks, Joan. *The Genetic Connection.* New York: Signet, 1979.

Kennell, John J.; Slyter, Howard; and Klaus, Marshall H. "The Mourning Response of Parents to the Death of a Newborn." *The New England Journal of Medicine* 283, no. 7 (August 13, 1970): 344–349.

Schiff, Harriett S. *The Bereaved Parent.* (See Chapter One.)

Wiener, Jerry M. "Reaction of the Family to the Fatal Illness of a Child." *Loss and Grief: Psychological Management in Medical Practice.* Edited by Bernard Schoenberg et al. New York: Columbia University Press, 1970.

8. SINGLE WOMEN

Barglow, Peter; Istiphan, Isis; Bedger, Jean E.; and Welbourne, Claudia. "Response of Unmarried Adolescent Mothers to Infant or Fetal Death." *Adolescent Psychiatry, Vol. 2.* Edited by Sherman C. Feinstein and Peter Giovacchini. New York: Basic Books, 1973 285–300.

Fallaci, Oriana. *Letter to a Child Never Born.* (See References for Chapter Two.)

Geronimus, Arlene. "The Effects of Race, Residence and Prenatal Care on the Relationship of Maternal Age to Neonatal Mortality." *American Journal of Public Health* 76 (1986): 1416–1421.

Hollingsworth, Dorothy R., and Felice, Marianne. "Teenage Pregnancy: A Multiracial Sociologic Problem." *American Journal of Obstetrics and Gynecology* 155 (1986): 741–46.

Horowitz, Nancy H. "Adolescent Mourning Reactions to Infant and Fetal Loss." *Social Casework* 59, no. 9 (November 1978): 551–559.

Kandell, Netta. "The Unwed Adolescent Pregnancy: An Accident?" *American Journal of Nursing* 79, no. 12 (December 1979): 2112–2114.

Klein, Carole. *The Single Parent Experience.* New York: Walker, 1973.

Leppert, Phyllis; Namerow, Pearila; and Barner, Doris. "Pregnancy Outcomes Among Adolescent and Older Women Receiving Comprehensive Prenatal Care." *Journal of Adolescent Health Care* 7 (1986): 112–117.

Rosenstock, Harvey A. "Recognizing the Teen-ager Who Needs to Be Pregnant: A Clinical Perspective." *Southern Medical Journal* 73 (February 1980): 134–136.

Schwartz, David B. "Perspectives on Adolescent Pregnancy." *Wisconsin Medical Journal* 79 (March 1980): 35–36.

Sukanich, Aurapin; Rogers, Kenneth; and McDonald, Hugh. "Physical Maturity and Outcome of Pregnancy in Primiparas Younger Than 16 Years of Age." *Pediatrics* 78 (1986): 31–36.

9. CHILDREN AT HOME

Bluebond-Langner, Myra. "Meanings of Death to Children." *New Meanings of Death*. Edited by Herman Feifel. New York: McGraw-Hill, 1977.

Cain, Albert; Fast, Irene; and Erickson, Mary. "Children's Disturbed Reactions to the Death of a Sibling." *American Journal of Ortho-psychiatry* 34 (1964): 741–752.

Cain, Albert; Erickson, Mary; Fast, Irene; and Vaughan, Rebecca. "Children's Disturbed Reactions to Their Mother's Miscarriage." (See References for Chapter Two.)

Cain, Albert, and Cain, Barbara. "On Replacing a Child." *Journal of American Child Psychiatry* 3 (1964): 443–455.

Dodge, Nancy. *Thumpy's Story*. Prairie Lark Press, P. O. Box 699-B, Springfield, IL 62705, n.d.

Dodge, Nancy C., and Lamb, Sister Jane Marie. *Sharing with Thumpy (Workbook), My Story of Love and Grief* by (child's name). Prairie Lark Press, P. O. Box 699-B, Springfield, IL 62705, 1985.

Fox, Sandra S. *Books and Films on Death and Dying for Children and Adolescents: An Annotated Bibliography*. The Good Grief Program, 295 Longwood Avenue, Boston, MA 02115, 1985.

Furman, Erna. *A Child's Parent Dies: Studies in Childhood Bereavement*. New Haven: Yale University Press, 1974.

Grollman, Earl A. "Children and Death." *Concerning Death: A Practical Guide for the Living*. Edited by Earl Grollman. Boston: Beacon Press, 1974.

Grollman, Earl A., ed. *Explaining Death to Children*. Boston: Beacon Press, 1967.

Hardgrove, Carol, and Warrick, Louise H. "How Shall We Tell the Children?" *American Journal of Nursing* 74, no. 3 (March 1974): 450.

Johnson, Joy, and Johnson, Marvin. *Where's Jess?* Omaha: Centering Corporation, 1982.

Kreimentz, Jill. *How it Feels When a Parent Dies*. New York: Knopf, 1981.

Kubler-Ross, Elizabeth. *On Children and Death*. New York: Macmillan, 1983.

Lasker, Arnold A. "Telling Children the Facts of Death." *National Jewish Monthly* 83, no. 6 (February 1969). Reprinted in *Your Child* (Winter 1972).

Lasker, Arnold A. "When Children Face Bereavement." *Conservative Judaism* 18 (Winter 1964): 53–58.

LeShan, Eda. *Learning to Say Good-by*. New York: Avon, 1978.

Moriarty, Irene. "Mourning the Death of an Infant: The Siblings' Story." *The Journal of Pastoral Care* 32, no. 1 (March 1978): 22–33.

Nagy, Maria. "The Child's View of Death." *The Meaning of Death*. Edited by Herman Feifel. New York: McGraw-Hill, 1965.

Poznanski, Elva O. "The 'Replacement Child': A Saga of Unresolved Parental Grief." *Journal of Pediatrics* 81 (1972): 1190–1193.

Scrimshaw, Susan, and March, Daniel. "I Had a Baby Sister, But She Lasted Only One Day." *Journal of the American Medical Association* 251 (1984): 732–73.

Smialek, Zoe. "Observations on Immediate Reactions of Families to Sudden Infant Death." *Pediatrics* 62, no. 2 (August 1978): 160–165.

Szybist, Carolyn. "Epilogue." *The Child and Death*, by O. J. Sahler. St. Louis: C. V. Mosby, 1978.

Times, Roberta. *Living with an Empty Chair—A Guide Through Grief.* Amherst, Mass.: Mandala Press, 1977.

10. GRANDPARENTS

Earl, W. J. H. "Help for Parents after Stillbirth." *British Medical Journal* 1, no. 6111 (February 25, 1978): 505–506.

Friedman, Stanford B.; Chodoff, Paul; Mason, John W.; and Hamburg, David A. "Behavioral Observations on Parents Anticipating the Death of a Child." (See References for Chapter Six.)

Lifton, Robert J. "Advocacy and Corruption in the Healing Professions." *Nourishing the Humanistic in Medicine.* Edited by William R. Rogers and David Barnard. Pittsburgh: University of Pittsburgh Press, 1979, pp. 53–72.

Smialek, Zoe. "Observations on Immediate Reactions of Families to Sudden Infant Death." (See References for Chapter Nine.)

11. FRIENDS AND RELATIVES

Cadden, Vivian. *Crisis in the Family.* Chicago: National Research Bureau, 1973.

Freese, Arthur. *Help for Your Grief: Turning Emotional Loss into Growth.* New York: Shocken, 1977.

Guerry, Vincent. *Life with the Baoule.* Translated by Nora Hodges. Washington, D. C.: Three Continents Press, 1975.

Helmrath, Thomas A., and Steinitz, Elaine M. "Death of an Infant: Parental Grieving and the Failure of Social Support." (See References for Chapter Seven.)

Kamien, Marcia. "The Death of a New Baby: The Grief No One Wants to Talk About." *Glamour* (May 1979): 187–189.

Vernon, Glenn. *Sociology of Death: An Analysis of Death Related Behavior.* New York: Ronald Press, 1970.

Walker, Kenni. "Easing the Pain of Bereaved Parents." *Nursing* (April 1986): 49–50.

12. MEDICAL CARE

Becker, Rita, et al. "Development of a Perinatal Grief Checklist." *Journal of Obstetric, Gynecologic and Neonatal Nursing* 14 (1985): 194–199.

Benfield, Gary D.; Lieb, Susan A.; and Reuter, Jeanette. "Grief Response of Parents after Referral of the Critically Ill Newborn to a Regional Center." *New England Journal of Medicine* 294 (April 29, 1976): 975–978.

Bergman, Abraham B. "Psychological Aspects of Sudden Unexpected Death in Infants and Children." *Pediatric Clinics of North America* 21 (February 1974): 115–121.

Bourne, S. "The Psychological Effects of Stillbirths on the Doctor." *Proceedings of the Third International Congress of Psychosomatic Medicine in Obstetrics and Gynaecology.* Basel, Switzerland: Karger, 1972, pp. 333–334.

Caplan, Gerald. "Practical Steps for the Family Physician in the Prevention of Emotional Disorder." *Journal of the American Medical Association* 1970 (July 25, 1959): 1497–1506.

Carr, Donna, and Knupp, Chaplain Samuel F. "Grief and Perinatal Loss: A Community Hospital Response to Support." *Journal of Obstetric, Gynecologic and Neonatal Nursing* (March/April 1985).

Chez, Ronald, et al. "Helping Patients and Doctors Cope with Perinatal Death." *Contemporary OB/GYN* 20 (1982): 98.

Clyman, R. I., et al. "Do Parents Utilize Physician Follow-up after the Death of Their Newborn?" *Pediatrics* 64 (1979): 665.

Darling, Rosalyn B. *Families Against Society: Reactions to Children with Birth Defects.* Beverly Hills, Calif.: Sage, 1979.

Easson, William M. "The Family of the Dying Child." *Pediatric Clinics of North America* 19 (November 1972): 1157–1165.

Elliott, Barbara A., and Hein, Herman A. "Neonatal Death: Reflections for Physicians." *Pediatrics* 62 (July 1978): 96–99.

Forrest, G. C.; Standish, E.; and Baum, J. D. "Support after Perinatal Death: A Study of Support and Counselling after Perinatal Bereavement," *British Medical Journal* 285 (1982): 1475–1479.

Francis, Vida; Korsch, Barbara M.; and Morris, Marie J. "Gaps in Doctor-Patient Communications: Patients' Response to Medical Advice." *The New England Journal of Medicine* 280 (March 6, 1978): 535–540.

Hagan, Joan. "Nursing Interaction and Intervention with Grieving Families." *Nursing Forum* 13 (1974): 371–385.

Hall, Lee. "Social Workers Play Vital Role in Perinatal Care." *NASW News* (January 1979): 4.

Jimenez, Sherry Lynn Mims. "Grief Counseling: When Doctors Are Too Distraught, Educators Can Help Grieving Parent." *Childbirth Educator* (Fall 1983): 42.

Kellner, Kenneth; Donnelly, William; and Gould, Sharon. "Parental Behavior after Perinatal Death: Lack of Predictive Demographic and Obstetric Variables." *Obstetrics and Gynecology* 63 (June 1984): 809–814.

Kirk, E. Paul. "Psychological Effects and Management of Perinatal Loss." *American Journal of Obstetrics and Gynecology* 149 (May 1984): 46–51.

Knapp, Ronald, and Peppers, Larry. "Doctor-Patient Relationships in Fetal/Infant Death Encounters." *Journal of Medical Education* 54 (October 1979): 775–780.

Kohlsaat, Barbara. "The Psychosocial Impact of Tertiary Care: Neonatal Intensive Care and the Social Worker." *Quarterly Review Bulletin* (September 1978): 28–32.

Lake, Marion, et al. "The Role of a Grief Support Team Following Still-birth." *American Journal of Obstetrics and Gynecology* 146 (August 1983): 877–881.

Lehman, Darrin R.; Ellard, John H.; and Wortman, Camille B. "Social Support for the Bereaved Recipients and Providing Perspectives on What Is Helpful." *Journal of Consulting and Clinical Psychology* 54 (1986): 438–441.

Lifton, Robert J. "Advocacy and Corruption in the Healing Professions." (See References for Chapter Ten.)

Meier, Paula. "A Crisis Group for Parents of High-Risk Infants." *Maternal-Child Nursing Journal* 7 (Spring 1978): 21–31.

O'Donohue, Nancy. "Perinatal Bereavement: The Role of the Health Care Professional." *Quarterly Review Bulletin* 4 (September 1978): 30–32.

Opirhory, Gloria. "Counseling the Parents of a Critically Ill Newborn." *Journal of Obstetric, Gynecologic and Neonatal Nursing* 8 (May/June 1979): 179–182.

Solnit, Albert J., and Green, Morris. "Psychological Considerations in the Management of Deaths on Pediatric Hospital Services." *Pediatrics* 24 (July 1959): 106–112.

Taylor, Paul, and Hall, Barbara Lee. "Parent-Infant Bonding: Problems and Opportunities in a Perinatal Center." *Seminars in Perinatology* 3 (January 1979): 73–84.

Whited, Linda. "Helping the Parents of a Stillborn." *Nursing* (May 1985): 63.

13. RELIGION

Case, Ronna. "When Birth Is Also a Funeral." *Journal of Pastoral Care* 32 (March 1978): 6–21.

Catholic Hospital Association. *Religious Aspects of Medical Care: A Handbook of Religious Practices of All Faiths.* St. Louis: Catholic Hospital Association, 1975.

Feldman, David. *Marital Relations, Birth Control, and Abortion in Jewish Law.* New York: Schocken, 1978.

Freese, Arthur. "Religion, Afterlife, Burial, Cremation and Mourning Practices: The Help They Offer." *Help for Your Grief.* (See References for Chapter Eleven).

Irion, Paul. *The Funeral: Vestige or Value?* New York: Arno Press, 1977.

Kubler-Ross, Elizabeth, ed. *Death: The Final Stage of Growth.* Englewood Cliffs, N.J.: Prentice-Hall, 1975.

Kushner, Harold. *When Bad Things Happen to Good People.* New York: Schocken, 1981.

Lapsley, James N. "Death and Bereavement in Mercer County, New Jersey: A Study in Ethnic Diversity." *Pastoral Psychology* 25, no. 3 (Spring 1977): 173–185.

Lasker, Arnold. "Meeting the Needs of the Bereaved." *Proceedings of the Rabbinical Assembly* 27, 1963.

Mandelbaum, David. "Social Uses of Funeral Rites." *The Meaning of Death*. Edited by Herman Feifel. New York: McGraw-Hill, 1965, pp. 189–217.

Massanari, Jared, and Massanari, Alice. *Our Life with Caleb*. (See References for Chapter Five.)

Pine, Vanderlyn R. *Acute Grief and the Funeral*. Springfield, Il.: Charles C. Thomas, 1976.

Reeves, Robert B., Jr.; Neele, Robert E.; and Kutscher, Austin H., eds. *Pastoral Care of the Dying and Bereaved: Selected Readings*. New York: Health Sciences Publishing Corp., 1973.

Selby, James W.; Calhoun, Lawrence G.; and Parrott, Gertrude. "Attitudes Toward Seeking Pastoral Help in the Event of the Death of a Close Friend or Relative." *American Journal of Community Psychology* 6, no. 4 (1978): 399–403.

14. LAW

Dallek, Geraldine. "Labor and Delivery as a Medical Emergency." *Clearinghouse Review* 10 (March 1977): 947–953.

Hayes, John. "The Patient's Right of Access to His Hospital and Medical Records." *Medical Trial Technique Quarterly*, 1978.

Justice V. Booth Maternity Center 498 A. 2nd 950, 1986.

Lobdell V. Tarrant County Hospital District, 710 S.W. 2nd 811, 1986.

Law, Sylvia, and Polan, Steven. *Pain and Profit—The Politics of Malpractice*. New York: Harper & Row, 1978.

Martindale-Hubbell Law Directory, 112th Annual Edition. Summit, N.J.: Martindale-Hubbell, 1980.

Modaber V. Kelly, 348 S. E. 2nd 233, 1986.

Niswander, Kenneth E. "The Obstetrician, Fetal Asphyxia, and Cerebral Palsy." *American Journal of Obstetrics and Gynecology* 133 (February 15, 1979): 358–361.

Seiden, Dena. "The Malpractice Muddle." *Commonweal* (17 January 1986): 8–13.

Volk, Michael D. and Morgan, Melvin D. *Medical Malpractice: Obstetric and Neonatal Cases*. New York: Shepards-McGraw, 1986.

15. POSSIBLE CAUSES

"ACLU Sues American Cyanamid: Charges Sex Discrimination in Forced Sterilization of Women." *Civil Liberties Record* (American Civil Liberties Union of Pennsylvania) 30 March 1980.

Baldwin, Deborah. "The War Comes Home." *Environmental Action* 11 (April 1980): 3–8, 31–32.

Barbanel, Josh. "At Love Canal, Despair Is the Pervasive Affliction." *The New York Times* (May 19, 1980): A1, B3.

Barnes, Anne B.; Colton, Theodore; et al. "Fertility and Outcome of Pregnancy in Women Exposed in Utero to Diethylstilbestrol." *New England Journal of Medicine* 302, no. 11 (March 13, 1980): 609–613.

Birnbaum, David A. "The Iatrogenesis of Damaged Mothers and Newborns." *Twenty-first Century Obstetrics Now, Vol. 1.* Edited by Lee Stewart and David Steward. Chapel Hill, N.C.: NAPSAC, 1977, pp. 105–114.

Boffey, Philip M. "Limits Are Advised on Viewing Fetuses Through Ultrasound." *The New York Times,* February 9, 1984, A1, A29.

Brewer, Gail Sforza, and Brewer, Thomas. *What Every Pregnant Woman Should Know: The Truth About Diet and Drugs in Pregnancy.* New York: Penguin, 1979.

Brody, Jane. "Sperm Found Especially Vulnerable to Environment." *The New York Times* (March 10, 1981): C1, C3.

Brown, Michael. *Laying Waste: The Poisoning of America by Toxic Chemicals,* New York: Pantheon, 1980.

Clendinen, Dudley. "How Love Canal Mothers Became a Political Force." *The New York Times* (May 26, 1980): B1–B2.

Corea, Gena. *The Hidden Malpractice.,* rev. ed. New York: Harper and Row, 1984.

Corbett, Thomas H. "Cancer, Miscarriages, and Birth Defects Associated with Operating Room Exposure." *Proceedings, Conference on Women and the Workplace.* Edited by Eula Bingham. Washington, D.C.: Society for Occupational and Environmental Health, 1977.

Gaffron, Margie. "A Fear We Are Just Learning to Live With." *The Progressive* 44 (June 1980): 24.

Kline, Jennie; Stein, Zena; Strobino, Barbara; Susser, Mervyn; and Warburton, Dorothy. "Surveillance of Spontaneous Abortions: Power in Environmental Monitoring." *American Journal of Epidemiology* 106 (1977): 345–350.

Lens, Sidney. "Dead on the Job." *The Progressive* 43, no. 11 (November 1979): 50–52.

Levine, Adeline Gordon. *Love Canal: Science, Politics, and People.* Lexington, MA: Lexington Books, 1982.

Lieberman, Sharon. "Die-ox-in." *Health Right: A Women's Health Newsletter* 6 (Spring 1979): 7, 14–17.

MacLeod, Gordon. "Health Decisions in the Nuclear Age." *Bulletin of the Allegheny County Medical Society* 69, no. 8 (April 26, 1980): 155–159.

Meier, Barry. "Companies Wrestle with Threats to Workers' Reproductive Health." *Wall Street Journal,* February 5, 1987.

Morgan, Robert W. et al., "Fetal Loss and Work in a Waste Water Treatment Plant." *American Journal of Public Health* 14 (1984): 499–501.

Nader, Ralph, and Brownstein, Ronald. "Beyond the Love Canal." *The Progressive* 44, no. 5 (May 1980): 28–31.

Norwood, Christopher. *At Highest Risk: Environmental Hazards to Young and Unborn Children.* New York: McGraw-Hill, 1980.

———. "Terata." *Mother Jones* (January 1985): 15–22.

Pawlick, Thomas. "The Silent Toll." *Harrowsmith* (June 1980): 33–49.

"Pregnancy Testing Urged for Women Entering Hospitals." *Medical World News* 19 (May 29, 1978): 22.

Robinson, Gail. "Organizing Against Workplace Pollution." *Environmental Action* 12, no. 3 (September 1980): 4–10.

"Six Deformed Babies in India Linked to Bhopal Gas Leak." *The New York Times,* July 16, 1985.

"Spray 2,4-D and See," *Mother Jones* (February/March 1981): 9.

Stein, Zena, and Kline, Jennie. "Smoking, Alcohol and Reproduction." *American Journal of Public Health* 73 (1983): 1154–1156.

Stellman, Jeanne. *Women's Work, Women's Health.* New York: Pantheon, 1977.

Streissguth, Ann Pytkowicz; Landesman-Dwyer, Sharon; Martin, Joan C.; and Smith, David W. "Teratogenic Effects of Alcohol in Humans and Laboratory Animals." *Science* 209, no. 4454 (July 18, 1980): 353–361.

Vaughan, Thomas; Daling, Janet; and Starzyk, Patricia. "Fetal Death and Maternal Occupation." *Journal of Occupational Medicine* 26 (1984) 676–678.

Wachtel, Eleanor. "Pregnancy Guilt Trips." *Maclean's* 94 (December 21, 1981): 39.

16. RECOVERING

Bereavement Support Groups: Leadership Manual. Grief Education Institute, 2422 South Downing St., Denver, CO 80210.

Cohen, Marion. "What I Do with Kerin." *Mothering* (Fall 1980): 89–93.

Estok, P., and Lehman, A. "Perinatal Death: Grief Support for Families." *Birth* 10 (1983): 17–25.

Moers, Ellen. "Female Gothic." *Literary Women.* Garden City, N.Y.: Doubleday, 1976.

SHARE. "Starting Your Own SHARE Group," 4th edition. St. John's Hospital, 800 East Carpenter, Springfield, IL 62769.

Staudacher, Carol. *Beyond Grief: A Guide for Recovering from the Death of a Loved One.* Oakland, CA: New Harbinger Publications, 1987.

Szybist, Carolyn. "Epilogue." (See References for Chapter Nine.)

Videka-Sherman, L., and M. Lieberman. "The Effects of Self-Help and Psychotherapy Intervention on Child Loss: The Limits of Recovery." *American Journal of Orthopsychiatry* 55 (Jan. 1985): 70–82.

Wilson, A., and Soule, D. J. "The Role of a Self-Help Group in Working with Parents of a Stillborn Baby." *Death Education* (1981): 175–186.

17. ANOTHER BABY

Cain, Albert, and Cain, Barbara. "On Replacing a Child." (See References for Chapter Nine.)

Cooper, Beatrice, and Ekstein, Rudolf. "Concerning Parental Vulnerability: Issues Around Child and Infant Loss." *The Child in His Family: Vulnerable Children.* Edited by E. James Anthony, Cyrille Koupernik, and Colette Chiland. New York: John Wiley, 1978, pp. 219–230.

Frederick, J. "Preceding Pregnancy Loss as an Index of Risk of Stillbirth or Neonatal Death in the Present Pregnancy." *Biology of the Neonate* 31, nos. 1–2, 1977.

Hales, Diane, and Creasy, Robert. *New Hope for Problem Pregnancies*. New York: Berkley, 1984.

Harlap, Susan; Shiono, Patricia H.; Ramcharan, Savitri; Berendes, Heinz; and Pellegrin, Frederick. "A Prospective Study of Spontaneous Fetal Losses after Induced Abortions." *New England Journal of Medicine* 301, no. 13 (September 27, 1979): 677–681.

Poznanski, Elva D. "The 'Replacement Child': A Saga of Unresolved Parental Grief." (See References for Chapter Nine.)

Schweibert, Pat, and Kirk, Paul. "Still to be Born: A Guide for Bereaved who are Making Decisions about their Future," 1986, Perinatal Loss, 2116 N.E. 18th Ave., Portland, OR 97212.

Stray-Pedersen, Babill, and Stray-Pedersen, Sverre. "Etiologic Factors and Subsequent Reproductive Performance in 195 Couples with a Prior History of Habitual Abortion." *American Journal of Obstetrics and Gynecology* 14k8 (1984): 140–146.

Szybist, Carolyn. "The Subsequent Child." Chicago: National Foundation for Sudden Infant Death, 1973.

VII. REPORT OF NEW RESEARCH

Lasker, Judith; Potvin, Louise; Toedter, Lori; and Alhadeff, Janice. "Measuring Grief: A Short Version of the Perinatal Grief Scale." Submitted for publication.

Toedter, Lori; Lasker, Judith; and Alhadeff, Janice. "The Perinatal Grief Scale: Development and Initial Validation." Presented at Eastern Psychological Association meetings, Arlington, VA, April 1987.

Glossary

Abortion, complete. A miscarriage in which all of the products of conception have been expelled and the cervix has closed.

Abortion, incomplete. A miscarriage in which all of the products of conception have not been expelled from the uterus.

Abortion, induced. Intentional termination of a pregnancy.

Abortion, inevitable. A miscarriage that cannot be halted.

Abortion, missed. A miscarriage in which a dead fetus and other products of conception remain in the uterus for four or more weeks.

Abortion, selective. The term often used to refer to intentional termination of a pregnancy after a finding of deformity in the fetus.

Abortion, spontaneous. Miscarriage; unintended ending of a pregnancy before the twentieth week.

Abortion, therapeutic. The intentional termination of a pregnancy for the purpose of preserving the life of the mother.

Abortion, threatened. Symptoms such as vaginal bleeding with or without pain, which may either end with a miscarriage or with the continuation of a normal pregnancy.

Abruptio placentae. A condition in which the placenta detaches itself prematurely from the uterus, cutting off the fetus's supply of oxygen.

Adhesions. Scar tissue which binds two surfaces together that are usually apart from each other.

AIDS (Acquired Immune Deficiency Syndrome). A fatal disease affecting the immune system, which can be transmitted through sexual contact or exchange of blood.

Alpha feto protein. A protein normally produced by a fetus, which can be measured prenatally to identify possible birth defects.

Amniocentesis. A procedure for removing a sample of amniotic fluid from the uterus by way of a needle inserted through the mother's abdominal wall in order to obtain information about the fetus.

Amniotic fluid. The fluid surrounding the fetus in the uterus which protects it during pregnancy and labor.

Amencephaly. A congenital condition characterized by absence of brain and spinal cord.

Anesthesia. A drug or gas that gives partial or complete loss of sensation with or without loss of consciousness.

Anomaly. A malformation or abnormality in any part of the body.

Anoxia. The lack or absence of oxygen.

Artificial insemination. The mechanical injection of viable semen into the vagina in order to fertilize an egg.

Bereavement. The state of having experienced a significant loss.

Bonding. The process of attachment between infant and parents; this relationship can start even before conception.

Breech birth. Delivery of an infant's feet or buttocks first instead of the head.

Catheter. A tube for evacuating or injecting fluids.

Cerclage. A surgical technique for closing the cervix during pregnancy so that a woman with an incompetent cervix will not deliver prematurely.

Cervix. The lower section of the uterus, which protrudes into the vagina and dilates during labor to allow the passage of the infant.

Caesarean section. The surgical removal of the fetus by means of an incision through the abdominal wall into the uterus.

Childbirth educator. An individual, usually a nurse, who prepares expectant parents for childbirth by practicing relaxation techniques and reviewing what can be expected during labor and delivery.

Chorionic Biopsy. (See Chorionic Villus Sampling.)

Chorionic Villus Sampling. A technique for obtaining a sample of pre-placental tissue from the uterus in order to look for chromosomal abnormalities.

Conception. The union between the egg and sperm to create a new life.

Congenital. Present at birth, although not necessarily hereditary.

Crib death. (See Sudden Infant Death Syndrome.)

D & C (Dilation and Curettage). A procedure involving the expansion of the cervix and the insertion of a loop-shaped instrument to scrape the inner lining of the uterus.

D & E (Dilation and Evacuation). A procedure in which the cervix is dilated and the uterine contents are removed, either by a suction device or with curettage.

DES (Diethylstilbestrol). Synthetic estrogen used sometimes as a "morning-after pill," formerly thought to prevent miscarriage.

Down's syndrome. A genetic abnormality, formerly known as mongolism, characterized by the prsence of an extra chromosome 21 and moderate to severe retardation.

Ectopic pregnancy. A pregnancy that occurs outside the uterine cavity.

Embryo. The term used to describe the early stages of fetal growth, from the fourth to the ninth week of pregnancy.

Endometriosis. A condition characterized by pieces of the uterine lining locating themselves anywhere outside the uterine cavity.

Episiotomy. A surgical incision made in order to enlarge the external vaginal opening during delivery to prevent tearing.

Estrogen. A hormone responsible for developing the female reproductive cycle.

Euthanasia. Killing a person with an incurable and painful disease mercifully.

Fallopian tube. The tube that carries the egg from the ovary to the uterus.

Fetal blood sampling. A procedure to get fetal blood by inserting a needle into the umbilical cord.

Fetal death. The term often used to include both miscarriage and stillbirth.

Fetoscopy. A technique for directly visualizing a fetus while in the uterus and extracting a fetal blood sample; placental aspiration.

Fetus. The developing baby from approximately the ninth week of pregnancy until the moment of birth.

Forceps. An instrument sometimes used to assist in the delivery of an infant.

Genetic abnormality. A disorder arising from an anomaly in the chromosomal structure which may or may not be hereditary.

Genetic counseling. Advice and information provided, usually by a team of experts, on the detection and risk of recurrence of genetic disorders.

Gestation. The period of fetal development in the uterus from conception to birth.

Gonorrhea. A sexually transmitted disease.

Grief. The emotional reaction to the loss of a significant person or object.

Habitual abortion. Miscarriages occurring in three or more pregnancies.

HCG (Human Chorionic Gonadotropin). A hormone manufactured by the fertilized egg. Its presence is an indication of a pregnancy.

Hemophilia. A hereditary blood disease characterized by failure of the blood to clot and the occurrence of abnormal bleeding.

Hemorrhage. Excessive bleeding.

Hereditary. Transmitted from one's ancestors by way of genes within the chromosomes of the fertilizing sperm and egg.

Hysterotomy. A surgical procedure for the removal of a fetus; a type of induced abortion used occasionally during the second trimester.

Incompetent cervix. A weakened cervix that is unable to hold the fetus in the uterus the full nine months, sometimes a cause of late miscarriage or premature birth.

Induction of labor. The use of agents to stimulate the onset of labor or to increase the speed and intensity of labor.

Intrauterine device (IUD). A birth control device inserted in the uterus.

In vitro fertilization (IVF). A procedure in which eggs are removed from a woman and mixed with sperm in a petri dish. After two days the fertilized eggs are inserted back into the woman's uterus.

Isolette. An incubator for infants in distress, providing controlled temperature and oxygen supply.

IUD. (See Intrauterine device.)

Klinefelter's syndrome. A genetic abnormality which appears only in males. Characterized by an extra X chromosome, it causes secondary female characteristics, infertility, and possible retardation.

La Leche League. An international organization for the promotion of breast-feeding.

Lamaze. A commonly used approach to prepared childbirth.

Laparoscopy. Surgical procedure for visualizing the ovaries and fallopian tubes.

Low birth weight. The weight of a baby at birth if it is under 2500 grams (five and one-half pounds).

Maternal Serum Alpha Fetoprotein (MSAFP). A blood test that checks to see if the fetus has neural tube defects.

Midwife. An individual, now usually a nurse, who is specially trained in the practice of obstetrics.

Miscarriage. (See Abortion, spontaneous.)

Mutagen. A substance that alters the genetic structure of the sperm or ovum before conception.

Neonatal. Referring to the first twenty-eight days after birth.

Neonatal death. The death of a live-born infant within twenty-eight days of birth.

Neonatal intensive care unit. Also called intensive care nursery (I.C.N.). A special-care nursery for seriously ill newborns, usually located in regional medical centers.

Neonatologist. A pediatrician who is specially trained in the care of newborns.

Ovum. Female reproductive cell.

Perinatal. Referring to the period of time from the twentieth week of pregnancy through the first twenty-eight days after birth.

PID (Pelvic Inflammatory Disease). Any inflammation of a woman's pelvic organs. Symptoms may include pain, fever, and vaginal discharge.

Placenta. Spongy organ attached to the wall of the uterus through which nourishment and oxygen pass from the bloodstream of the mother through the umbilical cord into the bloodstream of the fetus.

Placental Aspiration. A technique that allows a direct view of the fetus and extracts a small sample of blood from the fetus.

Placenta previa. Abnormally low implantation of the placenta in the uterus.

Postmaturity. The birth of an infant after forty-two weeks of gestation.

Prematurity. The birth of an infant before thirty-eight weeks of gestation.

Progesterone. A hormone responsible for changes in the reproductive cycle that allow the embryo to implant.

Prolapsed cord. Expulsion of a loop of umbilical cord after the membranes have ruptured but prior to delivery. Pressure on the cord from the emerging baby will cut off the baby's blood supply.

Prostaglandin. A hormone which, when injected into the amniotic sac surrounding the fetus or given in the form of a vaginal suppository, induces labor; it is often used in second trimester abortions.

Saline. A salt solution which, when injected into the amniotic sac, leads to the death of the fetus; it is sometimes used during second trimester abortions.

Salpingectomy. Surgical removal of one or both fallopian tubes.

Sonography. (See ultrasound.)

Salpingostomy. An operation to make an opening in the fallopian tube. Can be done to remove an embryo without severing the tube.

Sperm. Male reproductive cell.

Spina bifida. An abnormality in the development of the spine, sometimes characterized by severe neurological impairment and paralysis.

Stillbirth. Death before birth of a fetus that is at least twenty weeks of gestation.

Sudden Infant Death Syndrome (SIDS). Unexplained death of infants usually during sleep.

Teratogen. A substance that alters fetal growth and development and causes birth abnormalities.

Term. Forty weeks' gestation; the baby's due date.

Toxemia. Often referred to as pre-eclampsia, an abnormal condition of late pregnancy characterized by swelling, high blood pressure, and protein in the urine.

Trimester. One of the three-month periods into which pregnancy is divided.

Trisomy 18. A genetic abnormality characterized by an extra chromosome 18 and severe mental retardation and physical anomalies.

Tubal ligation. A surgical procedure, involving tying off or cauterizing the fallopian tubes, which is used for sterilization of women.

Ultrasound. A technique for visualizing the fetus in the uterus which allows for estimating the size and detecting some abnormalities; also called pulse-echo sonography.

Umbilical cord. The lifeline through which nourishment, oxygen, and waste products pass between the placenta and the fetus.

Uterus. Womb; the female organ in which the fetus grows during pregnancy.

Vernix. An oily substance covering the fetus due to secretion of skin glands.

Viability. Capability of surviving outside the uterus; usually after twenty weeks gestation.

Index

About the Authors

Susan Borg is an architect in New Jersey, where she lives with her husband and two daughters. Daniel, her first child, died shortly after birth.

Judith Lasker, Ph.D., is associate professor of sociology and associate dean of the College of Arts and Science at Lehigh University. She lives in Pennsylvania with her husband and two daughters. Her first child, Elana, was stillborn.